Python Machine Learning By Example

Second Edition

Implement machine learning algorithms and techniques to build intelligent systems

Yuxi (Hayden) Liu

BIRMINGHAM - MUMBAI

Python Machine Learning By Example
Second Edition

Commissioning Editor: Sunith Shetty
Acquisition Editor: Reshma Amare
Content Development Editor: Athikho Sapuni Rishana
Technical Editor: Vibhuti Gawde
Copy Editor: Safis Editing
Project Coordinator: Kirti Pisat
Proofreader: Safis Editing
Indexer: Pratik Shirodkar
Graphics: Jisha Chirayil
Production Coordinator: Jisha Chirayil

First published: May 2017
Second edition: February 2019

Production reference: 1270219

Published by Packt Publishing Ltd.
Livery Place
35 Livery Street
Birmingham
B3 2PB, UK.

ISBN 978-1-78961-672-9

www.packtpub.com

mapt.io

Mapt is an online digital library that gives you full access to over 5,000 books and videos, as well as industry leading tools to help you plan your personal development and advance your career. For more information, please visit our website.

Why subscribe?

- Spend less time learning and more time coding with practical eBooks and Videos from over 4,000 industry professionals

- Improve your learning with Skill Plans built especially for you

- Get a free eBook or video every month

- Mapt is fully searchable

- Copy and paste, print, and bookmark content

Packt.com

Did you know that Packt offers eBook versions of every book published, with PDF and ePub files available? You can upgrade to the eBook version at www.packt.com and as a print book customer, you are entitled to a discount on the eBook copy. Get in touch with us at customercare@packtpub.com for more details.

At www.packt.com, you can also read a collection of free technical articles, sign up for a range of free newsletters, and receive exclusive discounts and offers on Packt books and eBooks.

I would like to thank all of the great people that made this book possible. Without any of you, this book would only exist in my mind. I would like to especially thank all of my editors at Packt Publishing: Vibhuti, Athikho, Martin, and so many more, as well as my reviewer, Vadim, a renowned machine learning researcher from MIT. I would also like to thank all of the reviewers of the code of this book. Without them, this book would be harder to read and apply to real-world problems. Last but not least, I'd like to thank all the readers for the support they provided, which encourages me to continue with the second edition of this book.

Foreword

This book is a deep dive into the exciting world of machine learning. What's unique about this book is the clarity with which it explains concepts from first principles and teaches by example in a way that is accessible to a wide audience. You will learn how to implement key algorithms from scratch and compare your code against proven machine learning libraries.

The discussion in this book is backed by mathematical principles and includes from-scratch coding exercises that help you gain a deeper understanding of the subject. By reading this book, you will be learning something new, whether you are a beginner or an experienced machine learning practitioner.

True to its title, you will learn about a number of interesting applications, such as predicting click-through rates for targeted advertisements, mining text data for patterns, and predicting the stock price of a major exchange index. Throughout the book, you will find exercises and links to help you better understand the material.

I encourage you to turn the page and dive into the exciting world of machine learning.

Vadim Smolyakov

Contributors

About the author

Yuxi (Hayden) Liu is an author of a series of machine learning books and an education enthusiast. His first book, the first edition of *Python Machine Learning By Example*, was a #1 bestseller in Amazon India in 2017 and 2018. His other books include *R Deep Learning Projects* and *Hands-On Deep Learning Architectures with Python* published by Packt.

He is an experienced data scientist who's focused on developing machine learning and deep learning models and systems. He has worked in a variety of data-driven domains and has applied his machine learning expertise to computational advertising, recommendation, and network anomaly detection. He published five first-authored IEEE transaction and conference papers during his master's research at the University of Toronto.

About the reviewer

Vadim Smolyakov is currently pursuing his PhD at MIT in the areas of computer science and artificial intelligence. His primary research interests include Bayesian inference, deep learning, and optimization. Prior to coming to MIT, Vadim received his undergraduate degree in engineering science at the University of Toronto. He previously worked as a data scientist in the e-commerce space. Vadim is passionate about machine learning and data science, and is interested in making the field accessible to a broad audience and inspiring readers to innovate and pursue research in artificial intelligence.

Packt is searching for authors like you

If you're interested in becoming an author for Packt, please visit authors.packtpub.com and apply today. We have worked with thousands of developers and tech professionals, just like you, to help them share their insight with the global tech community. You can make a general application, apply for a specific hot topic that we are recruiting an author for, or submit your own idea.

Table of Contents

Preface

The surge in interest in machine learning is due to the fact that it revolutionizes automation by learning patterns in data and using them to make predictions and decisions. If you're interested in machine learning, this book will serve as your entry point.

This edition of *Python Machine Learning By Example* begins with an introduction to important concepts and implementations using Python libraries. Each chapter of the book walks you through an industry-adopted application. You'll implement machine learning techniques in areas such as exploratory data analysis, feature engineering, and natural language processing (NLP) in a clear and easy-to-follow way.

With the help of this extended and updated edition, you'll learn how to tackle data-driven problems and implement your solutions with the powerful yet simple Python language, and popular Python packages and tools such as TensorFlow, scikit-learn, Gensim, and Keras. To aid your understanding of popular machine learning algorithms, this book covers interesting and easy-to-follow examples such as news topic modeling and classification, spam email detection, and stock price forecasting.

By the end of the book, you'll have put together a broad picture of the machine learning ecosystem and will be well-versed with the best practices of applying machine learning techniques to make the most out of new opportunities.

Who this book is for

If you're a machine learning aspirant, data analyst, or a data engineer who's highly passionate about machine learning and wants to begin working on machine learning assignments, this book is for you. Prior knowledge of Python coding is assumed, and basic familiarity with statistical concepts will be beneficial, although not necessary.

What this book covers

Chapter 1, *Getting Started with Machine Learning and Python*, will be the starting point for readers who are looking forward to entering the field of machine learning with Python. It will introduce the essential concepts of machine learning, which we will dig deeper into throughout the rest of the book. In addition, it will discuss the basics of Python for machine learning and explain how to set it up properly for the upcoming examples and projects.

Chapter 2, *Exploring the 20 Newsgroups Dataset with Text Analysis Techniques*, will start developing the first project of the book, exploring and mining the 20 newsgroups dataset, which will be split into two parts—Chapter 2, *Exploring the 20 Newsgroups Dataset with Text Analysis Techniques*, and Chapter 3, *Mining the 20 Newsgroups Dataset with Clustering and Topic Modeling Algorithms*. In this chapter, readers will get familiar with NLP and various NLP libraries that will be used for this project. We will explain several important NLP techniques implementing them in NLTK. We will also cover the dimension reduction technique, especially t-SNE and its use in text data visualization.

Chapter 3, *Mining the 20 Newsgroups Dataset with Clustering and Topic Modeling Algorithms*, will continue our newsgroups project after exploring the 20 newsgroups dataset. In this chapter, readers will learn about unsupervised learning and clustering algorithms, as well as some advanced NLP techniques, such as LDA and word embedding. We will cluster the newsgroups data using the k-means algorithm, and detect topics using NMF and LDA.

Chapter 4, *Detecting Spam Emails with Naive Bayes*, will start our supervised learning journey. In this chapter, we focus on classification with Naïve Bayes, and we'll look at an in-depth implementation. We will also cover other important machine learning concepts, such as classification performance evaluation, model selection and tuning, and cross-validation. Examples including spam email detection will be demonstrated.

Chapter 5, *Classifying Newsgroup Topics with a Support Vector Machine*, will reuse the newsgroups dataset we used in Chapter 2, *Exploring the 20 Newsgroups Dataset with Text Analysis Techniques*, and Chapter 3, *Mining the 20 Newsgroups Dataset with Clustering and Topic Modeling Algorithms*. We will cover multiclass classification, as well as SVM and how they are applied in topic classification. Other important concepts, such as kernel machines, overfitting, and regularization, will be discussed as well.

Chapter 6, *Predicting Online Ad Click-Through with Tree-Based Algorithms*, will introduce and explain decision trees and random forests in depth throughout the course of solving the advertising click-through rate problem. Important concepts of tree-based models such as ensemble, feature importance, and feature selection will also be covered.

Chapter 7, *Predicting Online Ads Click-Through with Logistic Regression*, will introduce and explain logistic regression classifiers on the same project from the previous chapters. We will also cover other concepts, such as categorical variable encoding, L1 and L2 regularization, feature selection, online learning and stochastic gradient descent, and, of course, how to work with large datasets.

`Chapter 8`, *Scaling Up Prediction to Terabyte Click Logs*, covers online advertising click-through prediction, where we have millions of labeled samples in a typical large-scale machine learning problem. In this chapter, we will explore a more scalable solution than the previous chapters, utilizing powerful parallel computing tools such as Apache Hadoop and Spark. We will cover the essential concepts of Spark, such installation, RDD, and core programming, as well as its machine learning components. We will work with the entire dataset of millions of samples, explore the data, build classification models, perform feature engineering, and performance evaluation using Spark, which scales up the computation.

`Chapter 9`, *Stock Price Prediction with Regression Algorithms*, introduces the aim of this project, which is to analyze and predict stock market prices using the Yahoo/Google Finance data, and maybe additional data.

We will start the chapter by covering the challenges in finance and looking at a brief explanation of the related concepts. The next step is to obtain and explore the dataset and start feature engineering after exploratory data analysis. The core section, looking at regression and regression algorithms, linear regression, decision tree regression, SVR, and neural networks, will follow. Readers will also practice solving regression problems using scikit-learn and the TensorFlow API.

`Chapter 10`, *Machine Learning Best Practices*, covers best practices in machine learning. After covering multiple projects in this book, you will have gathered a broad picture of the machine learning ecosystem using Python. However, there will be issues once you start working on projects in the real world. This chapter aims to foolproof your learning and get you ready for production by providing 21 best practices throughout the entire machine learning workflow.

To get the most out of this book

You are expected to have basic knowledge of Python, the basic machine learning algorithms, and some basic Python libraries, such as TensorFlow and Keras, to create smart cognitive actions for your projects.

Download the example code files

You can download the example code files for this book from your account at `www.packt.com`. If you purchased this book elsewhere, you can visit `www.packt.com/support` and register to have the files emailed directly to you.

You can download the code files by following these steps:

1. Log in or register at www.packt.com.
2. Select the **SUPPORT** tab.
3. Click on **Code Downloads & Errata**.
4. Enter the name of the book in the **Search** box and follow the onscreen instructions.

Once the file is downloaded, please make sure that you unzip or extract the folder using the latest version of:

- WinRAR/7-Zip for Windows
- Zipeg/iZip/UnRarX for Mac
- 7-Zip/PeaZip for Linux

The code bundle for the book is also hosted on GitHub at https://github.com/PacktPublishing/Python-Machine-Learning-By-Example-Second-Edition. In case there's an update to the code, it will be updated on the existing GitHub repository.

We also have other code bundles from our rich catalog of books and videos available at https://github.com/PacktPublishing/. Check them out!

Download the color images

We also provide a PDF file that has color images of the screenshots/diagrams used in this book. You can download it here: https://www.packtpub.com/sites/default/files/downloads/9781789616729_ColorImages.pdf.

Conventions used

There are a number of text conventions used throughout this book.

CodeInText: Indicates code words in text, database table names, folder names, filenames, file extensions, pathnames, dummy URLs, user input, and Twitter handles. Here is an example: "Then, we'll load the en_core_web_sm model and parse the sentence using this model."

When we wish to draw your attention to a particular part of a code block, the relevant lines or items are set in bold:

```
[default]
exten => s,1,Dial(Zap/1|30)
exten => s,2,Voicemail(u100)
exten => s,102,Voicemail(b100)
exten => i,1,Voicemail(s0)
```

Any command-line input or output is written as follows:

```
sudo pip install -U nltk
```

Bold: Indicates a new term, an important word, or words that you see onscreen. For example, words in menus or dialog boxes appear in the text like this. Here is an example: "A new window will pop up and ask us which collections (the **Collections** tab in the following screenshot) or corpus (the identifiers in the **Corpora** tab in the following screenshot) to download and where to keep the data."

Warnings or important notes appear like this.

Tips and tricks appear like this.

Get in touch

Feedback from our readers is always welcome.

General feedback: If you have questions about any aspect of this book, mention the book title in the subject of your message and email us at customercare@packtpub.com.

Errata: Although we have taken every care to ensure the accuracy of our content, mistakes do happen. If you have found a mistake in this book, we would be grateful if you would report this to us. Please visit www.packt.com/submit-errata, selecting your book, clicking on the Errata Submission Form link, and entering the details.

Piracy: If you come across any illegal copies of our works in any form on the Internet, we would be grateful if you would provide us with the location address or website name. Please contact us at copyright@packt.com with a link to the material.

If you are interested in becoming an author: If there is a topic that you have expertise in and you are interested in either writing or contributing to a book, please visit `authors.packtpub.com`.

Reviews

Please leave a review. Once you have read and used this book, why not leave a review on the site that you purchased it from? Potential readers can then see and use your unbiased opinion to make purchase decisions, we at Packt can understand what you think about our products, and our authors can see your feedback on their book. Thank you!

For more information about Packt, please visit `packt.com`.

Section 1: Fundamentals of Machine Learning

In this section, readers will learn about the essential concepts in machine learning, including types of machine learning tasks, the core of machine learning, and an overview of data processing and modeling. Readers will also have a chance to set up the working environment of the rest of the book, and will learn how to install Python machine learning packages properly.

The following chapter is in this section:

- Chapter 1, *Getting Started with Machine Learning and Python*

Getting Started with Machine Learning and Python

1

We kick off our Python and machine learning journey with the basic, yet important, concepts of machine learning. We'll start with what machine learning is about, why we need it, and its evolution over a few decades. We'll then discuss typical machine learning tasks and explore several essential techniques of working with data and working with models. It's a great starting point for the subject and we'll learn it in a fun way. Trust me. At the end, we'll also set up the software and tools needed for this book.

We'll go into detail on the following topics:

- Overview of machine learning and the importance of machine learning
- The core of machine learning—generalizing with data
- Overfitting
- Underfitting
- Bias variance trade-off
- Techniques to avoid overfitting
- Techniques for data preprocessing
- Techniques for feature engineering
- Techniques for model aggregation
- Software installing
- Python package setup

Defining machine learning and why we need it

Machine learning is a term coined around 1960, composed of two words—**machine** corresponds to a computer, robot, or other device, and **learning** refers to an activity intended to acquire or discover event patterns, which we humans are good at.

So, why do we need machine learning and why do we want a machine to learn as a human? First and foremost, of course, computers and robots can work 24/7 and don't get tired, need breaks, call in sick, or go on strike. Their maintenance is much lower than a human's and costs a lot less in the long run. Also, for sophisticated problems that involve a variety of huge datasets or complex calculations, for instance, it's much more justifiable, not to mention intelligent, to let computers do all of the work. Machines driven by algorithms designed by humans are able to learn latent rules and inherent patterns and to fulfill tasks desired by humans. Learning machines are better suited than humans for tasks that are routine, repetitive, or tedious. Beyond that, automation by machine learning can mitigate risks caused by fatigue or inattention. Self-driving cars, as shown in the following photograph, are a great example: a vehicle capable of navigating by sensing its environment and making its decision without human input. Another example is the use of robotic arms in production lines, capable of causing a significant reduction in injuries and costs:

Assume humans don't fatigue or we have resources to hire enough shift workers, would machine learning still have a place? Of course it would; there are many cases, reported and unreported, where machines perform comparably or even better than domain experts. As algorithms are designed to learn from the ground truth, and the best-thought decisions made by human experts, machines can perform just as well as experts. In reality, even the best expert makes mistakes. Machines can minimize the chance of making wrong decisions by utilizing collective intelligence from individual experts. A major study that found machines are better than doctors at diagnosing some types of cancer proves this philosophy, for instance. **AlphaGo** is probably the best known example of machines beating human masters. Also, it's much more scalable to deploy learning machines than to train individuals to become experts, economically and socially. We can distribute thousands of diagnostic devices across the globe within a week but it's almost impossible to recruit and assign the same number of qualified doctors.

Now you may argue: what if we have sufficient resources and capacity to hire the best domain experts and later aggregate their opinions—would machine learning still have a place? Probably not—learning machines might not perform better than the joint efforts of the most intelligent humans. However, individuals equipped with learning machines can outperform the best group of experts. This is actually an emerging concept called **AI-based Assistance** or **AI Plus Human Intelligence**, which advocates combining the efforts of machine learners and humans. We can summarize the previous statement in the following inequality:

human + machine learning → most intelligent tireless human $\gtrless$ machine learning > human

A medical operation involving robots is one example of the best human and machine learning synergy. The following photograph presents robotic arms in an operation room alongside the surgery doctor:

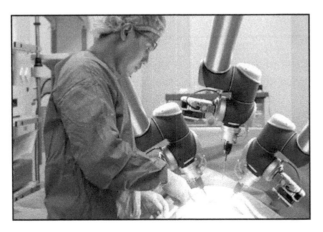

So, does machine learning simply equate to automation that involves the programming and execution of human-crafted or human-curated rule sets? A popular myth says that the majority of code in the world has to do with simple rules possibly programmed in Common Business Oriented Language (COBOL), which covers the bulk of all of the possible scenarios of client interactions. So, if the answer to that question is yes, why can't we just hire many software programmers and continue programming new rules or extending old rules?

One reason is that defining, maintaining, and updating rules becomes more and more expensive over time. The number of possible patterns for an activity or event could be enormous and, therefore, exhausting all enumeration isn't practically feasible. It gets even more challenging when it comes to events that are dynamic, ever-changing, or evolving in real time. It's much easier and more efficient to develop learning algorithms that command computers to learn and extract patterns and to figure things out themselves from abundant data.

The difference between machine learning and traditional programming can be described using the following diagram:

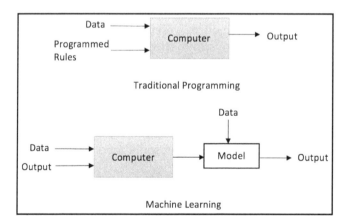

Another reason is that the volume of data is exponentially growing. Nowadays, the floods of textual, audio, image, and video data are hard to fathom. The **Internet of Things** (**IoT**) is a recent development of a new kind of internet, which interconnects everyday devices. The IoT will bring data from household appliances and autonomous cars to the forefront. The average company these days has mostly human clients but, for instance, social media companies tend to have many bot accounts. This trend is likely to continue and we'll have more machines talking to each other. Besides the quantity, the quality of data available has kept increasing in the past years due to cheaper storage. This has empowered the evolution of machine learning algorithms and data-driven solutions.

Jack Ma, co-founder of the e-commerce company Alibaba, explained in a speech that IT was the focus of the past 20 years but, for the next 30 years, we'll be in the age of **Data Technology** (**DT**). During the age of IT, companies grew larger and stronger thanks to computer software and infrastructure. Now that businesses in most industries have already gathered enormous amounts of data, it's presently the right time to exploit DT to unlock insights, derive patterns, and boost new business growth. Broadly speaking, machine learning technologies enable businesses to better understand customer behavior, engage with customers, and optimize operations management. As for us individuals, machine learning technologies are already making our lives better every day.

An application of machine learning with which we're all familiar is spam email filtering. Another is online advertising, where ads are served automatically based on information advertisers have collected about us. Stay tuned for the next chapters, where we'll learn how to develop algorithms in solving these two problems and more. A search engine is an application of machine learning we can't imagine living without. It involves information retrieval, which parses what we look for, queries related to records, and applies contextual ranking and personalized ranking, which sorts pages by topical relevance and user preference. E-commerce and media companies have been at the forefront of employing recommendation systems, which help customers to find products, services, and articles faster. The application of machine learning is boundless and we just keep hearing new examples everyday: credit card fraud detection, disease diagnosis, presidential election prediction, instant speech translation, and robot advisors—you name it!

In the 1983 *War Games* movie, a computer made life-and-death decisions that could have resulted in Word War III. As far as we know, technology wasn't able to pull off such feats at the time. However, in 1997, the Deep Blue supercomputer did manage to beat a world chess champion. In 2005, a Stanford self-driving car drove by itself for more than 130 kilometers in a desert. In 2007, the car of another team drove through regular traffic for more than 50 kilometers. In 2011, the Watson computer won a quiz against human opponents. In 2016, the AlphaGo program beat one of the best Go players in the world. If we assume that computer hardware is the limiting factor, then we can try to extrapolate into the future. Ray Kurzweil did just that and, according to him, we can expect human level intelligence around 2029. What's next?

A very high-level overview of machine learning technology

Machine learning mimicking human intelligence is a subfield of AI—a field of computer science concerned with creating systems. Software engineering is another field in computer science. Generally, we can label Python programming as a type of software engineering. Machine learning is also closely related to linear algebra, probability theory, statistics, and mathematical optimization. We usually build machine learning models based on statistics, probability theory, and linear algebra, then optimize the models using mathematical optimization. The majority of you reading this book should have a good, or at least sufficient, command of Python programming. Those who aren't feeling confident about mathematical knowledge might be wondering how much time should be spent learning or brushing up on the aforementioned subjects. Don't panic: we'll get machine learning to work for us without going into any mathematical details in this book. It just requires some basic 101 knowledge of probability theory and linear algebra, which helps us to understand the mechanics of machine learning techniques and algorithms. And it gets easier as we'll be building models both from scratch and with popular packages in Python, a language we like and are familiar with.

For those who want to learn or brush up on probability theory and linear algebra, feel free to search for *basic probability theory* and *basic linear algebra*. There are a lot of resources online, for example, `https://people.ucsc.edu/~abrsvn/intro_prob_1.pdf` on probability 101 and `http://www.maths.gla.ac.uk/~ajb/dvi-ps/2w-notes.pdf` about basic linear algebra.

Those who want to study machine learning systematically can enroll into computer science, **Artificial Intelligence** (**AI**), and, more recently, data science masters programs. There are also various data science boot camps. However, the selection for boot camps is usually stricter as they're more job-oriented and the program duration is often short, ranging from 4 to 10 weeks. Another option is the free **Massive Open Online Courses** (**MOOCs**), Andrew Ng's popular course on machine learning. Last but not least, industry blogs and websites are great resources for us to keep up with the latest developments.

Machine learning isn't only a skill but also a bit of sport. We can compete in several machine learning competitions, such as Kaggle (`www.kaggle.com`)—sometimes for decent cash prizes, sometimes for joy, and most of the time to play our strengths. However, to win these competitions, we may need to utilize certain techniques, which are only useful in the context of competitions and not in the context of trying to solve a business problem. That's right, the **no free lunch** theorem applies here.

Types of machine learning tasks

A machine learning system is fed with input data—this can be numerical, textual, visual, or audiovisual. The system usually has an output—this can be a floating-point number, for instance, the acceleration of a self-driving car, or can be an integer representing a category (also called a **class**), for example, a cat or tiger from image recognition.

The main task of machine learning is to explore and construct algorithms that can learn from historical data and make predictions on new input data. For a data-driven solution, we need to define (or have it defined to us by an algorithm) an evaluation function called **loss** or **cost function**, which measures how well the models are learning. In this setup, we create an optimization problem with the goal of learning in the most efficient and effective way.

Depending on the nature of the learning data, machine learning tasks can be broadly classified into the following three categories:

- **Unsupervised learning**: When the learning data only contains indicative signals without any description attached, it's up to us to find the structure of the data underneath, to discover hidden information, or to determine how to describe the data. This kind of learning data is called **unlabeled** data. Unsupervised learning can be used to detect anomalies, such as fraud or defective equipment, or to group customers with similar online behaviors for a marketing campaign.
- **Supervised learning**: When learning data comes with a description, targets, or desired output besides indicative signals, the learning goal becomes to find a general rule that maps input to output. This kind of learning data is called **labeled** data. The learned rule is then used to label new data with unknown output. The labels are usually provided by event-logging systems and human experts. Besides, if it's feasible, they may also be produced by members of the public, through crowd-sourcing, for instance. Supervised learning is commonly used in daily applications, such as face and speech recognition, products or movie recommendations, and sales forecasting.

  We can further subdivide supervised learning into regression and classification. **Regression** trains on and predicts continuous-valued response, for example, predicting house prices, while **classification** attempts to find the appropriate class label, such as analyzing a positive/negative sentiment and prediction loan default.

If not all learning samples are labeled, but some are, we'll have **semi-supervised learning**. It makes use of unlabeled data (typically a large amount) for training, besides a small amount of labeled data. Semi-supervised learning is applied in cases where it's expensive to acquire a fully labeled dataset and more practical to label a small subset. For example, it often requires skilled experts to label hyperspectral remote sensing images and lots of field experiments to locate oil at a particular location, while acquiring unlabeled data is relatively easy.

- **Reinforcement learning**: Learning data provides feedback so that the system adapts to dynamic conditions in order to achieve a certain goal in the end. The system evaluates its performance based on the feedback responses and reacts accordingly. The best known instances include self-driving cars and the chess master, AlphaGo.

The following diagram depicts types of machine learning tasks:

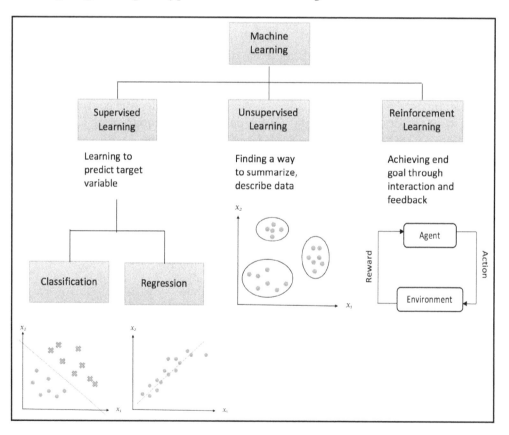

Feeling a little bit confused by the abstract concepts? Don't worry. We'll encounter many concrete examples of these types of machine learning tasks later in this book. In Chapter 2, *Exploring the 20 Newsgroups Dataset with Text Analysis Techniques*, and Chapter 3, *Mining the 20 Newsgroups Dataset with Clustering and Topic Modeling Algorithms*, we'll explore unsupervised techniques and algorithms; in Chapter 4, *Detecting Spam Email with Naive Bayes*, and Chapter 8, *Scaling Up Prediction to Terabyte Click Logs*, we'll work on supervised learning tasks and several classification algorithms; in Chapter 9, *Stock Price Prediction with Regression Algorithms*, we'll continue with another supervised learning task, regression, and assorted regression algorithms.

A brief history of the development of machine learning algorithms

In fact, we have a whole zoo of machine learning algorithms that have experienced varying popularity over time. We can roughly categorize them into four main approaches such as logic-based learning, statistical learning, artificial neural networks, and genetic algorithms.

The logic-based systems were the first to be dominant. They used basic rules specified by human experts and, with these rules, systems tried to reason using formal logic, background knowledge, and hypotheses. In the mid-1980s, **artificial neural networks** (**ANNs**) came to the foreground, to be then pushed aside by statistical learning systems in the 1990s. ANNs imitate animal brains and consist of interconnected neurons that are also an imitation of biological neurons. They try to model complex relationships between input and output values and to capture patterns in data. Genetic algorithms (GA) were popular in the 1990s. They mimic the biological process of evolution and try to find the optimal solutions using methods such as mutation and crossover.

We are currently seeing a revolution in **deep learning**, which we might consider a rebranding of neural networks. The term deep learning was coined around 2006 and refers to deep neural networks with many layers. The breakthrough in deep learning is caused by the integration and utilization of **Graphical Processing Units** (**GPUs**), which massively speed up computation. GPUs were originally developed to render video games and are very good in parallel matrix and vector algebra. It's believed that deep learning resembles the way humans learn, therefore, it may be able to deliver on the promise of sentient machines.

Some of us may have heard of **Moore's law**—an empirical observation claiming that computer hardware improves exponentially with time. The law was first formulated by Gordon Moore, the co-founder of Intel, in 1965. According to the law, the number of transistors on a chip should double every two years. In the following diagram, you can see that the law holds up nicely (the size of the bubbles corresponds to the average transistor count in GPUs):

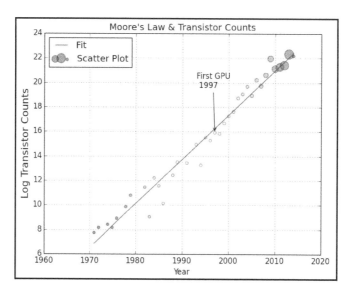

The consensus seems to be that Moore's law should continue to be valid for a couple of decades. This gives some credibility to Ray Kurzweil's predictions of achieving true machine intelligence in 2029.

Core of machine learning – generalizing with data

The good thing about data is that there's a lot of it in the world. The bad thing is that it's hard to process this data. The challenges stem from the diversity and noisiness of the data. We humans usually process data coming into our ears and eyes. These inputs are transformed into electrical or chemical signals. On a very basic level, computers and robots also work with electrical signals. These electrical signals are then translated into ones and zeroes. However, we program in Python in this book and, on that level, normally we represent the data either as numbers, images, or texts. Actually, images and text aren't very convenient, so we need to transform images and text into numerical values.

Especially in the context of supervised learning, we have a scenario similar to studying for an exam. We have a set of practice questions and the actual exams. We should be able to answer exam questions without knowing the answers to them. This is called **generalization**—we learn something from our practice questions and, hopefully, are able to apply the knowledge to other similar questions. In machine learning, these practice questions are called **training sets** or **training samples**. They're where the models derive patterns from. And the actual exams are **testing sets** or **testing samples**. They're where the models eventually apply and how compatible they are is what it's all about. Sometimes, between practice questions and actual exams, we have mock exams to assess how well we'll do in actual ones and to aid revision. These mock exams are called **validation sets** or **validation samples** in machine learning. They help us to verify how well the models will perform in a simulated setting, then we fine-tune the models accordingly in order to achieve greater hits.

An old-fashioned programmer would talk to a business analyst or other expert, then implement a rule that adds a certain value multiplied by another value corresponding, for instance, to tax rules. In a machine learning setting, we give the computer example input values and example output values. Or if we're more ambitious, we can feed the program the actual tax texts and let the machine process the data further, just like an autonomous car doesn't need a lot of human input.

This means implicitly that there's some function, for instance, a tax formula, we're trying to figure out. In physics, we have almost the same situation. We want to know how the universe works and formulate laws in a mathematical language. Since we don't know the actual function, all we can do is measure the error produced and try to minimize it. In supervised learning tasks, we compare our results against the expected values. In unsupervised learning, we measure our success with related metrics. For instance, we want clusters of data to be well defined; the metrics could be how similar the data points within one cluster are, and how different the data points from two clusters are. In reinforcement learning, a program evaluates its moves, for example, using some predefined function in a chess game.

Other than the normal generalizing with data, there can be two levels of generalization, over and under generalization, which we'll explore in the next section.

Overfitting, underfitting, and the bias-variance trade-off

Overfitting is a very important concept, hence, we're discussing it here, early in this book.

If we go through many practice questions for an exam, we may start to find ways to answer questions that have nothing to do with the subject material. For instance, given only five practice questions, we find that if there are two occurrences of *potatoes*, one *tomato*, and three occurrences of *banana* in a question, the answer is always *A* and if there is one *potato*, three occurrences of *tomato*, and two occurrences of banana in a question, the answer is always *B*, then we conclude this is always true and apply such a theory later on, even though the subject or answer may not be relevant to potatoes, tomatoes, or bananas. Or even worse, you may memorize the answers to each question verbatim. We can then score high on the practice questions; we do so with the hope that the questions in the actual exams will be the same as the practice questions. However, in reality, we'll score very low on the exam questions as it's rare that the exact same questions will occur in the exams.

The phenomenon of memorization can cause overfitting. This can occur when we're over extracting too much information from the training sets and making our model just work well with them, which is called **low bias** in machine learning. In case you need a quick recap of bias, here it is: *Bias* is the difference between the average prediction and the true value. It's computed as follows:

$$Bias[\hat{y}] = E[\hat{y} - y]$$

Here, $\hat{y}$ is the prediction. At the same time, however, overfitting won't help us to generalize with data and derive true patterns from it. The model, as a result, will perform poorly on datasets that weren't seen before. We call this situation **high variance** in machine learning. Again, a quick recap of variance: *Variance* measures the spread of the prediction, which is the variability of the prediction. It can be calculated as follows:

$$Variance[\hat{y}] = E[\hat{y}^2] - E[\hat{y}]^2$$

The following example demonstrates what a typical instance of overfitting looks like, where the regression curve tries to flawlessly accommodate all samples:

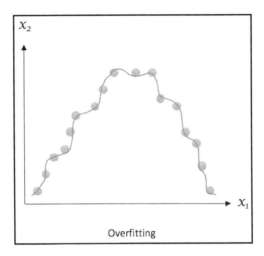

Overfitting

Overfitting occurs when we try to describe the learning rules based on too many parameters relative to the small number of observations, instead of the underlying relationship, such as the preceding example of potato and tomato where we deduced three parameters from only five learning samples. Overfitting also takes place when we make the model excessively complex so that it fits every training sample, such as memorizing the answers for all questions, as mentioned previously.

The opposite scenario is **underfitting**. When a model is underfit, it doesn't perform well on the training sets and won't do so on the testing sets, which means it fails to capture the underlying trend of the data. Underfitting may occur if we aren't using enough data to train the model, just like we'll fail the exam if we don't review enough material; it may also happen if we're trying to fit a wrong model to the data, just like we'll score low in any exercises or exams if we take the wrong approach and learn it the wrong way. We call any of these situations **high bias** in machine learning; although its variance is low as performance in training and test sets are pretty consistent, in a bad way.

The following example shows what a typical underfitting looks like, where the regression curve doesn't fit the data well enough or capture enough of the underlying pattern of the data:

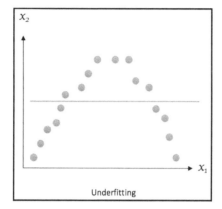

Underfitting

After the overfitting and underfitting example, let's look at what a well-fitting example should look like:

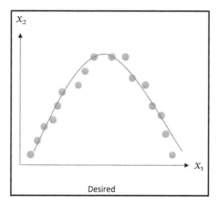

Desired

We want to avoid both overfitting and underfitting. **Recall bias** is the error stemming from incorrect assumptions in the learning algorithm; high bias results in underfitting, and variance measures how sensitive the model prediction is to variations in the datasets. Hence, we need to avoid cases where either bias or variance is getting high. So, does it mean we should always make both bias and variance as low as possible? The answer is yes, if we can. But, in practice, there's an explicit trade-off between them, where decreasing one increases the other. This is the so-called **bias-variance trade-off**. Sounds abstract? Let's take a look at the next example.

Let's say we're asked to build a model to predict the probability of a candidate being the next president based on phone poll data. The poll was conducted using zip codes. We randomly choose samples from one zip code and we estimate there's a 61% chance the candidate will win. However, it turns out he loses the election. Where did our model go wrong? The first thing we think of is the small size of samples from only one zip code. It's a source of high bias also, because people in a geographic area tend to share similar demographics, although it results in a low variance of estimates. So, can we fix it simply by using samples from a large number of zip codes? Yes, but don't get happy so early. This might cause an increased variance of estimates at the same time. We need to find the optimal sample size—the best number of zip codes to achieve the lowest overall bias and variance.

Minimizing the total error of a model requires a careful balancing of bias and variance. Given a set of training samples $x_1, x_2, ..., x_n$ and their targets $y_1, y_2, ..., y_n$, we want to find a regression function $\hat{y}(x)$ that estimates the true relation $y(x)$ as correctly as possible. We measure the error of estimation, how good (or bad) the regression model is **mean squared error** (**MSE**):

$$MSE = E\left[(y(x) - \hat{y}(x))^2\right]$$

The E denotes the expectation. This error can be decomposed into bias and variance components following the analytical derivation as shown in the following formula (although it requires a bit of basic probability theory to understand):

$$MSE = E\left[(y - \hat{y})^2\right]$$
$$= E\left[(y - E[\hat{y}] + E[\hat{y}] - \hat{y})^2\right]$$
$$= E\left[(y - E[\hat{y}])^2\right] + E\left[(E[\hat{y}] - \hat{y})^2\right] + E\left[2(y - E[\hat{y}])(E[\hat{y}] - \hat{y})\right]$$
$$= E\left[(y - E[\hat{y}])^2\right] + E\left[(E[\hat{y}] - \hat{y})^2\right] + 2(y - E[\hat{y}])(E[\hat{y}] - E[\hat{y}])$$
$$= \left(E[\hat{y} - y]\right)^2 + E[\hat{y}^2] - E[\hat{y}]^2$$
$$= Bias[\hat{y}]^2 + Variance[\hat{y}]$$

The *Bias* term measures the error of estimations and the *Variance* term describes how much the estimation $\hat{y}$ moves around its mean. The more complex the learning model $\hat{y}(x)$ is and the larger size of training samples, the lower the bias will be. However, these will also create more shift on the model in order to better fit the increased data points. As a result, the variance will be lifted.

We usually employ cross-validation technique as well as regularization and feature reduction to find the optimal model balancing bias and variance and to diminish overfitting.

 You may ask why we only want to deal with overfitting: how about underfitting? This is because underfitting can be easily recognized: it occurs as long as the model doesn't work well on a training set. And we need to find a better model or tweak some parameters to better fit the data, which is a must under all circumstances. On the other hand, overfitting is hard to spot. Sometimes, when we achieve a model that performs well on a training set, we're overly happy and think it ready for production right away. This happens all of the time despite how dangerous it could be. We should instead take extra step to make sure the great performance isn't due to overfitting and the great performance applies to data excluding the training data.

Avoiding overfitting with cross-validation

Recall that between practice questions and actual exams, there are mock exams where we can assess how well we'll perform in actual exams and use that information to conduct necessary revision. In machine learning, the validation procedure helps evaluate how the models will generalize to independent or unseen datasets in a simulated setting. In a conventional validation setting, the original data is partitioned into three subsets, usually 60% for the training set, 20% for the validation set, and the rest (20%) for the testing set. This setting suffices if we have enough training samples after partitioning and we only need a rough estimate of simulated performance. Otherwise, cross-validation is preferable.

In one round of cross-validation, the original data is divided into two subsets, for **training** and **testing** (or **validation**) respectively. The testing performance is recorded. Similarly, multiple rounds of cross-validation are performed under different partitions. Testing results from all rounds are finally averaged to generate a more reliable estimate of model prediction performance. Cross-validation helps to reduce variability and, therefore, limit overfitting.

 When the training size is very large, it's often sufficient to split it into training, validation, and testing (three subsets) and conduct a performance check on the latter two. Cross-validation is less preferable in this case since it's computationally costly to train a model for each single round. But if you can afford it, there's no reason not to use cross-validation. When the size isn't so large, cross-validation is definitely a good choice.

There are mainly two cross-validation schemes in use, exhaustive and non-exhaustive. In the exhaustive scheme, we leave out a fixed number of observations in each round as testing (or validation) samples and the remaining observations as training samples. This process is repeated until all possible different subsets of samples are used for testing once. For instance, we can apply **Leave-One-Out-Cross-Validation (LOOCV)** and let each datum be in the testing set once. For a dataset of the size n, LOOCV requires n rounds of cross-validation. This can be slow when n gets large. This following diagram presents the workflow of LOOCV:

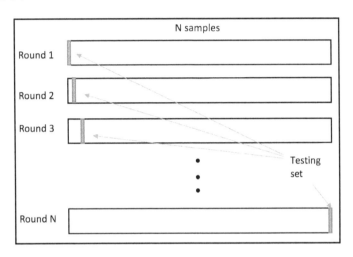

A non-exhaustive scheme, on the other hand, as the name implies, doesn't try out all possible partitions. The most widely used type of this scheme is **k-fold cross-validation**. The original data first randomly splits the data into **k equal-sized** folds. In each trial, one of these folds becomes the testing set, and the rest of the data becomes the training set. We repeat this process k times, with each fold being the designated testing set once. Finally, we average the k sets of test results for the purpose of evaluation. Common values for k are 3, 5, and 10. The following table illustrates the setup for five-fold:

Round	Fold 1	Fold 2	Fold 3	Fold 4	Fold 5
1	Testing	Training	Training	Training	Training
2	Training	Testing	Training	Training	Training
3	Training	Training	Testing	Training	Training
4	Training	Training	Training	Testing	Training
5	Training	Training	Training	Training	Testing

K-fold cross-validation often has a lower variance compared to LOOCV, since we're using a chunk of samples instead a single one for validation.

We can also randomly split the data into training and testing sets numerous times. This is formally called the **holdout** method. The problem with this algorithm is that some samples may never end up in the testing set, while some may be selected multiple times in the testing set.

Last but not the least, **nested cross-validation** is a combination of cross-validations. It consists of the following two phases:

- **Inner cross-validation**: This phase is conducted to find the best fit and can be implemented as a k-fold cross-validation
- **Outer cross-validation**: This phase is used for performance evaluation and statistical analysis

We'll apply cross-validation very intensively throughout this entire book. Before that, let's look at cross-validation with an analogy next, which will help us to better understand it.

A data scientist plans to take his car to work and his goal is to arrive before 9 a.m. every day. He needs to decide the departure time and the route to take. He tries out different combinations of these two parameters on some Mondays, Tuesdays, and Wednesdays and records the arrival time for each trial. He then figures out the best schedule and applies it every day. However, it doesn't work quite as well as expected. It turns out the scheduling **model** is overfit with data points gathered in the first three days and may not work well on Thursdays and Fridays. A better solution would be to test the best combination of parameters derived from Mondays to Wednesdays on Thursdays and Fridays and similarly repeat this process based on different sets of learning days and testing days of the week. This analogized cross-validation ensures the selected schedule works for the whole week.

In summary, cross-validation derives a more accurate assess of model performance by combining measures of prediction performance on different subsets of data. This technique not only reduces variances and avoids overfitting, but also gives an insight into how the model will generally perform in practice.

Avoiding overfitting with regularization

Another way of preventing overfitting is **regularization.** Recall that the unnecessary complexity of the model is a source of overfitting. Regularization adds extra parameters to the error function we're trying to minimize, in order to penalize complex models.

According to the principle of Occam's Razor, simpler methods are to be favored. William Occam was a monk and philosopher who, in around the year 1320, came up with the idea that the simplest hypothesis that fits data should be preferred. One justification is that we can invent fewer simple models than complex models. For instance, intuitively, we know that there are more high-polynomial models than linear ones. The reason is that a line ($y=ax+b$) is governed by only two parameters—the intercept b and slope a. The possible coefficients for a line span two-dimensional space. A quadratic polynomial adds an extra coefficient for the quadratic term, and we can span a three-dimensional space with the coefficients. Therefore, it is much easier to find a model that perfectly captures all training data points with a **High order polynomial function**, as its search space is much larger than that of a linear function. However, these easily obtained models generalize worse than linear models, which are more prompt to overfitting. And, of course, simpler models require less computation time. The following diagram displays how we try to fit a **Linear function** and a **High order polynomial function** respectively to the data:

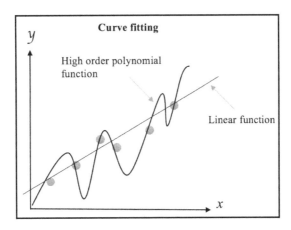

The linear model is preferable as it may generalize better to more data points drawn from the underlying distribution. We can use regularization to reduce the influence of the high orders of polynomial by imposing penalties on them. This will discourage complexity, even though a less accurate and less strict rule is learned from the training data.

We'll employ regularization quite often starting from Chapter 7, *Predicting Online Ads Click-Through with Logistic Regression*. For now, next let's see an analogy to help us to understand it better.

A data scientist wants to equip his robotic guard dog with the ability to identify strangers and his friends. He feeds it with the the following learning samples:

Male	Young	Tall	With glasses	In grey	**Friend**
Female	Middle	Average	Without glasses	In black	**Stranger**
Male	Young	Short	With glasses	In white	**Friend**
Male	Senior	Short	Without glasses	In black	**Stranger**
Female	Young	Average	With glasses	In white	**Friend**
Male	Young	Short	Without glasses	In red	**Friend**

The robot may quickly learn the following rules:

- Any middle-aged female of average height without glasses and dressed in black is a stranger
- Any senior short male without glasses and dressed in black is a stranger
- Anyone else is his friend

Although these perfectly fit the training data, they seem too complicated and unlikely to generalize well to new visitors. In contrast, the data scientist limits the learning aspects. A loose rule that can work well for hundreds of other visitors could be: anyone without glasses dressed in black is a stranger.

Besides penalizing complexity, we can also stop a training procedure early as a form of regularization. If we limit the time a model spends learning or we set some internal stopping criteria, it's more likely to produce a simpler model. The model complexity will be controlled in this way and hence overfitting becomes less probable. This approach is called **early stopping** in machine learning.

Last but not least, it's worth noting that regularization should be kept at a moderate level or, to be more precise, fine-tuned to an optimal level. Too small a regularization doesn't make any impact; too large a regularization will result in underfitting, as it moves the model away from the ground truth. We'll explore how to achieve optimal regularization in Chapter 7, *Predicting Online Ads Click-Through with Logistic Regression*, and Chapter 9, *Stock Price Prediction with Regression Algorithms*.

Avoiding overfitting with feature selection and dimensionality reduction

We typically represent data as a grid of numbers (a **matrix**). Each column represents a variable, which we call a **feature** in machine learning. In supervised learning, one of the variables is actually not a feature, but the label that we're trying to predict. And in supervised learning, each row is an example that we can use for training or testing.

The number of features corresponds to the dimensionality of the data. Our machine learning approach depends on the number of dimensions versus the number of examples. For instance, text and image data are very high dimensional, while stock market data has relatively fewer dimensions.

Fitting high-dimensional data is computationally expensive and is prone to overfitting due to the high complexity. Higher dimensions are also impossible to visualize, and therefore we can't use simple diagnostic methods.

Not all of the features are useful and they may only add randomness to our results. It's therefore often important to do good feature selection. **Feature selection** is the process of picking a subset of significant features for use in better model construction. In practice, not every feature in a dataset carries information useful for discriminating samples; some features are either redundant or irrelevant, and hence can be discarded with little loss.

In principle, feature selection boils down to multiple binary decisions about whether to include a feature or not. For n features, we get 2^n feature sets, which can be a very large number for a large number of features. For example, for 10 features, we have 1,024 possible feature sets (for instance, if we're deciding what clothes to wear, the features can be temperature, rain, the weather forecast, where we're going, and so on). At a certain point, brute force evaluation becomes infeasible. We'll discuss better methods in Chapter 6, *Predicting Online Ads Click-Through with Tree-Based Algorithms*. Basically, we have two options: we either start with all of the features and remove features iteratively or we start with a minimum set of features and add features iteratively. We then take the best feature sets for each iteration and compare them.

We'll explore how to perform feature selection mainly in Chapter 7, *Predicting Online Ads Click-Through with Logistic Regression*.

Another common approach of reducing dimensionality is to transform high-dimensional data in lower-dimensional space. It's called **dimensionality reduction** or **feature projection**. This transformation leads to information loss, but we can keep the loss to a minimum.

We'll talk about and implement dimensionality reduction in `Chapter 2`, *Exploring the 20 Newsgroups Dataset with Text Analysis Techniques,* `Chapter 3`, *Mining the 20 Newsgroups Dataset with Clustering and Topic Modeling Algorithms,* and `chapter 10`, *Machine Learning Best Practices*

Preprocessing, exploration, and feature engineering

Data mining, a buzzword in the 1990s, is the predecessor of data science (the science of data). One of the methodologies popular in the data mining community is called **Cross-Industry Standard Process for Data Mining** (**CRISP-DM**). CRISP-DM was created in 1996 and is still used today. I'm not endorsing CRISP-DM, however, I do like its general framework.

The CRISP DM consists of the following phases, which aren't mutually exclusive and can occur in parallel:

- **Business understanding**: This phase is often taken care of by specialized domain experts. Usually, we have a business person formulate a business problem, such as selling more units of a certain product.
- **Data understanding**: This is also a phase that may require input from domain experts, however, often a technical specialist needs to get involved more than in the business understanding phase. The domain expert may be proficient with spreadsheet programs, but have trouble with complicated data. In this book, it's usually termed as **phase exploration**.
- **Data preparation**: This is also a phase where a domain expert with only Microsoft Excel knowledge may not be able to help you. This is the phase where we create our training and test datasets. In this book, it's usually termed as **phase preprocessing**.
- **Modeling**: This is the phase most people associate with machine learning. In this phase, we formulate a model and fit our data.
- **Evaluation**: In this phase, we evaluate how well the model fits the data to check whether we were able to solve our business problem.
- **Deployment**: This phase usually involves setting up the system in a production environment (it's considered good practice to have a separate production system). Typically, this is done by a specialized team.

When we learn, we require high-quality learning material. We can't learn from gibberish, so we automatically ignore anything that doesn't make sense. A machine learning system isn't able to recognize gibberish, so we need to help it by cleaning the input data. It's often claimed that cleaning the data forms a large part of machine learning. Sometimes cleaning is already done for us, but you shouldn't count on it.

To decide how to clean the data, we need to be familiar with the data. There are some projects that try to automatically explore the data and do something intelligent, such as produce a report. For now, unfortunately, we don't have a solid solution, so you need to do some manual work.

We can do two things, which aren't mutually exclusive: first, scan the data and second, visualize the data. This also depends on the type of data we're dealing with—whether we have a grid of numbers, images, audio, text, or something else. In the end, a grid of numbers is the most convenient form, and we'll always work toward having numerical features. Let's pretend that we have a table of numbers in the rest of this section.

We want to know whether features have missing values, how the values are distributed, and what type of features we have. Values can approximately follow a normal distribution, a binomial distribution, a Poisson distribution, or another distribution altogether. Features can be binary: either yes or no, positive or negative, and so on. They can also be categorical: pertaining to a category, for instance, continents (Africa, Asia, Europe, Latin America, North America, and so on). Categorical variables can also be ordered, for instance, high, medium, and low. Features can also be quantitative, for example, temperature in degrees or price in dollars.

Feature engineering is the process of creating or improving features. It's more of a dark art than a science. Features are often created based on common sense, domain knowledge, or prior experience. There are certain common techniques for feature creation, however, there's no guarantee that creating new features will improve your results. We're sometimes able to use the clusters found by unsupervised learning as extra features. **Deep neural networks** are often able to derive features automatically. We'll briefly look at several techniques such as polynomial features, power transformations, and binning, as appetizers in this chapter.

Missing values

Quite often we miss values for certain features. This could happen for various reasons. It can be inconvenient, expensive, or even impossible to always have a value. Maybe we weren't able to measure a certain quantity in the past because we didn't have the right equipment or just didn't know that the feature was relevant. However, we're stuck with missing values from the past.

Sometimes, it's easy to figure out we're missing values and we can discover this just by scanning the data or counting the number of values we have for a feature and comparing to the number of values we expect based on the number of rows. Certain systems encode missing values with, for example, values such as 999,999 or -1. This makes sense if the valid values are much smaller than 999,999. If you're lucky, you'll have information about the features provided by whoever created the data in the form of a data dictionary or metadata.

Once we know that we're missing values, the question arises of how to deal with them. The simplest answer is to just ignore them. However, some algorithms can't deal with missing values, and the program will just refuse to continue. In other circumstances, ignoring missing values will lead to inaccurate results. The second solution is to substitute missing values with a fixed value—this is called **imputing**. We can impute the arithmetic **mean**, **median,** or **mode** of the valid values of a certain feature. Ideally, we'll have a relation between features or within a variable that's somewhat reliable. For instance, we may know the seasonal averages of temperature for a certain location and be able to impute guesses for missing temperature values given a date. We'll talk about dealing with missing data in detail in `Chapter 10`, *Machine Learning Best Practices*. Similarly, techniques in the following sections will be discussed and employed in later chapters, in case you feel lost.

Label encoding

Humans are able to deal with various types of values. Machine learning algorithms (with some exceptions) need numerical values. If we offer a string such as `Ivan`, unless we're using specialized software, the program won't know what to do. In this example, we're dealing with a categorical feature—names, probably. We can consider each unique value to be a label. (In this particular example, we also need to decide what to do with the case—is `Ivan` the same as `ivan`?). We can then replace each label with an integer—**label encoding**.

The following example shows how label encoding works:

Label	Encoded Label
Africa	1
Asia	2
Europe	3
South America	4
North America	5
Other	6

This approach can be problematic, because the learner may conclude that there's an order. For example, `Asia` and `North America` in the preceding case differ by 4 after encoding, which is a bit counter-intuitive.

One hot encoding

The **one-of-K** or **one hot encoding** scheme uses dummy variables to encode categorical features. Originally, it was applied to digital circuits. The dummy variables have binary values such as bits, so they take the values zero or one (equivalent to true or false). For instance, if we want to encode continents, we'll have dummy variables, such as `is_asia`, which will be true if the continent is `Asia` and false otherwise. In general, we need as many dummy variables as there are unique labels minus one. We can determine one of the labels automatically from the dummy variables, because the dummy variables are exclusive. If the dummy variables all have a false value, then the correct label is the label for which we don't have a dummy variable. The following table illustrates the encoding for continents:

	is_africa	is_asia	is_europe	is_sam	is_nam
Africa	1	0	0	0	0
Asia	0	1	0	0	0
Europe	0	0	1	0	0
South America	0	0	0	1	0
North America	0	0	0	0	1
Other	0	0	0	0	0

The encoding produces a matrix (grid of numbers) with lots of zeroes (false values) and occasional ones (true values). This type of matrix is called a **sparse matrix**. The sparse matrix representation is handled well by the the `scipy` package and shouldn't be an issue. We'll discuss the `scipy` package later in this chapter.

Scaling

Values of different features can differ by orders of magnitude. Sometimes, this may mean that the larger values dominate the smaller values. This depends on the algorithm we're using. For certain algorithms to work properly, we're required to scale the data.

There are following several common strategies that we can apply:

- Standardization removes the mean of a feature and divides by the standard deviation. If the feature values are normally distributed, we'll get a **Gaussian**, which is centered around zero with a variance of one.
- If the feature values aren't normally distributed, we can remove the median and divide by the interquartile range. The **interquartile range** is a range between the first and third quartile (or 25th and 75th percentile).
- Scaling features to a range is a common choice of range between zero and one.

Polynomial features

If we have two features, a and b, we can suspect that there's a polynomial relation, such as $a2 + ab + b2$. We can consider each term in the sum to be a feature—in this example, we have three features. The product ab in the middle is called an **interaction**. An interaction doesn't have to be a product—although this is the most common choice—it can also be a sum, a difference, or a ratio. If we're using a ratio to avoid dividing by zero, we should add a small constant to the divisor and dividend.

The number of features and the order of the polynomial for a polynomial relation aren't limited. However, if we follow Occam's razor, we should avoid higher-order polynomials and interactions of many features. In practice, complex polynomial relations tend to be more difficult to compute and tend to overfit, but if you really need better results, they may be worth considering.

Power transform

Power transforms are functions that we can use to transform numerical features into a more convenient form to conform better to a normal distribution. A very common transform for value, which vary by orders of magnitude, is to take the logarithm. Taking the logarithm of a zero and negative values isn't defined, so we may need to add a constant to all of the values of the related feature before taking the logarithm. We can also take the square root for positive values, square the values, or compute any other power we like.

Another useful transform is the **Box-Cox transformation**, named after its creators. The Box-Cox transformation attempts to find the best power needed to transform the original data into data that's closer to the normal distribution. The transform is defined as follows:

$$y_i^{(\lambda)} = \begin{cases} \frac{y_i^\lambda - 1}{\lambda} & if \lambda \neq 0, \\ 1n(y_i) & if \lambda = 0, \end{cases}$$

Binning

Sometimes, it's useful to separate feature values into several bins. For example, we may be only interested whether it rained on a particular day. Given the precipitation values, we can binarize the values, so that we get a true value if the precipitation value isn't zero and a false value otherwise. We can also use statistics to divide values into high, low, and medium bins. In marketing, we often care more about the age group, such as 18 to 24, than a specific age such as 23.

The binning process inevitably leads to loss of information. However, depending on your goals, this may not be an issue, and actually reduces the chance of overfitting. Certainly, there will be improvements in speed and reduction of memory or storage requirements and redundancy.

Combining models

In high school, we sit together with other students and learn together, but we aren't supposed to work together during the exam. The reason is, of course, that teachers want to know what we've learned, and if we just copy exam answers from friends, we may not have learned anything. Later in life, we discover that teamwork is important. For example, this book is the product of a whole team or possibly a group of teams.

Clearly, a team can produce better results than a single person. However, this goes against Occam's razor, since a single person can come up with simpler theories compared to what a team will produce. In machine learning, we nevertheless prefer to have our models cooperate with the following schemes:

- Voting and averaging
- Bagging
- Boosting
- Stacking

Voting and averaging

This is probably the most easily understood type of model aggregation. It just means the final output will be the majority or average of prediction output values from multiple models. It's also possible to assign different weights to each model in the ensemble, for example, some models might consider two votes. However, combining the results of models that are highly correlated to each other doesn't guarantee spectacular improvements. It's better to somehow diversify the models by using different features or different algorithms. If we find that two models are strongly correlated, we may, for example, decide to remove one of them from the ensemble and increase proportionally the weight of the other model.

Bagging

Bootstrap aggregating or **bagging** is an algorithm introduced by Leo Breiman in 1994, which applies **bootstrapping** to machine learning problems. Bootstrapping is a statistical procedure that creates datasets from existing data by sampling with replacement. Bootstrapping can be used to analyze the possible values that arithmetic mean, variance, or other quantity can assume.

The algorithm aims to reduce the chance of overfitting with the following steps:

1. We generate new training sets from input train data by sampling with replacement
2. For each generated training set, we fit a new model
3. We combine the results of the models by averaging or majority voting

The following diagram illustrates the steps for bagging, using classification as an example:

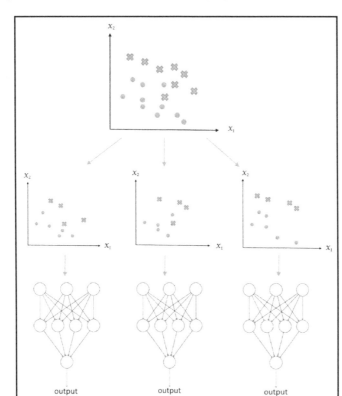

We'll explore how to employ bagging mainly in `Chapter 6`, *Predicting Online Ads Click-Through with Tree-Based Algorithms*.

Boosting

In the context of supervised learning, we define **weak learners** as learners that are just a little better than a baseline, such as randomly assigning classes or average values. Much like ants, weak learners are weak individually but together they have the power to do amazing things.

It makes sense to take into account the strength of each individual learner using weights. This general idea is called **boosting**. In boosting, all models are trained in sequence, instead of in parallel as in bagging. Each model is trained on the same dataset, but each data sample is under a different weight factoring, in the previous model's success. The weights are reassigned after a model is trained, which will be used for the next training round. In general, weights for mispredicted samples are increased to stress their prediction difficulty.

The following diagram illustrates the steps for boosting, again using classification as an example:

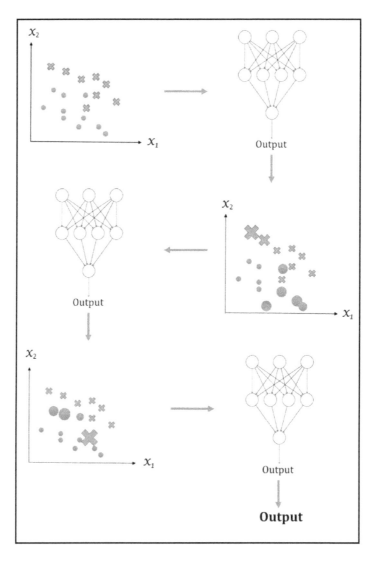

There are many boosting algorithms; boosting algorithms differ mostly in their weighting scheme. If you've studied for an exam, you may have applied a similar technique by identifying the type of practice questions you had trouble with and focusing on the hard problems.

Face detection in images is based on a specialized framework that also uses boosting. Detecting faces in images or videos is supervised learning. We give the learner examples of regions containing faces. There's an imbalance, since we usually have far more regions (about 10,000 times more) that don't have faces.

A cascade of classifiers progressively filters out negative image areas stage by stage. In each progressive stage, the classifiers use progressively more features on fewer image windows. The idea is to spend the most time on image patches, which contain faces. In this context, boosting is used to select features and combine results.

Stacking

Stacking takes the output values of machine learning estimators and then uses those as input values for another algorithm. You can, of course, feed the output of the higher-level algorithm to another predictor. It's possible to use any arbitrary topology but, for practical reasons, you should try a simple setup first as also dictated by Occam's razor.

Installing software and setting up

As the title says, Python is the language used to implement all machine learning algorithms and techniques throughout this entire book. We'll also use many popular Python packages and tools such as NumPy, SciPy, TensorFlow, and Scikit-learn. So at the end of this kick-off chapter, let's make sure we set up the tools and working environment properly, even though some of you are already experts in Python or might be familiar with some tools.

Setting up Python and environments

We'll be using Python 3 in this book. As you may know, Python 2 will no longer be supported after 2020, so starting with or switching to Python 3 is strongly recommended. Trust me, the transition is pretty smooth. But if you're stuck with Python 2, you still should be able to modify the codes to work for you. The Anaconda Python 3 distribution is one of the best options for data science and machine learning practitioners.

Anaconda is a free Python distribution for data analysis and scientific computing. It has its own package manager, `conda`. The distribution (`https://docs.anaconda.com/anaconda/packages/pkg-docs/`, depending on your operating system, or version 3.6, 3.7, or 2.7) includes more than 500 Python packages (as of 2018), which makes it very convenient. For casual users, the **Miniconda** (`https://conda.io/miniconda.html`) distribution may be the better choice. Miniconda contains the `conda` package manager and Python. Obviously, Miniconda takes more disk space than Anaconda.

The procedures to install Anaconda and Miniconda are similar. You can follow the instructions from `http://conda.pydata.org/docs/install/quick.html`. First, you have to download the appropriate installer for your operating system and Python version, as follows:

Regular installation

Follow the instructions for your operating system:

- Windows.
- macOS.
- Linux.

Sometimes, you can choose between a GUI and a CLI. I used the Python 3 installer although my system Python version was 2.7 at the time I installed it. This is possible since Anaconda comes with its own Python. On my machine, the Anaconda installer created an `anaconda` directory in my home directory and required about 900 MB. Similarly, the Miniconda installer installs a `miniconda` directory in your home directory.

Feel free to play around with it after you set it up. One way to verify you set up Anaconda properly is by entering the following command line in your Terminal on Linux/Mac or Command Prompt on Windows (from now on, I'll just mention terminal):

```
python
```

The preceding command line will display your Python running environment, as shown in the following screenshot:

```
Python 3.6.1 |Anaconda 4.4.0 (x86_64)| (default, May 11 2017, 13:04:09)
[GCC 4.2.1 Compatible Apple LLVM 6.0 (clang-600.0.57)] on darwin
Type "help", "copyright", "credits" or "license" for more information.
>>>
```

If this isn't what you're seeing, please check the system path or the path Python is running from.

The next step is setting up some of the common packages used throughout this book.

Installing the various packages

For most projects in this book, we'll be using NumPy (`http://www.numpy.org/`), `scikit-learn` (`http://scikit-learn.org/stable/`), and TensorFlow (`https://www.tensorflow.org/`). In the sections that follow, we'll cover the installation of the Python packages that we'll be using in this book.

NumPy

NumPy is the fundamental package for machine learning with Python. It offers powerful tools including the following:

- The N-dimensional array `ndarray` class and several subclasses representing matrices and arrays
- Various sophisticated array functions
- Useful linear algebra capabilities

Installation instructions for NumPy are at `http://docs.scipy.org/doc/numpy/user/install.html`. Alternatively, an easier method is installing it with `pip` in the command line as follows:

```
pip install numpy
```

To install `conda` for Anaconda users, run the following command line:

```
conda install numpy
```

A quick way to verify your installation is to import it in the shell as follows:

```
>>> import numpy
```

It's installed nicely if there's no error message.

SciPy

In machine learning, we mainly use NumPy arrays to store data vectors or matrices composed of feature vectors. SciPy (`https://www.scipy.org/scipylib/index.html`) uses NumPy arrays and offers a variety of scientific and mathematical functions. Installing SciPy in the terminal is similar, again as follows:

```
pip install scipy
```

Pandas

We also use the `pandas` library (`https://pandas.pydata.org/`) for data wrangling later in this book. The best way to get `pandas` is via `pip` or `conda`:

```
conda install pandas
```

Scikit-learn

The `scikit-learn` library is a Python machine learning package (probably the most well-designed machine learning package I've personally ever seen) optimized for performance as a lot of the code runs almost as fast as equivalent C code. The same statement is true for NumPy and SciPy. Scikit-learn requires both NumPy and SciPy to be installed. As the installation guide in `http://scikit-learn.org/stable/install.html` states, the easiest way to install `scikit-learn` is using `pip` or `conda` as follows:

```
pip install -U scikit-learn
```

TensorFlow

As for TensorFlow, it's a Python-friendly open source library invented by the Google Brain team for high-performance numerical computation. It makes machine learning faster and deep learning easier with the Python-based convenient frontend API and high-performance C++ based backend execution. Plus, it allows easy deployment of computation across CPUs and GPUs, which empowers expensive and large-scale machine learning. In this book, we focus on CPU as our computation platform. Hence, according to `https://www.tensorflow.org/install/`, installing TensorFlow is done via the following command line:

```
pip install tensorflow
```

There are many other packages we'll be using intensively, for example, **Matplotlib** for plotting and visualization, **Seaborn** for visualization, **NLTK** for natural language processing, and **PySpark** for large-scale machine learning. We'll provide installation details for any package when we first encounter it in this book.

Summary

We just finished our first mile on the Python and machine learning journey! Throughout this chapter, we became familiar with the basics of machine learning. We started with what machine learning is all about, the importance of machine learning (DT era) and its brief history, and looked at recent developments as well. We also learned typical machine learning tasks and explored several essential techniques of working with data and working with models. Now that we're equipped with basic machine learning knowledge and we've set up the software and tools, let's get ready for the real-world machine learning examples ahead.

In particular, we will be exploring newsgroups text data in our first ML project coming up next chapter.

Exercises

- Can you tell the difference between machine learning and traditional programming (rule-based automation)?
- What's overfitting and how do we avoid it?
- Name two feature engineering approaches.
- Name two ways to combine multiple models.
- Install Matplotlib if you're interested.

Section 2: Practical Python Machine Learning By Example

2

In this section, readers will learn several important machine learning algorithms and techniques through the process of solving real-world problems. The journey of learning machine learning by example includes mining natural language text data with dimensionality reduction and clustering algorithms, content topic discovery and categorization, online ad click-through prediction with various supervised learning algorithms, scaling up learning to a million records, and predicting stock prices with various regression algorithms.

This section includes the following chapters:

- Chapter 2, *Exploring the 20 Newsgroups Dataset with Text Analysis Techniques*
- Chapter 3, *Mining the 20 Newsgroups Dataset with Clustering and Topic Modeling Algorithms*
- Chapter 4, *Detecting Spam Email with Naive Bayes*
- Chapter 5, *Classifying News Topic with Support Vector Machine*
- Chapter 6, *Predicting Online Ads Click-Through with Tree-Based Algorithms*
- Chapter 7, *Predicting Online Ads Click-Through with Logistic Regression*
- Chapter 8, *Scaling Up Prediction to Terabyte Click Logs*
- Chapter 9, *Stock Price Prediction with Regression Algorithms*

2

Exploring the 20 Newsgroups Dataset with Text Analysis Techniques

We went through a bunch of fundamental machine learning concepts in the previous chapter. We learned about them along with analogies, in a fun way, such as studying for exams and designing a driving schedule. Starting from this chapter as the second step of our learning journal, we will be discovering in detail several important machine learning algorithms and techniques. Beyond analogies, we will be exposed to and solve real-world examples, which makes our journey more interesting. We will start with a natural language processing problem—exploring newsgroups data. We will gain hands-on experience in working with text data, especially how to convert words and phrases into machine-readable values and how to clean up words with little meaning. We will also visualize text data by mapping it into a two-dimensional space in an unsupervised learning manner.

We will go into detail for each of the following topics:

- What is NLP and its applications
- NLP basics
- Touring Python NLP libraries
- Tokenization
- Part-of-speech tagging
- Named entities recognition
- Stemming and lemmatization
- Getting and exploring the newsgroups data

- Data visualization using seaborn and matplotlib
- The Bag of words (BoW) model and token count vectorization
- Text preprocessing
- Stop words removal
- Dimensionality reduction
- T-SNE
- T-SNE for text visualization

How computers understand language - NLP

In `Chapter 1`, *Getting Started with Machine Learning and Python*, it was mentioned that machine learning driven programs or computers are good at discovering event patterns by processing and working with data. When the data is well structured or well defined, such as in a Microsoft Excel spreadsheet table and relational database table, it is intuitively obvious why machine learning is better at dealing with it than humans. Computers read such data the same way as humans, for example, `revenue: 5,000,000` as the revenue being 5 million and `age: 30` as age being 30; then computers crunch assorted data and generate insights. However, when the data is unstructured, such as words with which humans communicate, news articles, or someone's speech in French, it seems computers cannot understand words as well as human do (yet).

There is a lot of information in the world is words or raw text, or broadly speaking, **natural language**. This refers to any language humans use to communicate with each other. Natural language can take various forms, including, but not limited to, the following:

- Text, such as a web page, SMS, email, and menus
- Audio, such as speech and commands to Siri
- Signs and gestures
- Many others such as songs, sheet music, and Morse code

The list is endless and we are all surrounded by natural language all of the time (that's right, right now as you are reading this book). Given the importance of this type of unstructured data, natural language data, we must have methods to get computers to understand and reason with natural language and to extract data from it. Programs equipped with natural language processing techniques can already do a lot in certain areas, which already seems magical!

Natural language processing (**NLP**) is a significant subfield of machine learning, which deals with the interactions between machines (computers) and human (natural) languages. Natural languages are not limited to speech and conversation; they can be in writing or sign languages as well. The data for NLP tasks can be in different forms, for example, text from social media posts, web pages, even medical prescriptions, or audio from voice mail, commands to control systems, or even a favorite song or movie. Nowadays, NLP has been broadly involved in our daily lives: we cannot live without machine translation; weather forecasts scripts are automatically generated; we find voice search convenient; we get the answer to a question (such as what is the population of Canada) quickly thanks to intelligent question-answering systems; speech-to-text technology helps people with special needs.

If machines are able to understand language like humans do, we consider them intelligent. In 1950, the famous mathematician Alan Turing proposed in an article, *Computing Machinery and Intelligence*, a test as a criterion of machine intelligence. It's now called the **Turing test**, and its goal is to examine whether a computer is able to adequately understand languages so as to fool humans into thinking that this machine is another human. It is probably no surprise to us that no computer has passed the Turing test yet. But the 1950s is considered when the history of NLP started.

Understanding language might be difficult, but would it be easier to automatically translate texts from one language to another? In my first ever programming course, the lab booklet had the algorithm for coarse machine translation. We could imagine that this type of translation involves looking something up in dictionaries and generating new text. A more practically feasible approach would be to gather texts that are already translated by humans and train a computer program on these texts. In 1954, scientists claimed, in the Georgetown experiment, that machine translation would be solved in three to five years. Unfortunately, a machine translation system that can beat human expert translators does not exist yet. But machine translation has been greatly evolving since the introduction of deep learning and has incredible achievements in certain areas, for example, social media (Facebook open sourced a neural machine translation system), real-time conversation (Skype, SwiftKey Keyboard, and Google Pixel Buds), and image-based translation.

Conversational agents, or chatbots, are another hot topic in NLP. The fact that computers are able to have a conversation with us has reshaped the way businesses are run. In 2016, **Microsoft's AI chatbot**, **Tay**, was unleashed to mimic a teenage girl and converse with users on Twitter in real time. She learned how to speak from all things users posted and commented on Twitter. However, she was overwhelmed by tweets from trolls, and automatically learned their bad behaviors and started to output inappropriate things on her feeds. She ended up being terminated within 24 hours.

There are also several tasks attempting to organize knowledge and concepts in such a way that they become easier for computer programs to manipulate. The way we organize and represent concepts is called **ontology**. An ontology defines concepts and relations between concepts. For instance, we can have a so-called triple representing the relation between two concepts, such as *Python is a language*.

An important use case for NLP at a much lower level, compared to the previous cases, is **part-of-speech** (**PoS**) **tagging**. A part of speech is a grammatical word category such as noun or verb. PoS tagging tries to determine the appropriate tag for each word in a sentence or a larger document. The following table gives examples of English POS:

Part of speech	Examples
Noun	David, machine
Pronoun	Then, her
Adjective	Awesome, amazing
Verb	Read, write
Adverb	Very, quite
Preposition	Out, at
Conjunction	And, but
Interjection	Unfortunately, luckily
Article	A, the

Picking up NLP basics while touring popular NLP libraries

After a short list of real-world applications of NLP, we'll be touring the essential stack of Python NLP libraries in this chapter. These packages handle a wide range of NLP tasks as mentioned previously as well as others such as sentiment analysis, text classification, and named entity recognition.

The most famous NLP libraries in Python include the **Natural Language Toolkit** (**NLTK**), **spaCy**, **Gensim**, and **TextBlob**. The scikit-learn library also has impressive NLP-related features. Let's take a look at the following popular NLP libraries in Python:

- `nltk`: This library (http://www.nltk.org/) was originally developed for educational purposes and is now being widely used in industries as well. It is said that you can't talk about NLP without mentioning NLTK. It is one of the most famous and leading platforms for building Python-based NLP applications. You can install it simply by running the following command line in terminal:

  ```
  sudo pip install -U nltk
  ```

  If you're using `conda`, then execute the following command line:

  ```
  conda install nltk
  ```

- `SpaCy`: This library (https://spacy.io/) is a more powerful toolkit in the industry than NLTK. This is mainly for two reasons: one, spaCy is written in Cython, which is much more memory-optimized (now you see where the *Cy* in *spaCy* comes from) and excels in NLP tasks; second, spaCy keeps using state-of-the-art algorithms for core NLP problems, such as, convolutional neural network (CNN) models for tagging and name entity recognition. But it could seem advanced for beginners. In case you're interested, here's the installation instructions.

  Run the following command line in the terminal:

  ```
  pip install -U spacy
  ```

  For `conda`, execute the following command line:

  ```
  conda install -c conda-forge spacy
  ```

- `Gensim`: This library (https://radimrehurek.com/gensim/), developed by Radim Rehurek, has been gaining popularity over recent years. It was initially designed in 2008 to generate a list of similar articles given an article, hence the name of this library (*generate similar*—> *Gensim*). It was later drastically improved by Radim Rehurek in terms of its efficiency and scalability. Again, we can easily install it via `pip` by running the following command line:

  ```
  pip install --upgrade gensim
  ```

In the case of `conda`, you can perform the following command line in terminal:

```
conda install -c conda-forge gensim
```

You should make sure the dependencies, NumPy and SciPy, are already installed before gensim.

- `TextBlob`: This library (`https://textblob.readthedocs.io/en/dev/`) is a relatively new one built on top of NLTK. It simplifies NLP and text analysis with easy-to-use built-in functions and methods, as well as wrappers around common tasks. We can install TextBlob by running the following command line in the terminal:

```
pip install -U textblob
```

TextBlob has some useful features that are not available in NLTK (currently), such as spell checking and correction, language detection, and translation.

Corpus

As of 2018, NLTK comes with over 100 collections of large and well-structured text datasets, which are called **corpora** in NLP. Corpora can be used as dictionaries for checking word occurrences and as training pools for model learning and validating. Some useful and interesting corpora include Web Text corpus, Twitter samples, Shakespeare corpus sample, Sentiment Polarity, Names corpus (it contains lists of popular names, which we will be exploring very shortly), WordNet, and the Reuters benchmark corpus. The full list can be found at `http://www.nltk.org/nltk_data`. Before using any of these corpus resources, we need to first download them by running the following codes in the Python interpreter:

```
>>> import nltk
>>> nltk.download()
```

A new window will pop up and ask us which collections (the **Collections** tab in the following screenshot) or corpus (the **Corpora** tab in the following screenshot) to download, and where to keep the data:

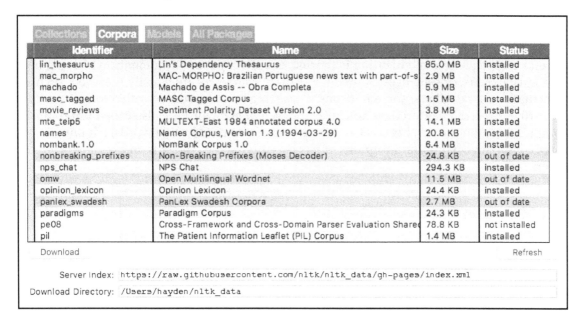

Installing the whole **popular** package is the quick solution, since it contains all important corpora needed for your current study and future research. Installing a particular corpora, as shown in the following screenshot, is also fine:

Once the package or corpus you want to explore is installed, we can now take a look at the Names corpus (make sure the `names` corpus is installed).

First, import the corpus `names`:

```
>>> from nltk.corpus import names
```

We can check out the first 10 names in the list:

```
>>> print(names.words()[:10])
['Abagael', 'Abagail', 'Abbe', 'Abbey', 'Abbi', 'Abbie',
'Abby', 'Abigael', 'Abigail', 'Abigale']
```

There are, in total, 7944 names, as shown in the following output derived by executing the following command:

```
>>> print(len(names.words()))
7944
```

Other corpora are also fun to explore.

Besides the easy-to-use and abundant corpora pool, more importantly, NLTK is also good at many NLP and text analysis tasks including tokenization, PoS tagging, named entities recognition, word stemming, and lemmatization.

Tokenization

Given a text sequence, **tokenization** is the task of breaking it into fragments, which can be words, characters, or sentences. Sometimes, certain characters are usually removed, such as punctuation marks, digits, and emoticons. These fragments are the so-called **tokens** used for further processing. Moreover, tokens composed of one word are also called **unigrams** in computational linguistics; **bigrams** are composed of two consecutive words; **trigrams** of three consecutive words; and **n-grams** of *n* consecutive words. Here is an example of tokenization:

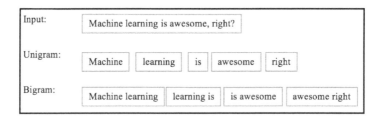

We can implement word-based tokenization using the `word_tokenize` function in NLTK. We will use the input text `'''I am reading a book.`, and in the next line, `It is Python Machine Learning By Example,`, then `2nd edition.'''`, as an example as shown in the following commands:

```
>>> from nltk.tokenize import word_tokenize
>>> sent = '''I am reading a book.
...             It is Python Machine Learning By Example,
...             2nd edition.'''
>>> print(word_tokenize(sent))
['I', 'am', 'reading', 'a', 'book', '.', 'It', 'is', 'Python', 'Machine',
'Learning', 'By', 'Example', ',', '2nd', 'edition', '.']
```

Word tokens are obtained.

> The `word_tokenize` function keeps punctuation marks and digits, and only discards whitespaces and newlines.

You might think word tokenization is simply splitting a sentence by space and punctuation. Here's an interesting example showing that tokenization is more complex than you think:

```
>>> sent2 = 'I have been to U.K. and U.S.A.'
>>> print(word_tokenize(sent2))
['I', 'have', 'been', 'to', 'U.K.', 'and', 'U.S.A', '.']
```

The tokenizer accurately recognizes the words `'U.K.'` and `'U.S.A'` as tokens instead of `'U'` and `'.'` followed by `'K'`, for example.

SpaCy also has an outstanding tokenization feature. It uses an accurately trained model that is constantly updated. To install it, we can run the following command:

```
python -m spacy download en_core_web_sm
```

Then, we'll load the `en_core_web_sm` model and parse the sentence using this model:

```
>>> import spacy
>>> nlp = spacy.load('en_core_web_sm')
>>> tokens2 = nlp(sent2)
>>> print([token.text for token in tokens2])
['I', 'have', 'been', 'to', 'U.K.', 'and', 'U.S.A.']
```

We can also segment text based on sentence. For example, on the same input text, using the `sent_tokenize` function from NLTK, we have the following commands:

```
>>> from nltk.tokenize import sent_tokenize
>>> print(sent_tokenize(sent))
['I am reading a book.', '...', 'It's Python Machine Learning By
Example,\n...          2nd edition.']
```

Two sentence-based tokens are returned, as there are two sentences in the input text regardless of a newline following a comma.

PoS tagging

We can apply an off-the-shelf tagger from NLTK or combine multiple taggers to customize the tagging process. It is easy to directly use the built-in tagging function, `pos_tag`, as in: `pos_tag(input_tokens)`, for instance. But behind the scene, it is actually a prediction from a pre-built supervised learning model. The model is trained based on a large corpus composed of words that are correctly tagged.

Reusing an earlier example, we can perform PoS tagging as follows:

```
>>> import nltk
>>> tokens = word_tokenize(sent)
>>> print(nltk.pos_tag(tokens))
[('I', 'PRP'), ('am', 'VBP'), ('reading', 'VBG'), ('a', 'DT'), ('book',
'NN'), ('.', '.'), ('It', 'PRP'), ('is', 'VBZ'), ('Python', 'NNP'),
('Machine', 'NNP'), ('Learning', 'NNP'), ('By', 'IN'), ('Example', 'NNP'),
(',', ','), ('2nd', 'CD'), ('edition', 'NN'), ('.', '.')]
```

The PoS tag following each token is returned. We can check the meaning of a tag using the `help` function. Looking up PRP and VBP, for example, gives us the following output:

```
>>> nltk.help.upenn_tagset('PRP')
PRP: pronoun, personal
    hers herself him himself hisself it itself me myself one oneself ours
ourselves ownself self she thee theirs them themselves they thou thy us
>>> nltk.help.upenn_tagset('VBP')
VBP: verb, present tense, not 3rd person singular
    predominate wrap resort sue twist spill cure lengthen brush terminate
appear tend stray glisten obtain comprise detest tease attract emphasize
mold postpone sever return wag ...
```

In spaCy, getting a PoS tag is also easy. The `token` object parsed from an input sentence has an attribute called `pos_`, which is the tag we are looking for:

```
>>> print([(token.text, token.pos_) for token in tokens2])
[('I', 'PRON'), ('have', 'VERB'), ('been', 'VERB'), ('to', 'ADP'), ('U.K.',
'PROPN'), ('and', 'CCONJ'), ('U.S.A.', 'PROPN')]
```

Named-entity recognition

Given a text sequence, the **named-entity recognition** (**NER**) task is to locate and identify words or phrases that are of definitive categories such as names of persons, companies, locations, and dates. We will briefly mention it again in `Chapter 4`, *Detecting Spam Email with Naive Bayes*.

As an appetizer, let's take a peep at an example of using spaCy for NER.

First, tokenize an input sentence, `The book written by Hayden Liu in 2018 was sold at $30 in America`, as usual as shown in the following command:

```
>>> tokens3 = nlp('The book written by Hayden Liu in 2018 was sold at $30
in America')
```

The resultant token object contains an attribute called `ents`, which is the named entities. We can extract the tagging for each recognized named entity as follows:

```
print([(token_ent.text, token_ent.label_) for token_ent in tokens3.ents])
[('Hayden Liu', 'PERSON'), ('2018', 'DATE'), ('30', 'MONEY'), ('America',
'GPE')]
```

We can see from the results that `Hayden Liu` is PERSON, 2018 is DATE, 30 is MONEY, and `America` is GPE (country). Please refer to `https://spacy.io/api/annotation#section-named-entities` for a full list of named entity tags.

Stemming and lemmatization

Word **stemming** is a process of reverting an inflected or derived word to its root form. For instance, *machine* is the stem of *machines*, and *learning* and *learned* are generated from *learn* as their stem.

The word **lemmatization** is a cautious version of stemming. It considers the PoS of a word when conducting stemming. We will discuss these two text preprocessing techniques, stemming and lemmatization, in further detail shortly. For now, let's take a quick look at how they're implemented respectively in NLTK by performing the following steps:

1. Import `porter` as one of the three built-in stemming algorithms (`LancasterStemmer` and `SnowballStemmer` are the other two) and initialize the stemmer as follows:

```
>>> from nltk.stem.porter import PorterStemmer
>>> porter_stemmer = PorterStemmer()
```

2. Stem `machines` and `learning`, as shown in the following codes:

```
>>> porter_stemmer.stem('machines')
'machin'
>>> porter_stemmer.stem('learning')
'learn'
```

 Stemming sometimes involves chopping of letters if necessary, as we can see in `machin` in the preceding command output.

3. Now import a lemmatization algorithm based on the built-in WordNet corpus and initialize a lemmatizer:

```
>>> from nltk.stem import WordNetLemmatizer
>>> lemmatizer = WordNetLemmatizer()
```

Similar to stemming, we lemmatize *machines, learning*:

```
>>> lemmatizer.lemmatize('machines')
'machine'
>>> lemmatizer.lemmatize('learning')
'learning'
```

Why is `learning` unchanged? It turns out that this algorithm only lemmatizes on nouns by default.

Semantics and topic modeling

Gensim is famous for its powerful semantic and topic modeling algorithms. Topic modeling is a typical text mining task of discovering the hidden semantic structures in a document. Semantic structure in plain English is the distribution of word occurrences. It is obviously an unsupervised learning task. What we need to do is to feed in plain text and let the model figure out the abstract "topics". We will study topic modeling in detail in `Chapter 3`, *Mining the 20 Newsgroups Dataset with Clustering and Topic Modeling Algorithms*.

In addition to robust semantic modeling methods, gensim also provides the following functionalities:

- **Word embedding**: Also known as **word vectorization**, this is an innovative way to represent words while preserving words' co-occurrence features. We will study word embedding in detail in `Chapter 10`, *Machine Learning Best Practices*.
- **Similarity querying**: This functionality retrieves objects that are similar to the given query object. It's a feature built on top of word embedding.
- **Distributed computing**: This functionality makes it possible to efficiently learn from millions of documents.

Last but not least, as mentioned in the first chapter, scikit-learn is the main package we use throughout this entire book. Luckily, it provides all text processing features we need, such as tokenization, besides comprehensive machine learning functionalities. Plus, it comes with a built-in loader for the 20 newsgroups dataset.

Now that the tools are available and properly installed, what about the data?

Getting the newsgroups data

The first project in this book is about the 20 newsgroups dataset. It's composed of text taken from newsgroup articles, as its name implies. It was originally collected by Ken Lang and now has been widely used for experiments in text applications of machine learning techniques, specifically NLP techniques.

The data contains approximately 20,000 documents across 20 online newsgroups. A newsgroup is a place on the internet where people can ask and answer questions about a certain topic. The data is already cleaned to a certain degree and already split into training and testing sets. The cutoff point is at a certain date.

The original data comes from `http://qwone.com/~jason/20Newsgroups/`, with 20 different topics listed, as follows:

- `comp.graphics`
- `comp.os.ms-windows.misc`
- `comp.sys.ibm.pc.hardware`
- `comp.sys.mac.hardware`
- `comp.windows.x`
- `rec.autos`
- `rec.motorcycles`
- `rec.sport.baseball`
- `rec.sport.hockey`
- `sci.crypt`
- `sci.electronics`
- `sci.med`
- `sci.space`
- `misc.forsale`
- `talk.politics.misc`
- `talk.politics.guns`
- `talk.politics.mideast`
- `talk.religion.misc`
- `alt.atheism`
- `soc.religion.christian`

All of the documents in the dataset are in English. And we can easily deduce the topics from the newsgroups names.

The dataset is labeled and each document is composed of text data and a group label. This also makes it a perfect fit for supervised learning, such as text classification. And we will explore it in detail in `Chapter 5`, *Classifying Newsgroup Topic with Support Vector Machine.*

Some of the newsgroups are closely related or even overlapping, for instance, those five computer groups (`comp.graphics`, `comp.os.ms-windows.misc`, `comp.sys.ibm.pc.hardware`, `comp.sys.mac.hardware`, and `comp.windows.x`), while some are not closely related to each other, such as Christian (`soc.religion.christian`) and baseball (`rec.sport.baseball`). Hence, it's a perfect use case for unsupervised learning such as clustering with which we can see whether similar topics are grouped together and unrelated ones are far apart. Moreover, we can even discover abstract topics beyond the original 20 labels using topic modeling techniques. We will explore clustering and topic modeling in detail in `Chapter 3`, *Mining the 20 Newsgroups Dataset with Clustering and Topic Modeling Algorithms*.

For now, let's focus on exploring and analyzing the text data. We shall get started with acquiring the data.

It is possible to download the dataset manually from the original website or many other online repositories. However, there are also many versions of the dataset—some are cleaned in a certain way and some are in raw form. To avoid confusion, it is best to use a consistent acquisition method. The scikit-learn library provides a utility function that loads the dataset. Once the dataset is downloaded, it's automatically cached. We don't need to download the same dataset twice.

 In most cases, caching the dataset, especially for a relatively small one, is considered a good practice. Other Python libraries also provide data download utilities, but not all of them implement automatic caching. This is another reason why we love scikit-learn.

As always, we first import the loader function for the 20 newsgroups data, as follows:

```
>>> from sklearn.datasets import fetch_20newsgroups
```

Then, we download the dataset with all default parameters as follows:

```
>>> groups = fetch_20newsgroups()
Downloading 20news dataset. This may take a few minutes.
Downloading dataset from https://ndownloader.figshare.com/files/5975967 (14
MB)
```

We can also specify one or more certain topic groups and particular sections (training, testing, or both) and just load such a subset of data in the program. The full list of parameters and options for the loader function is summarized in the following table:

Parameter	Default value	Example values	Description
subset	'train'	'train', 'test', 'all'	The dataset to load: the training set, the testing set or both.
data_home	~/scikit_learn_data	~/myfolder	Directory where the files are stored and cached
categories	None	['sci.space", alt.atheism']	List of newsgroups to load. If None, all newsgroups will be loaded.
shuffle	True	True, False	Boolean indicating whether to shuffle the data
random_state	42	7, 43	Random seed integer used to shuffle the data
remove	()	('headers', 'footers', 'quotes')	Tuple indicating part(s) among header, footer and quote of each newsgroup post to omit. Nothing is removed by default.
download_if_missing	True	True, False	Boolean indicating whether to download the data if it is not found locally

You might find `random_state` interesting. Why do we need to it and why do we need to fix it? It's actually used for the purpose of reproducibility. You are able to get the same dataset every time you run the script. Otherwise, working on datasets shuffled under different orders might bring in unnecessary variations.

Exploring the newsgroups data

After we download the 20 newsgroups dataset by whatever means we prefer, the `data` object of `groups` is now cached in memory. The `data` object is in the form of key-value dictionary. Its keys are as follows:

```
>>> groups.keys()
dict_keys(['data', 'filenames', 'target_names', 'target', 'DESCR'])
```

The `target_names` key gives the newsgroups names:

```
>>> groups['target_names']
    ['alt.atheism', 'comp.graphics', 'comp.os.ms-windows.misc',
'comp.sys.ibm.pc.hardware', 'comp.sys.mac.hardware', 'comp.windows.x',
'misc.forsale', 'rec.autos', 'rec.motorcycles', 'rec.sport.baseball',
'rec.sport.hockey', 'sci.crypt', 'sci.electronics', 'sci.med', 'sci.space',
'soc.religion.christian', 'talk.politics.guns', 'talk.politics.mideast',
'talk.politics.misc', 'talk.religion.misc']
```

The `target` key corresponds to a newsgroup but is encoded as an integer:

```
>>> groups.target
array([7, 4, 4, ..., 3, 1, 8])
```

Then what are the distinct values for these integers? We can use the `unique` function from NumPy to figure it out:

```
>>> import numpy as np
>>> np.unique(groups.target)
array([ 0, 1, 2, 3, 4, 5, 6, 7, 8, 9, 10, 11, 12, 13, 14, 15, 16, 17, 18,
19])
```

They're ranging from 0 to 19, representing the 1st, 2nd, 3rd, ..., 20th newsgroup topics in `groups['target_names']`.

In the context of multiple topics or categories, it is important to know what the distribution of topics is. A uniform class distribution is the easiest to deal with, because there are no under-represented or over-represented categories. However, frequently we have a skewed distribution with one or more categories dominating. We herein use the `seaborn` package (https://seaborn.pydata.org/) to compute the histogram of categories and plot it utilizing the `matplotlib` package (https://matplotlib.org/). We can install both packages via `pip` as follows:

```
python -m pip install -U matplotlib
pip install seaborn
```

In the case of `conda`, you can execute the following command line:

```
conda install -c conda-forge matplotlib
conda install seaborn
```

Remember to install `matplotlib` before `seaborn` as `matplotlib` is one of the dependencies of the `seaborn` package.

Now let's display the distribution of the classes as follows:

```
>>> import seaborn as sns
>>> sns.distplot(groups.target)
<matplotlib.axes._subplots.AxesSubplot object at 0x108ada6a0>
>>> import matplotlib.pyplot as plt
>>> plt.show()
```

Refer to the following screenshot for the end result:

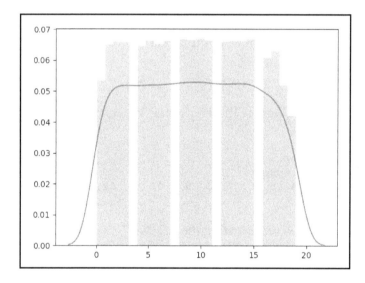

As we can see, the distribution is approximately uniform so that's one less thing to worry about.

 It's good to visualize to get a general idea of how the data is structured, what possible issues may arise, and whether there are any irregularities that we have to take care of.

Other keys are quite self-explanatory: `data` contains all newsgroups documents and `filenames` stores the path where each document is located in your filesystem.

Now, let's now have a look at the first document and its topic number and name by executing the following command:

```
>>> groups.data[0]
"From: lerxst@wam.umd.edu (where's my thing)\nSubject: WHAT car is
this!?\nNntp-Posting-Host: rac3.wam.umd.edu\nOrganization: University of
Maryland, College Park\nLines: 15\n\n I was wondering if anyone out there
could enlighten me on this car I saw\nthe other day. It was a 2-door sports
car, looked to be from the late 60s/\nearly 70s. It was called a Bricklin.
The doors were really small. In addition,\nthe front bumper was separate
from the rest of the body. This is \nall I know. If anyone can tellme a
model name, engine specs, years\nof production, where this car is made,
history, or whatever info you\nhave on this funky looking car, please e-
mail.\n\nThanks,\n- IL\n ---- brought to you by your neighborhood Lerxst --
--\n\n\n\n\n"
>>> groups.target[0]
7
>>> groups.target_names[groups.target[0]]
'rec.autos'
```

If `random_state` isn't fixed (`42` by default), you may get different results running the preceding scripts.

As we can see, the first document is from the `rec.autos` newsgroup, which was assigned the number 7. Reading this post, we can easily figure out it's about cars. The word `car` actually occurs a number of times in the document. Words such as `bumper` also seem very car-oriented. However, words such as `doors` may not necessarily be car related, as they may also be associated with home improvement or another topic. As a side note, it makes sense to not distinguish between `doors` and `door`, or the same word with different capitalization such as `Doors`. There are some rare cases where capitalization does matter, for instance, if we're trying to find out whether a document is about the band called `The Doors` or the more common concept, `the doors` (in wood).

Thinking about features for text data

From the preceding analysis, we can safely conclude that, if we want to figure out whether a document was from the `rec.autos` newsgroup, the presence or absence of words such as `car`, `doors`, and `bumper` can be very useful features. The presence or not of a word is a boolean variable, and we can also propose looking at the count of certain words. For instance, `car` occurs multiple times in the document. Maybe the more times such a word is found in a text, the more likely it is that the document has something to do with cars.

Counting the occurrence of each word token

It seems that we are only interested in the occurrence of certain words, their count, or a related measure and not in the order of the words. We can therefore view a text as a collection of words. This is called the **Bag of Words (BoW) model**. This is a very basic model, but it works pretty well in practice. We can optionally define a more complex model that takes into account the order of words and PoS tags. However, such a model is going to be more computationally expensive and more difficult to program. In reality, the basic BoW model in most cases suffices. Have a doubt? We can give it a shot and see whether the BoW model makes sense.

We start with converting documents into a matrix where each row represents each newsgroup document and each column represents a word token, or specifically, a unigram to begin with. And the value of each element in the matrix is the number of times the word (column) occurs in the document (row). We are utilizing the `CountVectorizer` class from scikit-learn to do the work:

```
>>> from sklearn.feature_extraction.text import CountVectorizer
```

The important parameters and options for the count conversion function are summarized in the following table:

Constructor parameter	Default value	Example values	Description
ngram_range	(1,1)	(1, 2), (2, 2)	Lower and upper bound of the n-grams to be extracted in the input text, for example (1, 1) means unigram, (1, 2) means unigram and bigram
stop_words	None	'english', or list ['a', 'the', 'of'] or None	Which stop word list to use, can be "english" referring to the built-in list, or a customized input list. If None, no word will be removed.
lowercase	True	True, False	Whether or not converting all characters to lowercase
max_features	None	None, 200, 500	The number of top (most frequent) tokens to consider, or all tokens if None
binary	False	True, False	If True, all non-zero counts become 1s.

We first initialize the count vectorizer with 500 top features (500 most frequent tokens):

```
>>>   count_vector = CountVectorizer(max_features=500)
```

Use it to fit on the raw text data as follows:

```
>>> data_count = count_vector.fit_transform(groups.data)
```

Now the count vectorizer captures the top 500 features and generates a token count matrix out of the original text input:

```
>>> data_count
<11314x500 sparse matrix of type '<class 'numpy.int64'>'
    with 798221 stored elements in Compressed Sparse Row format>
>>> data_count[0]
<1x500 sparse matrix of type '<class 'numpy.int64'>'
    with 53 stored elements in Compressed Sparse Row format>
```

The resulting count matrix is a sparse matrix where each row only stores non-zero elements (hence, only 798,221 elements instead of *11314 * 500 = 5,657,000*). For example, the first document is converted into a sparse vector composed of 53 non-zero elements. If you are interested in seeing the whole matrix, feel free to run the following:

```
>>> data_count.toarray()
```

If you just want the first row, run the following:

```
>>> data_count.toarray()[0]
```

Let's take a look at the following output derived from the preceding command:

```
array([0, 0, 0, 0, 0, 0, 0, 0, 0, 0, 0, 1, 0, 0, 0, 0, 0, 0, 0, 0, 0, 0,
       0, 0, 0, 0, 0, 0, 0, 0, 0, 0, 0, 0, 0, 0, 0, 0, 0, 0, 0, 0, 0, 0,
       0, 0, 0, 0, 0, 0, 0, 0, 0, 0, 0, 0, 0, 0, 0, 0, 0, 0, 0, 0, 0, 0,
       0, 0, 0, 0, 0, 0, 0, 0, 0, 0, 0, 0, 0, 0, 0, 0, 0, 0, 0, 0, 1, 0,
       0, 0, 0, 0, 1, 0, 0, 5, 0, 0, 0, 0, 0, 0, 0, 0, 0, 0, 0, 0, 0, 0,
       0, 0, 0, 0, 0, 0, 0, 0, 1, 0, 0, 0, 0, 0, 0, 0, 0, 0, 0, 0, 0, 0,
       0, 0, 0, 0, 0, 0, 0, 0, 0, 0, 1, 0, 0, 0, 0, 0, 0, 0, 0, 0, 0, 0,
       0, 0, 0, 0, 0, 0, 0, 0, 0, 0, 0, 0, 2, 0, 0, 0, 0, 0, 0, 0, 0, 0,
       0, 0, 0, 0, 0, 0, 0, 0, 0, 0, 0, 0, 0, 0, 0, 0, 0, 0, 0, 0, 0, 0,
       0, 0, 0, 0, 0, 0, 0, 0, 0, 0, 0, 0, 0, 0, 0, 0, 0, 0, 0, 0, 0, 1,
       0, 0, 0, 1, 0, 0, 0, 0, 0, 0, 0, 0, 0, 0, 1, 0, 0, 0, 0, 0, 0, 0, 0,
       0, 0, 0, 0, 0, 0, 0, 0, 0, 0, 0, 0, 0, 1, 0, 0, 0, 0, 0, 0, 0, 0, 0,
       0, 0, 0, 1, 0, 0, 0, 0, 0, 0, 1, 0, 0, 0, 0, 0, 0, 1, 0, 0, 0,
       0, 0, 0, 0, 0, 0, 0, 0, 0, 0, 0, 0, 0, 0, 0, 0, 0, 0, 0, 0, 0, 0, 0,
       0, 0, 0, 0, 0, 0, 0, 1, 0, 0, 0, 0, 0, 0, 0, 0, 0, 0, 0, 0, 1, 0,
       0, 0, 0, 0, 0, 0, 0, 0, 0, 0, 0, 0, 0, 0, 0, 0, 0, 0, 1, 0, 0, 0,
       0, 0, 0, 0, 0, 0, 0, 0, 0, 0, 0, 0, 0, 0, 0, 0, 0, 0, 0, 1, 0, 0, 0,
       0, 0, 0, 0, 0, 0, 0, 0, 0, 0, 1, 0, 0, 0, 0, 0, 0, 0, 0, 0, 0, 0,
       0, 0, 0, 0, 0, 0, 0, 0, 0, 1, 0, 0, 0, 0, 0, 0, 0, 0, 0, 0, 0, 0,
       0, 0, 0, 0, 0, 0, 1, 0, 0, 0, 0, 0, 0, 0, 0, 0, 0, 0, 0, 1, 1, 0,
       0, 0, 0, 0, 0, 0, 0, 0, 0, 0, 0, 0, 0, 0, 0, 0, 0, 0, 1, 0, 0, 0,
       0, 0, 0, 0, 0, 0, 0, 0, 0, 0, 0, 0, 0, 0, 0, 0, 0, 0, 0, 0, 0, 0,
       0, 0, 0, 0, 0, 0, 0, 0, 0, 0, 0, 0, 1, 0, 0], dtype=int64)
```

So what are those 500 top features? They can be found in the following output:

```
>>> print(count_vector.get_feature_names())
['00', '000', '10', '100', '11', '12', '13', '14', '145', '15', '16', '17',
'18', '19', '1993', '20', '21', '22', '23', '24', '25', '26', '27', '30',
'32', '34', '40', '50', '93', 'a86', 'able', 'about', 'above', 'ac',
'access', 'actually', 'address', 'after', 'again', 'against', 'ago', 'all',
'already', 'also', 'always', 'am', 'american', 'an', 'and', 'andrew',
'another', 'answer', 'any', 'anyone', 'anything', 'apple', 'apr', 'april',
'are', 'armenian', 'around', 'article', 'as', 'ask', 'at', 'au',
'available', 'away', 'ax', 'b8f', 'back', 'bad', 'based', 'be', 'because',
'been',
......
......
......
, 'that', 'the', 'their', 'them', 'then', 'there', 'these', 'they',
'thing', 'things', 'think', 'this', 'those', 'though', 'thought', 'three',
'through', 'time', 'times', 'to', 'today', 'told', 'too', 'true', 'try',
'trying', 'turkish', 'two', 'type', 'uiuc', 'uk', 'under', 'university',
'unix', 'until', 'up', 'us', 'usa', 'use', 'used', 'using', 'uucp', 've',
'version', 'very', 'vs', 'want', 'war', 'was', 'washington', 'way', 'we',
'well', 'were', 'what', 'when', 'where', 'whether', 'which', 'while',
'who', 'whole', 'why', 'will', 'win', 'window', 'windows', 'with',
'without', 'won', 'word', 'work', 'works', 'world', 'would', 'writes',
'wrong', 'wrote', 'year', 'years', 'yes', 'yet', 'you', 'your']
```

Our first trial doesn't look perfect. Obviously, the most popular tokens are numbers, or letters with numbers such as a86, which do not convey important information. Moreover, there are many words that have no actual meaning, such as you, the, them, and then. Also, some words contain identical information, for example, tell and told, use and used, and time and times. Let's tackle these issues.

Text preprocessing

We start with retaining letter-only words so that numbers such as 00 and 000 and combinations of letter and number such as b8f will be removed. The filter function is defined as follows:

```
>>> def is_letter_only(word):
...     for char in word:
...         if not char.isalpha():
...             return False
...     return True
...
>>> data_cleaned = []
```

```
>>> for doc in groups.data:
...     doc_cleaned = ' '.join(word for word in doc.split()
                                    if is_letter_only(word) )
...     data_cleaned.append(doc_cleaned)
```

It will generate a cleaned version of the newsgroups data.

Dropping stop words

We didn't talk about `stop_words` as an important parameter in `CountVectorizer`. **Stop words** are those common words that provide little value in helping documents differentiate themselves. In general, stop words add noise to the BoW model and can be removed.

There's no universal list of stop words. Hence, depending on the tools or packages you are using, you will remove different sets of stop words. Take scikit-learn as an example—you can check the list as follows:

```
>>> from sklearn.feature_extraction import stop_words
>>> print(stop_words.ENGLISH_STOP_WORDS)
frozenset({'most', 'three', 'between', 'anyway', 'made', 'mine', 'none',
'could', 'last', 'whenever', 'cant', 'more', 'where', 'becomes', 'its',
'this', 'front', 'interest', 'least', 're', 'it', 'every', 'four', 'else',
'over', 'any', 'very', 'well', 'never', 'keep', 'no', 'anything', 'itself',
'alone', 'anyhow', 'until', 'therefore', 'only', 'the', 'even', 'so',
'latterly', 'above', 'hereafter', 'hereby', 'may', 'myself', 'all',
'those', 'down',
......
......
'him', 'somehow', 'or', 'per', 'nowhere', 'fifteen', 'via', 'must',
'someone', 'from', 'full', 'that', 'beyond', 'still', 'to', 'get',
'himself', 'however', 'as', 'forty', 'whatever', 'his', 'nothing',
'though', 'almost', 'become', 'call', 'empty', 'herein', 'than', 'while',
'bill', 'thru', 'mostly', 'yourself', 'up', 'former', 'each', 'anyone',
'hundred', 'several', 'others', 'along', 'bottom', 'one', 'five',
'therein', 'was', 'ever', 'beside', 'everyone'})
```

To drop stop words from the newsgroups data, we simply just need to specify the `stop_words` parameter:

```
>>> count_vector_sw = CountVectorizer(stop_words="english",
max_features=500)
```

Besides stop words, you may notice names are included in the top features, such as `andrew`. We can filter names with the Name corpus from NLTK we just worked with.

Stemming and lemmatizing words

As mentioned earlier, we have two basic strategies to deal with words from the same root—stemming and lemmatization. Stemming is a quicker approach that involves, if necessary, chopping off letters, for example, *words* becomes *word* after stemming. The result of stemming doesn't have to be a valid word. For instance, *trying* and *try* become *tri*. Lemmatizing, on the other hand, is slower but more accurate. It performs a dictionary lookup and guarantees to return a valid word. Recall we have implemented both stemming and lemmatization using NLTK in a previous section.

Putting all of these (preprocessing, dropping stop words, lemmatizing, and count vectorizing) together, we obtain the following:

```
>>> from nltk.corpus import names
>>> all_names = set(names.words())
>>> count_vector_sw = CountVectorizer(stop_words="english",
max_features=500)
>>> from nltk.stem import WordNetLemmatizer
>>> lemmatizer = WordNetLemmatizer()
>>> data_cleaned = []
>>> for doc in groups.data:
...     doc = doc.lower()
...     doc_cleaned = ' '.join(lemmatizer.lemmatize(word)
                               for word in doc.split()
                               if is_letter_only(word) and
                               word not in all_names)
...     data_cleaned.append(doc_cleaned)
>>> data_cleaned_count = count_vector_sw.fit_transform(data_cleaned)
```

Now the features are much more meaningful:

```
>>> print(count_vector_sw.get_feature_names())
['able', 'accept', 'access', 'according', 'act', 'action', 'actually',
'add', 'address', 'ago', 'agree', 'algorithm', 'allow', 'american',
'anonymous', 'answer', 'anybody', 'apple', 'application', 'apr', 'april',
'arab', 'area', 'argument', 'armenian', 'article', 'ask', 'asked',
'assume', 'atheist', 'attack', 'attempt', 'available', 'away', 'bad',
'based', 'belief', 'believe', 'best', 'better', 'bible', 'big', 'bike',
'bit', 'black', 'board', 'body', 'book', 'box', 'build', 'bus', 'buy',
'ca', 'california', 'called', 'came', 'canada', 'car', 'card', 'care',
'carry', 'case', 'cause', 'center', 'certain', 'certainly', 'chance',
'change', 'check', 'child', 'chip', 'christian', 'church', 'city', 'claim',
'clear', 'clinton', 'clipper', 'code', 'college', 'color', 'come',
'coming', 'command', 'comment', 'common', 'communication', 'company',
'computer', 'consider', 'considered', 'contact', 'control', 'copy',
......
......
```

```
'short', 'shot', 'similar', 'simple', 'simply', 'single', 'site',
'situation', 'size', 'small', 'software', 'sort', 'sound', 'source',
'space', 'special', 'specific', 'speed', 'standard', 'start', 'started',
'state', 'statement', 'steve', 'stop', 'strong', 'study', 'stuff',
'subject', 'sun', 'support', 'sure', 'taken', 'taking', 'talk', 'talking',
'tape', 'tax', 'team', 'technical', 'technology', 'tell', 'term', 'test',
'texas', 'text', 'thanks', 'thing', 'think', 'thinking', 'thought', 'time',
'tin', 'today', 'told', 'took', 'total', 'tried', 'true', 'truth', 'try',
'trying', 'turkish', 'turn', 'type', 'understand', 'united', 'university',
'unix', 'unless', 'usa', 'use', 'used', 'user', 'using', 'usually',
'value', 'various', 'version', 'video', 'view', 'wa', 'want', 'wanted',
'war', 'water', 'way', 'weapon', 'week', 'went', 'western', 'white',
'widget', 'win', 'window', 'woman', 'word', 'work', 'working', 'world',
'worth', 'write', 'written', 'wrong', 'year', 'york', 'young']
```

Visualizing the newsgroups data with t-SNE

We have just converted text from each raw newsgroup document into a sparse vector of a size of 500. For a vector from a document, each element represents the number of times a word token occurring in this document. Also, these 500 word tokens are selected based on their overall occurrences after text preprocessing, removal of stop words, and lemmatization. Now you may ask questions such as, is such occurrence vector representative enough, or does such an occurrence vector convey enough information that can be used to differentiate the document itself from documents on other topics? We can answer these questions easily by visualizing those representation vectors—we did a good job if document vectors from the same topic are nearby. But how? They are of 500 dimensions, while we can visualize data of **at most** three dimensions. We can resort to t-SNE for dimensionality reduction.

What is dimensionality reduction?

Dimensionality reduction is an important machine learning technique that reduces the number of features and, at the same time, retains as much information as possible. It is usually performed by obtaining a set of new principal features.

As mentioned before, it is difficult to visualize data of high dimension. Given a three-dimensional plot, we sometimes don't even find it too straightforward to observe any findings, not to mention 10, 100, or 1,000 dimensions. Moreover, some of the features in high dimensional data may be correlated and, as a result, bring in redundancy. This is why we need dimensionality reduction.

Dimensionality reduction is not simply taking out a pair of two features from the original feature space. It is transforming the original feature space to a new space of fewer dimensions. The data transformation can be linear, such as the famous one **principal component analysis** (**PCA**), which maximizes the variance of projected data, or nonlinear, such as neural networks and t-SNE coming up shortly. For instance, in PCA, it maps the data in a higher dimensional space to a lower dimensional space where the variance of the data is maximized. **Non-negative matrix factorization** (**NMF**) is another powerful algorithm, which we'll study in detail in `Chapter 3`, *Mining the 20 Newsgroups Dataset with Clustering and Topic Modeling Algorithms*.

At the end of the day, most dimensionality reduction algorithms are in the family of **unsupervised learning** as the target or label information (if available) is not used in data transformation.

t-SNE for dimensionality reduction

t-SNE stands for **t-distributed Stochastic Neighbor Embedding**. It's a nonlinear dimensionality reduction technique developed by Laurens van der Maaten and Geoffrey Hinton. t-SNE has been widely used for data visualization in various domains, including computer vision, NLP, bioinformatics, and computational genomics.

As its name implies, t-SNE embeds high-dimensional data into a low-dimensional (usually two-dimensional or three-dimensional) space where similarity among data samples (neighbor information) is preserved. It first models a probability distribution over neighbors around data points by assigning a high probability to similar data points and an extremely small probability to dissimilar ones. Note that `similar` and `neighbor` are measured by Euclidean distance or other metrics. Then, it constructs a projection onto a low-dimensional space where the divergence between the input distribution and output distribution is minimized. The original high-dimensional space is modeled as Gaussian distribution, while the output low-dimensional space is modeled as t-distribution.

We'll herein implement t-SNE using the `TSNE` class from scikit-learn:

```
>>> from sklearn.manifold import TSNE
```

Now let's use t-SNE to verify our count vector representation.

We pick three distinct topics, `talk.religion.misc`, `comp.graphics`, and `sci.space`, and visualize documents vectors from these three topics.

First, just load documents of these three labels, as follows:

```
>>> categories_3 = ['talk.religion.misc', 'comp.graphics', 'sci.space']
>>> groups_3 = fetch_20newsgroups(categories=categories_3)
```

It goes through the same process and generates a count matrix, `data_cleaned_count_3`, with 500 features from the input, `groups_3`. You can refer to steps in previous sections as you just need to repeat the same code.

Next, we apply t-SNE to reduce the 500-dimensional matrix to two-dimensional matrix:

```
>>> tsne_model = TSNE(n_components=2, perplexity=40,
                      random_state=42, learning_rate=500)
>>> data_tsne = tsne_model.fit_transform(data_cleaned_count_3.toarray())
```

The parameters we specify in the `TSNE` object are as follows:

- `n_components`: The output dimension
- `perplexity`: The number of nearest data points considered neighbors in the algorithm with a typical value of between 5 and 50
- `random_state`: The random seed for program reproducibility
- `learning_rate`: The factor affecting the process of finding the optimal mapping space with a typical value of between 10 and 1,000

Note, the `TSNE` object only takes in dense matrix, hence we convert the sparse matrix, `data_cleaned_count_3`, into a dense one using `toarray()`.

We just successfully reduce the input dimension from 500 to 2. Finally, we can easily visualize it in a two-dimensional scatter plot where x axis is the first dimension, y axis is the second dimension, and the color, `c`, is based on the topic label of each original document:

```
>>> import matplotlib.pyplot as plt
>>> plt.scatter(data_tsne[:, 0], data_tsne[:, 1], c=groups_3.target)
>>> plt.show()
```

Refer to the following screenshot for the end result:

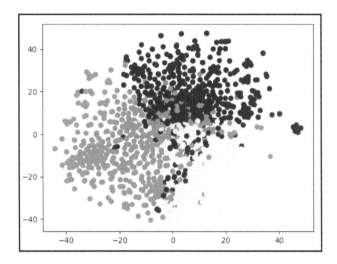

Data points from the three topics are in different colors such as green, purple, and yellow. We can observe three clear clusters. Data points from the same topic are close to each other while those from different topics are far away. Obviously, count vectors are great representations for original text data as they preserve distinction among three different topics.

You can also play around with the parameters and see whether you can obtain a nicer plot where the three clusters are better separated.

Count vectorization does well in keeping document disparity. How about maintaining similarity? We can also check that using documents from overlapping topics, such as five topics, comp.graphics, comp.os.ms-windows.misc, comp.sys.ibm.pc.hardware, comp.sys.mac.hardware, and comp.windows.x:

```
>>> categories_5 = ['comp.graphics', 'comp.os.ms-windows.misc',
'comp.sys.ibm.pc.hardware', 'comp.sys.mac.hardware', 'comp.windows.x']
>>> groups_5 = fetch_20newsgroups(categories=categories_5)
```

Similar processes (including text clean-up, count vectorization, and t-SNE) are repeated and the resulting plot is displayed as follows:

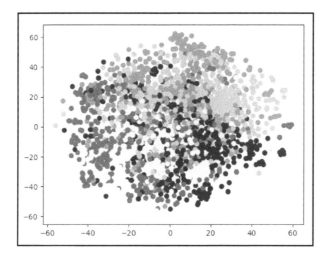

Data points from those five computer-related topics are all over the place, which means they are contextually similar. To conclude, count vectors are great representations for original text data as they are also good at preserving similarity among related topics.

Summary

In this chapter, we acquired the fundamental concepts of NLP as an important subfield in machine learning, including tokenization, stemming and lemmatization, and PoS tagging. We also explored three powerful NLP packages and realized some common tasks using NLTK and spaCy. Then, we continued with the main project exploring newsgroups data. We started with extracting features with tokenization techniques and went through text preprocessing, stop words removal, and stemming and lemmatization. We then performed dimensionality reduction and visualization with t-SNE and proved that count vectorization is a good representation for text data.

We had some fun mining the newsgroups data using dimensionality reduction as an unsupervised approach. Moving forward in the next chapter, we'll be continuing our unsupervised learning journey, specifically on topic modeling and clustering.

Exercises

- Do you think all of the top 500 word tokens contain valuable information? If not, can you impose another list of stop words?
- Can you use stemming instead of lemmatization to process the newsgroups data?
- Can you increase `max_features` in `CountVectorizer` from `500` to `5000` and see how the t-SNE visualization will be affected?
- Try visualizing documents from six topics (similar or dissimilar) and tweak parameters so that the formed clusters look reasonable.

3

Mining the 20 Newsgroups Dataset with Clustering and Topic Modeling Algorithms

In the previous chapter, we went through a text visualization using t-SNE. T-SNE, or any dimensionality reduction algorithm, is a type of unsupervised learning. Moving forward in this chapter, we will be continuing our unsupervised learning journey, specifically focusing specifically on clustering and topic modeling. We will start with how unsupervised learning learns without guidance and how it is good at discovering hidden information underneath data. Then we will talk about clustering as an important branch of unsupervised learning, which identifies different groups of observations from data. For instance, clustering is useful for market segmentation where consumers of similar behaviors are grouped into one segment for marketing purposes. We will perform clustering on the 20 newsgroups text dataset and see what clusters will be produced. Another unsupervised learning route we take is topic modeling, which is the process of extracting themes hidden in the dataset. You will be amused by how many interesting themes we are able to mine from the 20 newsgroups dataset.

We will cover the following topics:

- What is unsupervised learning?
- Types of unsupervised learning
- What is k-means clustering and how does it work?
- Implementing k-means clustering from scratch
- Implementing k-means with scikit-learn
- Optimizing k-means clustering models
- Term frequency-inverse document frequency

- Clustering newsgroups data using k-means
- What is topic modeling?
- Non-negative matrix factorization for topic modeling
- latent Dirichlet allocation for topic modeling
- Topic modeling on newsgroups data

Learning without guidance – unsupervised learning

In the previous chapter, we apply t-SNE to visualize the newsgroup text data in reduced 2 dimensions. T-SNE, or dimensionality reduction in general, is a type of **unsupervised learning**. Instead of having a teacher educating what particular output to produce, be it a class or membership (classification), be it a continuous value (regression), unsupervised learning identifies inherent structures or commonalities in the input data. Since there is no guidance in unsupervised learning, there is no clear answer on what is a right or wrong result. Unsupervised learning has the freedom to discover hidden information underneath input data.

An easy way to understand unsupervised learning is to think of going through many practice questions for an exam. In supervised learning, you are given answers to those practice questions. You basically figure out the relationship between the questions and answers and learn how to map the questions to the answers. Hopefully, you will do well in the actual exam in the end by giving the correct answers. However, in unsupervised learning, you are not provided with the answers to those practice questions. What you might do in this instance could include the following:

- Grouping similar practice questions so that you can later study related questions together at one time
- Finding questions that are highly repetitive so that you will not waste time on those
- Spotting rare questions so that you can be better prepared for them
- Extracting the key chunk of each question by removing boilerplate so you can cut to the point

You will notice that the outcomes of all these tasks are pretty open-ended. They are correct as long as they are able to describe the commonality, the structure underneath the data.

Practice questions are the **features** in machine learning, which are also often called **attributes**, **observations**, or **predictive variables**. Answers to questions are the labels in machine learning, which are also called **targets** or **target variables**. Practice questions with answers provided are **labeled data**. On the contrary, practice questions without answers are **unlabeled data**. Unsupervised learning works with unlabeled data and acts on that information without guidance.

Unsupervised learning can include the following types:

- **Clustering**: This means grouping data based on commonality, which is often used for exploratory data analysis. Grouping similar practice questions mentioned earlier is an example of clustering. Clustering techniques are widely used in customer segmentation or for grouping similar online behaviors for a marketing campaign.
- **Association**: This explores the co-occurrence of particular values of two or more features. Outlier detection (also called anomaly detection) is a typical case, where rare observations are identified. Spotting rare questions in the preceding example can be solved using outlier detection techniques.
- **Projection**: This maps the original feature space to a reduced dimensional space retaining or extracting a set of principal variables. Extracting the key chunk of practice questions is an example projection, or specifically a dimensionality reduction.

Unsupervised learning is extensively employed in the area of NLP mainly because of the difficulty of obtaining labeled text data. Unlike numerical data, such as house and stock data, online click streams, labeling text can sometimes be subjective, manual, and tedious. Unsupervised learning algorithms that do not require labels become effective when it comes to mining text data. In `chapter 2` *Exploring the 20 Newsgroups Dataset with Text Analysis Techniques*, we have experienced using t-SNE to reduce dimensionality of text data. Now, let's explore text mining with clustering algorithms and topic modeling techniques. We start with clustering the newsgroups data.

Clustering newsgroups data using k-means

The newsgroups data comes with labels, the categories of the newsgroups, and a number of categories that are closely related or even overlapping, for instance, the five computer groups: `comp.graphics`, `comp.os.ms-windows.misc`, `comp.sys.ibm.pc.hardware`, `comp.sys.mac.hardware`, and `comp.windows.x`, and the two religion-related ones, `alt.atheism` and `talk.religion.misc`.

Assuming those labels do not exist, will samples from related topics be clustered together? We, herein, resort to the k-means clustering algorithm.

How does k-means clustering work?

The goal of the k-means algorithm is to partition the data into k groups based on feature similarities. K is a predefined property of a k-means clustering model. Each of the k clusters are specified by a centroid (center of a cluster) and each data sample belongs to the cluster with the nearest centroid. During training, the algorithm iteratively updates the k centroids based on the data provided. Specifically, it involves the following steps:

1. **Specifying k**: The algorithm needs to know how many clusters to generate as an end result.
2. **Initializing centroids**: The algorithm starts with randomly selecting k samples from the dataset as centroids.
3. **Assigning clusters**: Now that we have k centroids, samples that share the same closest centroid constitute one cluster. K clusters are created as a result. Note that, **closeness** is usually measured by the **Euclidean distance**. Other metrics can also be used, such as the **Manhattan distance** and **Chebyshev distance**, which are listed in the following table:

Given two 2-dimension data points (x_1, y_1) and (x_2, y_2)	
Distance metric	**Calculation**
Euclidean distance	$\sqrt{(x_1 - x_2)^2 + (y_1 - y_2)^2}$
Manhattan distance	$|x_1 - x_2| + |y_1 - y_2|$
Chebyshev distance	$\max(|x_1 - x_2|, |y_1 - y_2|)$

4. **Updating centroids**: For each cluster, we need to recalculate its center point, which is the mean of all the samples in the cluster. K centroids are updated to be the means of corresponding clusters. This is why the algorithm is called **k-means**.
5. **Repeating step 3 and 4**: It keeps repeating assigning clusters and updating centroids until the model is converged where the centroids stop moving or move small enough, or enough iterations have been taken.

The outputs of a trained k-means clustering model include the following:

- The cluster ID of each training sample, ranging from 1 to k
- K centroids, which can be used to cluster new samples—the new sample will belong to the cluster of the closest centroid

It is very easy to understand the k-means clustering algorithm and its implementation is also straightforward, as we will discover next.

Implementing k-means from scratch

We use the `iris` dataset from scikit-learn as an example. Let's first load the data and visualize it. We herein only use two features out of the original four for simplicity:

```
>>> from sklearn import datasets
>>> iris = datasets.load_iris()
>>> X = iris.data[:, 2:4]
>>> y = iris.target
```

Since the dataset contains three iris classes, we plot it in three different colors, as follows:

```
>>> import numpy as np
>>> from matplotlib import pyplot as plt
>>> y_0 = np.where(y==0)
>>> plt.scatter(X[y_0, 0], X[y_0, 1])
>>> y_1 = np.where(y==1)
>>> plt.scatter(X[y_1, 0], X[y_1, 1])
>>> y_2 = np.where(y==2)
>>> plt.scatter(X[y_2, 0], X[y_2, 1])
>>> plt.show()
```

This will give you the following output for the origin data plot:

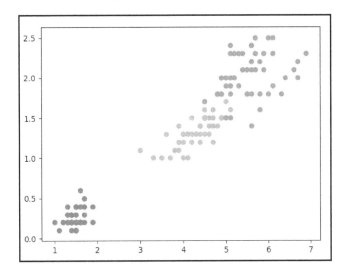

Assuming we know nothing about the label y, we try to cluster the data into three groups, as there seem to be three crows in the preceding plot (or you may say two, which we will come back to later). Let's perform *step 1, specifying k,* and *step 2, initializing centroids,* by randomly selecting three samples as initial `centroids`:

```
>>> k = 3
>>> random_index = np.random.choice(range(len(X)), k)
>>> centroids = X[random_index]
```

We visualize the data (without labels any more) along with the initial random `centroids`:

```
>>> def visualize_centroids(X, centroids):
...     plt.scatter(X[:, 0], X[:, 1])
...     plt.scatter(centroids[:, 0], centroids[:, 1], marker='*',
                                            s=200, c='#050505')
...     plt.show()
>>> visualize_centroids(X, centroids)
```

Refer to the following screenshot for the data, along with the initial random centroids:

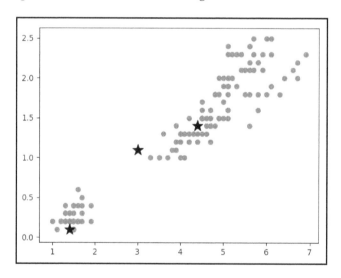

Now we perform *step 3*, which entails assigning clusters based on the nearest centroids. First, we need to define a function calculating distance that is measured by the Euclidean distance, as demonstrated herein:

```
>>> def dist(a, b):
...     return np.linalg.norm(a - b, axis=1)
```

Then, we develop a function that assigns a sample to the cluster of the nearest centroid:

```
>>> def assign_cluster(x, centroids):
...     distances = dist(x, centroids)
...     cluster = np.argmin(distances)
...     return cluster
```

With the clusters assigned, we perform *step 4*, which involves updating the centroids to the mean of all samples in the individual `clusters`:

```
>>> def update_centroids(X, centroids, clusters):
...     for i in range(k):
...         cluster_i = np.where(clusters == i)
...         centroids[i] = np.mean(X[cluster_i], axis=0)
```

Finally, we have *step 5*, which involves repeating *step 3* and *step 4* until the model converges and whichever of the following occurs:

- Centroids move small enough
- Sufficient iterations have been taken

We set the tolerance of the first condition and the maximum number of iterations as follows:

```
>>> tol = 0.0001
>>> max_iter = 100
```

Initialize their starting values, along with the starting clusters for all samples as follows:

```
>>> iter = 0
>>> centroids_diff = 100000
>>> clusters = np.zeros(len(X))
```

With all the components ready, we can train the model iteration by iteration where it first checks convergence, before performing *steps 3* and *step 4*, and visualizes the latest centroids:

```
>>> from copy import deepcopy
>>> while iter < max_iter and centroids_diff > tol:
...     for i in range(len(X)):
...         clusters[i] = assign_cluster(X[i], centroids)
```

```
...          centroids_prev = deepcopy(centroids)
...          update_centroids(X, centroids, clusters)
...          iter += 1
...          centroids_diff = np.linalg.norm(centroids -
                                             centroids_prev)
...          print('Iteration:', str(iter))
...          print('Centroids:\n', centroids)
...          print('Centroids move: {:5.4f}'.format(centroids_diff))
...          visualize_centroids(X, centroids)
```

Let's take a look at the following outputs generated from the preceding commands:

- **Iteration 1**: Take a look at the following output of iteration 1:

    ```
    Iteration: 1
    Centroids:
    [[5.01827957 1.72258065]
    [3.41428571 1.05714286]
    [1.464      0.244 ]]
    Centroids move: 0.8274
    ```

    The plot of centroids after iteration 1 is as follows:

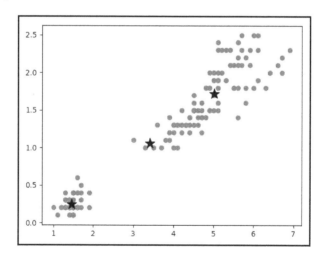

- **Iteration 2**: Take a look at the following output of iteration 2:

    ```
    Iteration: 2
    Centroids:
    [[5.20897436 1.81923077]
    [3.83181818 1.16818182]
    [1.464      0.244 ]]
    Centroids move: 0.4820
    ```

The plot of centroids after iteration 2 is as follows:

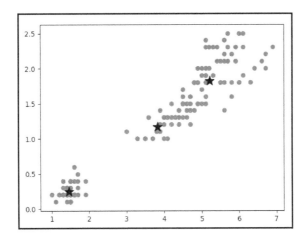

- **Iteration 3**: Take a look at the following output of iteration 3:

```
Iteration: 3
Centroids:
[[5.3796875  1.9125 ]
 [4.06388889 1.25555556]
 [1.464      0.244 ]]
Centroids move: 0.3152
```

The plot of centroids after iteration 3 is as follows:

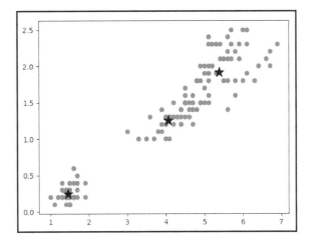

- **Iteration 4**: Take a look at the following output of iteration 4:

```
Iteration: 4
Centroids:
[[5.51481481 1.99444444]
 [4.19130435 1.30217391]
 [1.464      0.244 ]]
Centroids move: 0.2083
```

The plot of centroids after iteration 4 is as follows:

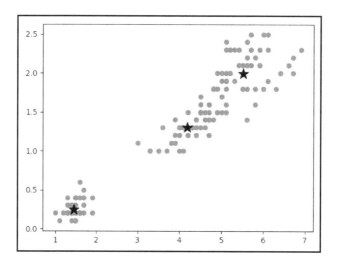

- **Iteration 5**: Take a look at the following output of iteration 5:

```
Iteration: 5
Centroids:
[[5.53846154 2.01346154]
 [4.22083333 1.31041667]
 [1.464      0.244 ]]
Centroids move: 0.0431
```

The plot of centroids after iteration 5 is as follows:

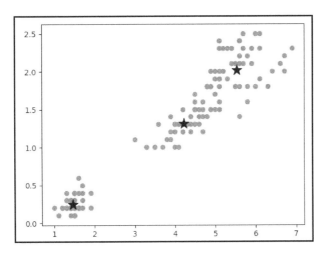

- **Iteration 6**: Take a look at the following output of iteration 6:

```
Iteration: 6
Centroids:
[[5.58367347 2.02653061]
[4.25490196 1.33921569]
[1.464 0.244 ]]
Centroids move: 0.0648
```

The plot of centroids after iteration 6 is as follows:

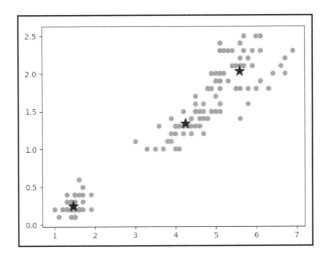

- **Iteration 7**: Take a look at the following output of iteration 7:

```
Iteration: 7
Centroids:
[[5.59583333 2.0375 ]
[4.26923077 1.34230769]
[1.464 0.244 ]]
Centroids move: 0.0220
```

The plot of centroids after iteration 7 is as follows:

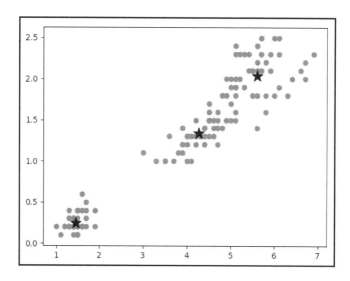

- **Iteration 8**: Take a look at the following output of iteration 8:

```
Iteration: 8
Centroids:
[[5.59583333 2.0375 ]
[4.26923077 1.34230769]
[1.464 0.244 ]]
Centroids move: 0.0000
```

The plot of centroids after iteration 8 is as follows:

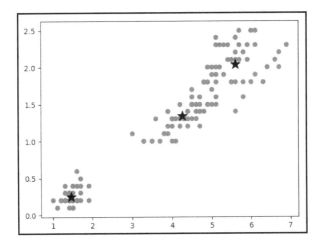

The model converges after eight iterations. The resulting centroids look promising, and we can also plot the clusters:

```
>>> for i in range(k):
...     cluster_i = np.where(clusters == i)
...     plt.scatter(X[cluster_i, 0], X[cluster_i, 1])
>>> plt.scatter(centroids[:, 0], centroids[:, 1], marker='*',
                                      s=200, c='#050505')
>>> plt.show()
```

Refer to the following screenshot for the end result:

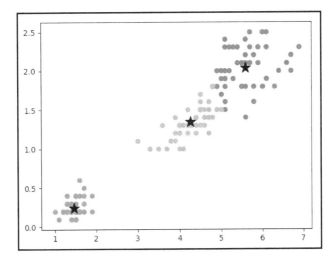

Implementing k-means with scikit-learn

Having developed our own k-means clustering model, we can now learn how to use scikit-learn for a quicker solution by performing the following steps:

1. First, import the `KMeans` class and initialize a model with three clusters as follows:

```
>>> from sklearn.cluster import KMeans
>>> kmeans_sk = KMeans(n_clusters=3, random_state=42)
```

The `KMeans` class takes in the following important parameters:

Constructor parameter	Default value	Example values	Description
n_clusters	8	3, 5, 10	K clusters
max_iter	300	10, 100, 500	Maximum number of iterations
tol	1e-4	1e-5, 1e-8	Tolerance to declare convergence
random_state	None	0, 42	Random seed for program reproducibility

2. We then fit the model on the data:

```
>>> kmeans_sk.fit(X)
```

3. After that, we can obtain the clustering results, including the clusters for data samples and centroids of individual clusters:

```
>>> clusters_sk = kmeans_sk.labels_
>>> centroids_sk = kmeans_sk.cluster_centers_
```

4. Similarly, we plot the clusters along with the centroids:

```
>>> for i in range(k):
...         cluster_i = np.where(clusters_sk == i)
...         plt.scatter(X[cluster_i, 0], X[cluster_i, 1])
>>> plt.scatter(centroids_sk[:, 0], centroids_sk[:, 1],
                           marker='*', s=200, c='#050505')
>>> plt.show()
```

This will result in the following output:

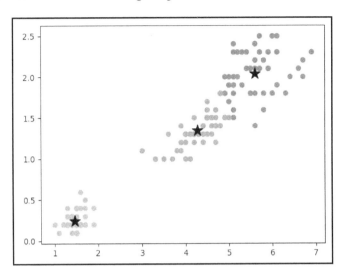

Choosing the value of k

Let's return to our earlier discussion on what is the right value for k. In the preceding example, it is more intuitive to set it to 3 since we know there are three classes in total. However, in most cases, we don't know how many groups are sufficient or efficient, while the algorithm needs a specific value of k to start with. So, how can we choose the value for k? There is a famous approach called the **Elbow method**.

In the Elbow method, different values of k are chosen and corresponding models are trained; for each trained model, the **sum of squared errors**, or **SSE** (also called the **sum of within-cluster distances**) to centroids is calculated and is plotted against k. Note, for one cluster, the squared error (or the within-cluster distance) is computed as the sum of the squared distances from individual samples in the cluster to the centroid. The optimal k is chosen where the marginal drop of SSE starts to decrease dramatically. It means further clustering does not provide any substantial gain.

Let's apply the Elbow method to the example we covered in the previous section (that's what this book is all about). We perform k-means clustering under different values of `k` on the `iris` data:

```
>>> iris = datasets.load_iris()
>>> X = iris.data
>>> y = iris.target
>>> k_list = list(range(1, 7))
>>> sse_list = [0] * len(k_list)
```

We, herein, use the whole feature space and `k` ranges from 1 to 6. Then, we train individual models and record the resulting SSE respectively:

```
>>> for k_ind, k in enumerate(k_list):
...     kmeans = KMeans(n_clusters=k, random_state=42)
...     kmeans.fit(X)
...     clusters = kmeans.labels_
...     centroids = kmeans.clustercenters
...     sse = 0
...     for i in range(k):
...         cluster_i = np.where(clusters == i)
...         sse += np.linalg.norm(X[cluster_i] - centroids[i])
...     print('k={}, SSE={}'.format(k, sse))
...     sse_list[k_ind] = sse
k=1, SSE=26.103076447039722
k=2, SSE=16.469773740281195
k=3, SSE=15.089477089696558
k=4, SSE=15.0307321707491
k=5, SSE=14.858930749063735
k=6, SSE=14.883090350867239
```

Finally, plot the SSE versus the various `k` ranges as follows:

```
>>> plt.plot(k_list, sse_list)
>>> plt.show()
```

This will result in the following output:

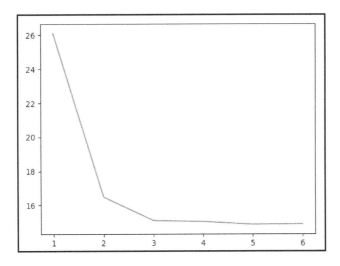

Apparently, the Elbow point is k=3, since the drop in SSE slows down dramatically right after 3. Hence, k=3 is an optimal solution in this case, which is consistent with the fact.

Clustering newsgroups data using k-means

Up to this point, you should be very familiar with k-means clustering. Let's see what we are able to mine from the newsgroups dataset using this algorithm. We, herein, use all data from four categories as an example.

We first load the data from those newsgroups and preprocess it as we did in Chapter 2, *Mining the 20 Newsgroups Dataset with Clustering and Topic Modeling Algorithms*:

```
>>> from sklearn.datasets import fetch_20newsgroups
>>> categories = [
...     'alt.atheism',
...     'talk.religion.misc',
...     'comp.graphics',
...     'sci.space',
... ]
>>> groups = fetch_20newsgroups(subset='all',
                                 categories=categories)
>>> labels = groups.target
>>> label_names = groups.target_names
>>> def is_letter_only(word):
...     for char in word:
...         if not char.isalpha():
```

```
...                  return False
...          return True
>>> from nltk.corpus import names
>>> all_names = set(names.words())
>>> from nltk.stem import WordNetLemmatizer
>>> lemmatizer = WordNetLemmatizer()
>>> data_cleaned = []
>>> for doc in groups.data:
...      doc = doc.lower()
...      doc_cleaned = ' '.join(lemmatizer.lemmatize(word) for
                     word in doc.split() if is_letter_only(word)
                     and word not in all_names)
...      data_cleaned.append(doc_cleaned)
```

We then convert the cleaned text data into count vectors using `CountVectorizer` of `scikit-learn`:

```
>>> from sklearn.feature_extraction.text import CountVectorizer
>>> count_vector = CountVectorizer(stop_words="english",
                        max_features=None, max_df=0.5, min_df=2)
>>> data = count_vector.fit_transform(data_cleaned)
```

Note the vectorizer we use here does not limit the number of features (word tokens), but the minimum and maximum document frequency, which are 2 and 50% of the dataset respectively. **Document frequency** of a word is measured by the fraction of documents (samples) in the dataset that contain this word.

With the input data ready, we now try to cluster them into four groups as follows:

```
>>> from sklearn.cluster import KMeans
>>> k = 4
>>> kmeans = KMeans(n_clusters=k, random_state=42)
>>> kmeans.fit(data)
```

Let's do a quick check on the sizes of the resulting clusters:

```
>>> clusters = kmeans.labels_
>>> from collections import Counter
>>> print(Counter(clusters))
Counter({3: 3360, 0: 17, 1: 7, 2: 3})
```

The clusters don't look absolutely correct, with most samples (3360 samples) congested in one big cluster (cluster 3). What could have gone wrong? It turns out that our count-based features are not sufficiently representative. A better numerical representation for text data is the term **frequency-inverse document frequency** (**tf-idf**). Instead of simply using the token count, or the so-called **term frequency** (**tf**), it assigns each term frequency a weighting factor that is inversely proportional to the document frequency. In practice, the **idf** factor of a term *t* in documents *D* is calculated as follows:

$$idf(t, D) = log\frac{n_D}{1 + n_t}$$

Here, n_D is the total number of documents, n_t is the number of documents containing the term *t*, and the *1* is added to avoid division by zero.

With the idf factor incorporated, the tf-idf representation diminishes the weight of common terms (such as *get*, and *make*) occurring frequently, and emphasizes terms that rarely occur, but that convey an important meaning.

To use the tf-idf representation, we just need to replace `CountVectorizer` with `TfidfVectorizer` from scikit-learn as follows:

```
>>> from sklearn.feature_extraction.text import TfidfVectorizer
>>> tfidf_vector = TfidfVectorizer(stop_words='english',
                       max_features=None, max_df=0.5, min_df=2)
```

Now, redo feature extraction using the tf-idf vectorizer and the k-means clustering algorithm on the resulting feature space:

```
>>> data = tfidf_vector.fit_transform(data_cleaned)
>>> kmeans.fit(data)
>>> clusters = kmeans.labels_
print(Counter(clusters))
Counter({1: 1560, 2: 686, 3: 646, 0: 495})
```

The clustering result becomes more reasonable.

We also take a closer look at the clusters by examining what they contain and the top 10 terms (the terms with the 10 highest tf-idf) representing each cluster:

```
>>> cluster_label = {i: labels[np.where(clusters == i)] for i in
                                         range(k)}
>>> terms = tfidf_vector.get_feature_names()
>>> centroids = kmeans.clustercenters
>>> for cluster, index_list in cluster_label.items():
...        counter = Counter(cluster_label[cluster])
...        print('cluster_{}: {} samples'.format(cluster, len(index_list)))
```

```
...          for label_index, count in sorted(counter.items(),
                                 key=lambda x: x[1], reverse=True):
...             print('{}: {} samples'.format(label_names[label_index], count))
...          print('Top 10 terms:')
...          for ind in centroids[cluster].argsort()[-10:]:
...             print(' %s' % terms[ind], end="")
...          print()

cluster_0: 495 samples
sci.space: 494 samples
comp.graphics: 1 samples
Top 10 terms:
toronto moon zoology nasa hst mission wa launch shuttle space
cluster_1: 1560 samples
sci.space: 459 samples
alt.atheism: 430 samples
talk.religion.misc: 352 samples
comp.graphics: 319 samples
Top 10 terms:
people new think know like ha just university article wa
cluster_2: 686 samples
comp.graphics: 651 samples
sci.space: 32 samples
alt.atheism: 2 samples
talk.religion.misc: 1 samples
Top 10 terms:
know thanks need format looking university program file graphic image
cluster_3: 646 samples
alt.atheism: 367 samples
talk.religion.misc: 275 samples
sci.space: 2 samples
comp.graphics: 2 samples
Top 10 terms:
moral article morality think jesus people say christian wa god
```

From what we observe in the preceding results:

- `cluster_0` is obviously about space and includes almost all `sci.space` samples and related terms such as `moon`, `nasa`, `launch`, `shuttle`, and `space`.
- `cluster_1` is more of a generic topic.

- cluster_2 is more about computer graphics and related terms, such as format, program, file, graphic, and image.
- cluster_3 is an interesting one, which successfully brings together two overlapping topics, atheism and religion, with key terms including moral, morality, jesus, christian, and god.

 Feel free to try different values of k, or use the Elbow method to find the optimal one (this is actually an exercise for this chapter).

It is quite interesting to find key terms for each text group via clustering. Topic modeling is another approach for doing so, but in a much more direct way. It does not simply search for the key terms in individual clusters generated beforehand. What it does do is that it directly extracts collections of key terms over documents. You will see how this works in the next section.

Discovering underlying topics in newsgroups

A **topic model** is a type of statistical model for discovering the probability distributions of words linked to the topic. The topic in topic modeling does not exactly match the dictionary definition, but corresponds to a nebulous statistical concept, an abstraction occurs in a collection of documents.

When we read a document, we expect certain words appearing in the title or the body of the text to capture the semantic context of the document. An article about Python programming will have words such as *class* and *function*, while a story about snakes will have words such as *eggs* and *afraid*. Documents usually have multiple topics; for instance, this recipe is about three things, topic modeling, non-negative matrix factorization, and latent Dirichlet allocation, which we will discuss shortly. We can therefore define an additive model for topics by assigning different weights to topics.

Topic modeling is widely used for mining hidden semantic structures in given text data. There are two popular topic modeling algorithms—non-negative matrix factorization, and latent Dirichlet allocation. We will go through both of these in the next two sections.

Topic modeling using NMF

Non-negative matrix factorization (**NMF**) relies heavily on linear algebra. It factorizes an input matrix, **V**, into a product of two smaller matrices, **W** and **H**, in such a way that these three matrices have no negative values. In the context of NLP, these three matrices have the following meanings:

- The input matrix **V** is the term counts or tf-idf matrix of size $n * m$, where n is the number of documents or samples, and m is the number of terms.
- The first decomposition output matrix W is the feature matrix of size $t * m$, where t is the number of topics specified. Each row of **W** represents a topic with each element in the row representing the rank of a term in the topic.
- The second decomposition output matrix H is the coefficient matrix of size $n * t$. Each row of **H** represents a document, with each element in the row representing the weight of a topic within the document.

How to derive the computation of **W** and **H** is beyond the scope of this book. However, you can refer to the following diagram to get a better sense of how NMF works:

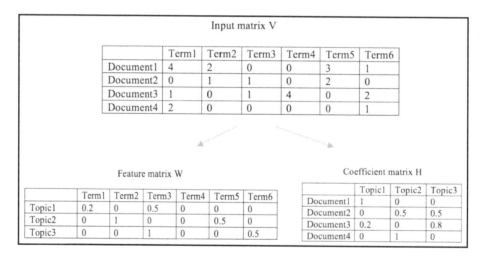

If you are interested in reading more about NMF, feel free to check out the original paper *Generalized Nonnegative Matrix Approximations with Bregman Divergences* by Inderjit S. Dhillon and Suvrit Sra in NIPS 2005.

Let's now apply NMF to our newsgroups data. Scikit-learn has a nice module for decomposition that includes NMF:

```
>>> from sklearn.decomposition import NMF
>>> t = 20
>>> nmf = NMF(n_components=t, random_state=42)
```

We specify 20 topics (n_components) as an example. Important parameters of the model are included in the following table:

Constructor parameter	Default value	Example values	Description
n_components	None	5, 10, 20	Number of components – in the context of topic modeling, this corresponds to the number of topics. If None, it becomes the number of input features.
max_iter	200	100, 200	Maximum number of iterations
tol	1e-4	1e-5, 1e-8	Tolerance to declare convergence

We use the term matrix as input to the NMF model, but you could also use the tf-idf one instead. We, herein, reuse count_vector, , as defined previously:

```
>>> data = count_vector.fit_transform(data_cleaned)
```

Now, fit the NMF model nmf on the term matrix data:

```
>>> nmf.fit(data)
```

We can obtain the resulting topic-feature rank **W** after the model is trained:

```
>>> nmf.components_
[[0.00000000e+00 0.00000000e+00 0.00000000e+00 ... 0.00000000e+00
  0.00000000e+00 1.81952400e-04]
 [0.00000000e+00 0.00000000e+00 0.00000000e+00 ... 0.00000000e+00
  7.35497518e-04 3.65665719e-03]
 [0.00000000e+00 0.00000000e+00 0.00000000e+00 ... 0.00000000e+00
  0.00000000e+00 0.00000000e+00]
 ...
 [0.00000000e+00 0.00000000e+00 0.00000000e+00 ... 2.69725134e-02
  0.00000000e+00 0.00000000e+00]
 [0.00000000e+00 0.00000000e+00 0.00000000e+00 ... 0.00000000e+00
  0.00000000e+00 4.26844886e-05]]
```

```
[0.00000000e+00 0.00000000e+00 0.00000000e+00 ... 0.00000000e+00
 0.00000000e+00 0.00000000e+00]]
```

For each topic, we display the top 10 terms based on their ranks:

```
>>> terms = count_vector.get_feature_names()
>>> for topic_idx, topic in enumerate(nmf.components_):
...         print("Topic {}:" .format(topic_idx))
...         print(" ".join([terms[i] for i in topic.argsort()[-10:]]))
Topic 0:
available quality program free color version gif file image jpeg
Topic 1:
ha article make know doe say like just people think
Topic 2:
include available analysis user software ha processing data tool image
Topic 3:
atmosphere kilometer surface ha earth wa planet moon spacecraft solar
Topic 4:
communication technology venture service market ha commercial space
satellite launch
Topic 5:
verse wa jesus father mormon shall unto mcconkie lord god
Topic 6:
format message server object image mail file ray send graphic
Topic 7:
christian people doe atheism believe religion belief religious god atheist
Topic 8:
file graphic grass program ha package ftp available image data
Topic 9:
speed material unified star larson book universe theory physicist physical
Topic 10:
planetary station program group astronaut center mission shuttle nasa space
Topic 11:
infrared high astronomical center acronym observatory satellite national
telescope space
Topic 12:
used occurs true form ha ad premise conclusion argument fallacy
Topic 13:
gospel people day psalm prophecy christian ha matthew wa jesus
Topic 14:
doe word hanging say greek matthew mr act wa juda
Topic 15:
siggraph graphic file information format isbn data image ftp available
Topic 16:
venera mar lunar surface space venus soviet mission wa probe
Topic 17:
april book like year time people new did article wa
Topic 18:
```

```
site retrieve ftp software data information client database gopher search
Topic 19:
use look xv color make program correction bit gamma image
```

There are a number of interesting topics, for instance, computer graphics-related topics, such as 0, 2, 6, and 8, space-related ones, such as 3, 4, and 9, and religion-related ones, such as 5, 7, and 13. There are also two topics, 1 and 12, that are hard to interpret, which is totally fine since topic modeling is a kind of free-form learning.

Topic modeling using LDA

Let's explore another popular topic modeling algorithm, **latent Dirichlet allocation** (LDA). LDA is a generative probabilistic graphical model that explains each input document by means of a mixture of topics with certain probabilities. Again, **topic** in topic modeling means a collection of words with a certain connection. In other words, LDA basically deals with two probability values, P(term | topic) and P(topic | document). This can be difficult to understand at the beginning. So, let's start from the bottom, the end result of an LDA model.

Let's take a look at the following set of documents:

```
Document 1: This restaurant is famous for fish and chips.
Document 2: I had fish and rice for lunch.
Document 3: My sister bought me a cute kitten.
Document 4: Some research shows eating too much rice is bad.
Document 5: I always forget to feed fish to my cat.
```

Now, let's say we want two topics. The topics derived from these documents may appear as follows:

```
Topic 1: 30% fish, 20% chip, 30% rice, 10% lunch, 10% restaurant (which we
can interpret Topic 1 to be food related)
Topic 2: 40% cute, 40% cat, 10% fish, 10% feed (which we can interpret
Topic 1 to be about pet)
```

Therefore, we find how each document is represented by these two topics:

```
Documents 1: 85% Topic 1, 15% Topic 2
Documents 2: 88% Topic 1, 12% Topic 2
Documents 3: 100% Topic 2
Documents 4: 100% Topic 1
Documents 5: 33% Topic 1, 67% Topic 2
```

After seeing a dummy example, we come back to its learning procedure:

1. Specify the number of topics, *T*. Now we have topic 1, 2, ..., and *T*.
2. For each document, randomly assign one of the topics to each term in the document.
3. For each document, calculate *P(topic=t | document)*, which is the proportion of terms in the document that are assigned to the topic *t*.
4. For each topic, calculate *P(term=w | topic)*, which is the proportion of term *w* among all terms that are assigned to the topic.
5. For each term *w*, reassign its topic based on the latest probabilities *P(topic=t | document)* and *P(term=w | topic=t)*.
6. Repeat *steps 3* to *step 5* under the latest topic distributions for each iteration. The training stops if the model converges or reaches the maximum number of iterations.

LDA is trained in a generative manner, where it tries to abstract from the documents a set of hidden topics that are likely to generate a certain collection of words.

With all this in mind, let's see LDA in action. The LDA model is also included in scikit-learn:

```
>>> from sklearn.decomposition import LatentDirichletAllocation
>>> t = 20
>>> lda = LatentDirichletAllocation(n_components=t,
                    learning_method='batch',random_state=42)
```

Again, we specify 20 topics (n_components). The key parameters of the model are included in the following table:

Constructor parameter	Default value	Example values	Description
n_components	10	5, 10, 20	Number of components – in the context of topic modeling, this corresponds to the number of topics.
learning_method	"batch"	"online", "batch"	In batch mode, all training data are used for each update. In online mode, mini-batch of training data is used for each update. In general, if the data size is large, the online mode is faster.
max_iter	10	10, 20	Maximum number of iterations
randome_state	None	0, 42	Seed used by the random number generator.

For the input data to LDA, remember that LDA only takes in term counts as it is a probabilistic graphical model. This is unlike NMF, which can work with both the term count matrix and the tf-idf matrix as long as they are non-negative data. Again, we use the term matrix defined previously as input to the lda model:

```
>>> data = count_vector.fit_transform(data_cleaned)
```

Now, fit the LDA model on the term matrix, data:

```
>>> lda.fit(data)
```

We can obtain the resulting topic-term rank after the model is trained:

```
>>> lda.components_
[[0.05      2.05      2.05      ...  0.05      0.05      0.05 ]
 [0.05      0.05      0.05      ...  0.05      0.05      0.05 ]
 [0.05      0.05      0.05      ...  4.0336285 0.05      0.05 ]
 ...
 [0.05      0.05      0.05      ...  0.05      0.05      0.05 ]
 [0.05      0.05      0.05      ...  0.05      0.05      0.05 ]
 [0.05      0.05      0.05      ...  0.05      0.05      3.05 ]]
```

Similarly, for each topic, we display the top 10 terms based on their ranks as follows:

```
>>> terms = count_vector.get_feature_names()
>>> for topic_idx, topic in enumerate(lda.components_):
...         print("Topic {}:".format(topic_idx))
...         print(" ".join([terms[i] for i in
                                 topic.argsort()[-10:]]))
Topic 0:
atheist doe ha believe say jesus people christian wa god
Topic 1:
moment just adobe want know ha wa hacker article radius
Topic 2:
center point ha wa available research computer data graphic hst
Topic 3:
objective argument just thing doe people wa think say article
Topic 4:
time like brian ha good life want know just wa
Topic 5:
computer graphic think know need university just article wa like
Topic 6:
free program color doe use version gif jpeg file image
Topic 7:
gamma ray did know university ha just like article wa
Topic 8:
tool ha processing using data software color program bit image
Topic 9:
```

```
apr men know ha think woman just university article wa
Topic 10:
jpl propulsion mission april mar jet command data spacecraft wa
Topic 11:
russian like ha university redesign point option article space station
Topic 12:
ha van book star material physicist universe physical theory wa
Topic 13:
bank doe book law wa article rushdie muslim islam islamic
Topic 14:
think gopher routine point polygon book university article know wa
Topic 15:
ha rocket new lunar mission satellite shuttle nasa launch space
Topic 16:
want right article ha make like just think people wa
Topic 17:
just light space henry wa like zoology sky article toronto
Topic 18:
comet venus solar moon orbit planet earth probe ha wa
Topic 19:
site format image mail program available ftp send file graphic
```

There are a number of interesting topics that we just mined, for instance, computer graphics-related topics, such as 2, 5, 6, 8, and 19, space-related ones, such as 10, 11, 12, and 15, and religion-related ones, such as 0 and 13. There are also topics involving noise, for example, 9 and 16, which may require some imagination to interpret. Again, this is not surprising at all, since LDA, or topic modeling in general, is a kind of free-form learning.

Summary

The project in this chapter was about finding hidden similarity underneath newsgroups data, be it semantic groups, be it themes, or word clouds. We started with what unsupervised learning does and the typical types of unsupervised learning algorithms. We then introduced unsupervised learning clustering and studied a popular clustering algorithm, k-means, in detail. We also talked about tf-idf as a more efficient feature extraction tool for text data. After that, we performed k-means clustering on the newsgroups data and obtained four meaningful clusters. After examining the key terms in each resulting cluster, we went straight to extracting representative terms among original documents using topic modeling techniques. Two powerful topic modeling approaches, NMF and LDA, were discussed and implemented. Finally, we had some fun interpreting the topics we obtained from both methods.

Hitherto, we have covered all the main categories of unsupervised learning, including dimensionality reduction in `Chapter 2`, *Mining the 20 Newsgroups Dataset with Clustering and Topic Modeling Algorithms,* clustering in this chapter, as well as topic modeling, which is also dimensionality reduction in a way. Starting from the next chapter, we will talk about supervised learning; specifically, binary classification will be our entry point.

Exercises

- Perform k-means clustering on newsgroups data using different values of k, or use the Elbow method to find the optimal one. See if you get better grouping results.
- Try different numbers of topics, in either NMF or LDA, and see which one produces more meaningful topics in the end. It should be a fun exercise.
- Can you experiment with NMF or LDA on the entire 20 groups of newsgroups data? Are the resulting topics full of noise or gems?

4
Detecting Spam Email with Naive Bayes

As promised, in this chapter, we kick off our supervised learning journey with machine learning classification, specifically, binary classification. We will be learning with the goal of building a high-performing spam email detector. It is a good starting point to learn classification with a real-life example—our email service providers are already doing this for us, and so can we. We will be learning the fundamental concepts of classification, including what it does and its various types and applications, with a focus on solving spam detection using a simple yet powerful algorithm, Naïve Bayes. One last thing: we will be demonstrating how to fine-tune a model, which is an important skill for every data science or machine learning practitioner to learn.

We will get into detail on the following topics:

- What is machine learning classification?
- Types of classification
- Applications of text classification
- The Naïve Bayes classifier
- The mechanics of Naïve Bayes
- The Naïve Bayes implementations
- Spam email detection with Naïve Bayes
- Classification performance evaluation
- Cross-validation
- Tuning a classification model

Getting started with classification

Spam email detection is basically a machine learning classification problem. Let's get started by learning important concepts of machine learning classification. **Classification** is one of the main instances of supervised learning. Given a training set of data containing observations and their associated categorical outputs, the goal of classification is to learn a general rule that correctly maps the **observations** (also called **features** or **predictive variables**) to the target **categories** (also called **labels** or **classes**). Put another way, a trained classification model will be generated after learning from features and targets of training samples, as shown in the first half of the following diagram. When new or unseen data comes in, the trained model will be able to determine their desired memberships. Class information will be predicted based on the known input features using the trained classification model, as displayed in the second half of the following diagram:

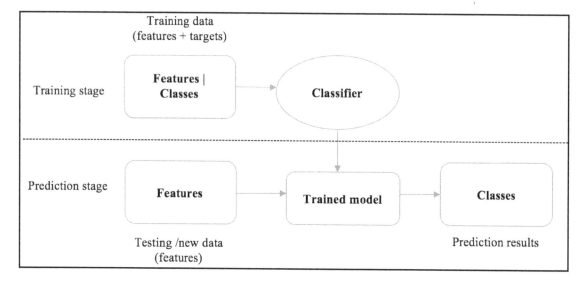

Types of classification

Based on the possibility of class output, machine learning classification can be categorized into binary classification, multiclass classification, and multilabel classification, as follows:

- **Binary classification**: This classifies observations into one of two possible classes. The example of spam email filtering we mentioned earlier is a typical use case of binary classification, which identifies email messages (input observations) as *spam* or *not spam* (output classes). Customer churn prediction is another frequently mentioned example, where the prediction system takes in customer segment data and activity data from CRM systems and identifies which customers are likely to churn. Another application in the marketing and advertising industry is click-through prediction for online ads—that is, whether or not an ad will be clicked, given users' cookie information and browsing history. Last, but not least, binary classification has also been employed in biomedical science, for example, in early cancer diagnosis, classifying patients into high or low risk groups based on MRI images. As demonstrated in the following example, binary classification tries to find a way to separate data from two classes:

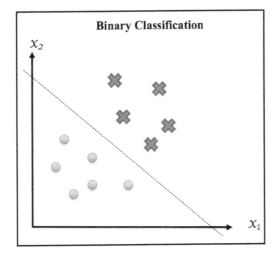

- **Multiclass classification**: This classification is also called **multinomial classification**, and allows more than two possible classes, as opposed to only two in binary cases. Handwritten digit recognition is a common instance of classification and has a long history of research and development since the early 1900s. A classification system, for example, learns to read and understand handwritten ZIP codes (digits from 0 to 9 in most countries) by which envelopes are automatically sorted. Handwritten digit recognition has become a *hello world* in the journey of studying machine learning, and the scanned document dataset constructed from the National Institute of Standards and Technology, called **MNIST** (short for Modified National Institute of Standards and Technology), is a benchmark dataset frequently used to test and evaluate multiclass classification models. The following screenshot shows the four samples taken from the MNIST dataset:

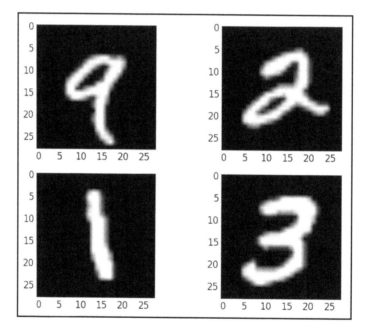

In the following example, the multiclass classification model tries to find segregation boundaries to separate data from the following three different classes:

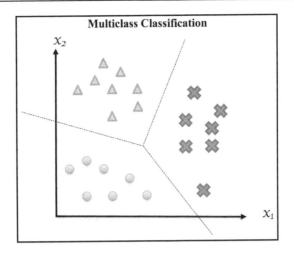

Multiclass Classification

- **Multi-label classification**: This classification is different from the first two types of classification, where target classes are disjointed. Research attention to this field has been increasingly drawn by the nature of the omnipresence of categories in modern applications. For example, a picture that captures a sea and sunset can simultaneously belong to both conceptual scenes, whereas it can only be an image of either cat or dog in a binary case, or one type of fruit among oranges, apples, and bananas in a multiclass case. Similarly, adventure films are often combined with other genres, such as fantasy, science fiction, horror, and drama. Another typical application is protein function classification, as a protein may have more than one function—storage, antibody, support, transport, and so on. One approach to solve an n label classification problem is to transform it into a set of n binary classifications problem, which is then handled by individual binary classifiers. Refer to the following diagram of restructuring a multi-label classification problem into multiple binary classification problems:

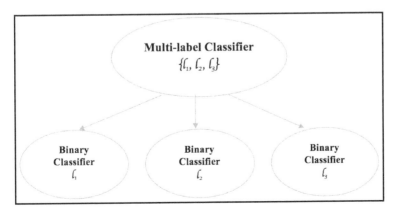

Applications of text classification

As was discussed in Chapter 3, *Mining the 20 Newsgroups Dataset with Clustering and Topic Modeling Algorithms*, unsupervised learning, including clustering and topic modeling, can be applied to text data. We will continue to see how supervised learning, specifically classification, is used in the text domain.

In fact, classification has been widely used in text analysis and news analytics. For instance, classification algorithms are used to identify news sentiment, positive or negative in a binary case, or positive, neutral, or negative in a multiclass classification case. News sentiment analysis provides a significant signal to trading in the stock market.

Another example that comes to mind is news topic classification, where classes may or may not be mutually exclusive. In the newsgroup example that we just worked on, classes are mutually exclusive (despite slight overlapping), such as computer graphics, motorcycles, baseball, hockey, space, and religion. We will demonstrate how to use machine learning algorithms to solve such multiclass classification problems in Chapter 5, *Classifying Newsgroup Topic with Support Vector Machine*. It is, however, good to realize that a news article is occasionally assigned multiple categories, where, properly speaking, multi-label classification is more suitable. For example, an article about the Olympic Games may be labeled as both sports and politics if there is an unexpected political involvement.

Finally, a text classification application that is perhaps difficult to realize is named-entity recognition (NER). Named entities are phrases of definitive categories, such as names of persons, companies, geographic locations, dates and times, quantities, and monetary values. NER is an important subtask of information extraction, to seek and identify such entities. For example, we can conduct NER on the following sentence: SpaceX[Organization], a California[Location]-based company founded by a famous tech entrepreneur Elon Musk[Person], announced that it would manufacture the next-generation, 9[Quantity]-meter-diameter launch vehicle and spaceship for the first orbital flight in 2020[Date].

To solve these problems, researchers have developed many power classification algorithms, among which Naïve Bayes and **support vector machine** (**SVM**) models are often used for text classification. In the following sections, we will cover the mechanics of Naïve Bayes and its in-depth implementation, along with other important concepts, including classifier tuning and classification performance evaluation.

Exploring Naïve Bayes

The **Naïve Bayes** classifier belongs to the family of probabilistic classifiers that computes the probabilities of each **predictive feature** (also called **attribute**) of the data belonging to each class in order to make a prediction of probability distribution over all classes (of course, including the most likely class that the data sample is associated with). What it does, as its name indicates, is as follows:

- **Bayes**: As in, it maps the probabilities of observing input features given belonging classes, to the probability distribution over classes based on Bayes' theorem. We will explain Bayes' theorem with the later examples in this chapter
- **Naïve**: As in, it simplifies probability computation by assuming that predictive features are mutually independent.

Learning Bayes' theorem by examples

It is important to understand Bayes' theorem before diving into the classifier. Let A and B denote two events. Events could be that *it will rain tomorrow; 2 kings are drawn from a deck of cards*; or *a person has cancer*. In Bayes' theorem, $P(A \mid B)$ is the probability that A occurs given that B is true. It can be computed as follows:

$$P(A \mid B) = \frac{P(B \mid A)P(A)}{P(B)}$$

Here, $P(B \mid A)$ is the probability of observing B given that A occurs, while $P(A)$ and $P(B)$ are the probability that A and B occur, respectively. Too abstract? Let's look at some of the following concrete examples:

- **Example 1**: Given two coins, one is unfair with 90% of flips getting a head and 10% getting a tail, while the other one is fair. Randomly pick one coin and flip it. What is the probability that this coin is the unfair one, if we get a head?

  We solve it by first denoting U for the event of picking the unfair coin, F for the fair coin, and H for the event of getting a head. So the probability that the unfair has been picked when we get a head, $P(U \mid H)$ can be calculated with the following:

$$P(U \mid H) = \frac{P(H \mid U)P(U)}{P(H)}$$

As we know P(H|U) is 90% . P(U) is 0.5 because we randomly pick a coin out of two. However, deriving the probability of getting a head *P(H)* is not that straightforward, as two events can lead to the following, where U is when the unfair one is picked and F is when the fair coin is picked:

$$P(H) = P(H|U)P(U) + P(H|F)P(F)$$

So *P(U |H)* becomes the following:

$$P(U|H) = \frac{P(H|U)P(U)}{P(H)} = \frac{P(H|U)P(U)}{P(H|U)P(U) + P(H|F)P(F)} = \frac{0.9 * 0.5}{0.9 * 0.5 + 0.5 * 0.5} = 0.64$$

- **Example 2**: Suppose a physician reported the following cancer screening test scenario among 10,000 people:

	Cancer	No cancer	Total
Text positive	80	900	980
Text negative	20	9,000	9,020
Total	100	9,900	10,000

It indicates for example **80** out of **100** cancer patients are correctly diagnosed, while the other **20** are not; cancer is falsely detected in **900** out of **9,900** healthy people.

If the result of this screening test on a person is positive, what is the probability that they actually has cancer?

Let's assign the event of having cancer and positive testing result as C and *Pos* respectively. Apply Bayes' theorem to calculate *P(C|Pos)*:

$$P(C|Pos) = \frac{P(Pos|C)P(C)}{P(Pos)} = \frac{\frac{80}{100} * \frac{100}{10000}}{\frac{980}{10000}} = 8.16\%$$

Given a positive screening result, the chance that the subject has cancer is 8.16%, which is significantly higher than the one under general assumption (100/10000=1%) without undergoing the screening.

- **Example 3**: Three machines A, B, and C in a factory account for 35%, 20%, and 45% of the bulb production. And the fraction of defective bulbs produced by each machine is 1.5%, 1%, and 2% respectively. A bulb produced by this factory was identified defective, which is denoted as event D. What are the probabilities that this bulb was manufactured by machine A, B, and C respectively?

Again, simply just follow Bayes' theorem, as follows:

$$P(A|D) = \frac{P(D|A)P(A)}{P(D)} = \frac{P(D|A)P(A)}{P(D|A)P(A) + P(D|B)P(B) + P(D|C)P(C)}$$
$$= \frac{0.015 * 0.35}{0.015 * 0.35 + 0.01 * 0.2 + 0.02 * 0.45} = 0.323$$

$$P(B|D) = \frac{P(D|B)P(B)}{P(D)} = \frac{P(D|B)P(B)}{P(D|A)P(A) + P(D|B)P(B) + P(D|C)P(C)}$$
$$= \frac{0.01 * 0.2}{0.015 * 0.35 + 0.01 * 0.2 + 0.02 * 0.45} = 0.123$$

$$P(C|D) = \frac{P(D|C)P(C)}{P(D)} = \frac{P(D|C)P(C)}{P(D|A)P(A) + P(D|B)P(B) + P(D|C)P(C)}$$
$$= \frac{0.02 * 0.45}{0.015 * 0.35 + 0.01 * 0.2 + 0.02 * 0.45} = 0.554$$

Also, either way, we do not even need to calculate $P(D)$ since we know that the following is the case:

$$P(A|D) : P(B|D) : P(C|D) = P(D|A)P(A) : P(D|B)P(B) : P(D|C)P(C) = 21 : 8 : 36$$

We too know the following concept:

$$P(A|D) + P(B|D) + P(C|D) = 1$$

So we have the following formula:

$$P(A|D) = \frac{21}{21 + 8 + 36} = 0.323, P(B|D) = \frac{8}{21 + 8 + 36} = 0.133$$

After making sense of Bayes' theorem as the backbone of Naïve Bayes, we can easily move forward with the classifier itself.

The mechanics of Naïve Bayes

Let's start with understanding the magic behind the algorithm—how Naïve Bayes works. Given a data sample x with n features, $x_1, x_2, ..., x_n$ (x represents a feature vector and $x = (x_1, x_2, ..., x_n)$), the goal of Naïve Bayes is to determine the probabilities that this sample belongs to each of K possible classes $y_1, y_2, ..., y_K$, that is $P(y_k | x)$ or $P(x_1, x_2, ..., x_n)$, where $k = 1, 2, ..., K$. It looks no different from what we have just dealt with: x, or $x_1, x_2, ..., x_n$, is a joint event that the sample has features with values $x_1, x_2, ..., x_n$ respectively, y_k is an event that the sample belongs to class k. We can apply Bayes' theorem right away:

$$P(y_k|x) = \frac{P(x|y_k)P(y_k)}{P(x)}$$

Let's look at each component in detail:

- $P(y_k)$ portrays how classes are distributed, provided with no further knowledge of observation features. Thus, it is also called **prior** in Bayesian probability terminology. Prior can be either predetermined (usually in a uniform manner where each class has an equal chance of occurrence) or learned from a set of training samples.
- $P(y_k | x)$, in contrast to prior $P(y_k)$, is the **posterior** with extra knowledge of observation.
- $P(x | y_k)$, or $P(x_1, x_2, ..., x_n | y_k)$ is the joint distribution of n features, given the sample belongs to class y_k. This is how likely the features with such values co-occur. This is named **likelihood** in Bayesian terminology. Obviously, the likelihood will be difficult to compute as the number of features increases. In Naïve Bayes, this is solved thanks to the feature independence assumption. The joint conditional distribution of n features can be expressed as the joint product of individual feature conditional distributions:

$$P(x|y_k) = P(x_1|y_k) * P(x_2|y_k) * \cdots * P(x_n|y_k)$$

  Each conditional distribution can be efficiently learned from a set of training samples.

- $P(x)$, also called **evidence**, solely depends on the overall distribution of features, which is not specific to certain classes and is therefore constant. As a result, **posterior** is proportional to **prior** and **likelihood**:

$$P(y_k|x) \propto P(x|y_k)P(y_k) = P(x_1|y_k) * P(x_2|y_k) * \cdots * P(x_n|y_k) * P(y_k)$$

The following diagram summarizes how a Naïve Bayes classification model is trained and applied to new data:

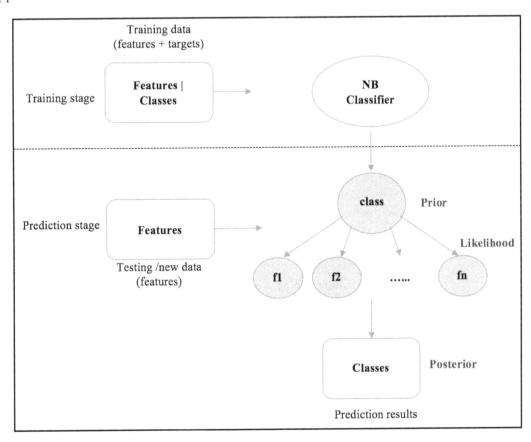

Let's see a Naïve Bayes classifier in action through an example before we jump to its implementations. Given four (pseudo) emails shown in the following table, we are asked to predict how likely it is that a new email is spam:

	ID	Terms in email	Is spam
Training data	1	click win prize	yes
	2	click meeting setup meeting	no
	3	prize free prize	yes
	4	click prize free	yes
Testing case	5	free setup meeting free	?

First, define the *S* and *NS* events as an email being spam or not spam respectively. From the training set, we can easily get the following:

$$P(S) = 3/4$$
$$P(NS) = 1/4$$

Or we can also impose an assumption of prior that $P(S) = 1\%$.

To calculate $P(S \mid x)$ where x = (*free, setup, meeting, free*), the first step is to compute $P(free \mid S)$, $P(setup \mid S)$, and $P(meeting \mid S)$ based on the training set; that is, the ratio of the occurrence of a term to that of all terms in the *S* class. However, as the term *free* was not seen in the *NS* class training set, $P(free \mid NS)$ will become 0, so will $P(x \mid NS)$ and $P(NS \mid x)$. It will be predicted as spam email, falsely. To eliminate the zero multiplication factor, the unseen term, we usually set each term frequency an initial value *1*, that is, we start counting term occurrence from one. This technique is also called **Laplace smoothing**. With this amendment, now we have the following:

$$P(free \mid S) = \frac{2+1}{9+6} = \frac{3}{15}$$
$$P(free \mid NS) = \frac{0+1}{4+6} = \frac{1}{10}$$

Here, *9* is the total number of term occurrences from the *S* class (3+3+3), *4* is the total term occurrences from the *NS* class, and *6* comes from the *1* additional count per term (*click, win, prize, meeting, setup, free*). Similarly, we can compute the following:

$$P(free \mid S) = \frac{0+1}{9+6} = \frac{1}{15}$$
$$P(free \mid NS) = \frac{1+1}{4+6} = \frac{2}{10}$$
$$P(meeting \mid S) = \frac{0+1}{9+6} = \frac{1}{15}$$
$$P(meeting \mid NS) = \frac{2+1}{4+6} = \frac{3}{10}$$

Hence we have the following formula:

$$\frac{P(S \mid x)}{P(NS \mid x)} = \frac{P(free \mid S) * P(setup \mid S) * P(meeting \mid S) * P(free \mid S) * P(S)}{P(free \mid NS) * P(setup \mid NS) * P(meeting \mid NS) * P(free \mid NS) * P(NS)} = 8/9$$

Also, remember this:

$$P(S|x) + P(NS|x) = 1$$

So, finally, we have the following:

$$P(S|x) = \frac{8}{8+9} = 47.1$$

There is *47.1%* chance that the new email is spam.

Implementing Naïve Bayes from scratch

After a hand-calculating spam email detection example, as promised, we are going to code it through a genuine dataset, taken from the Enron email dataset http://www.aueb.gr/users/ion/data/enron-spam/. The specific dataset we are using can be directly downloaded via http://www.aueb.gr/users/ion/data/enron-spam/preprocessed/enron1.tar.gz. You can either unzip it using software, or run the following command line on your terminal:

```
tar -xvz enron1.tar.gz
```

The uncompressed folder includes a folder of ham, or non-spam, email text files, and a folder of spam email text files, as well as a summary description of the database:

```
enron1/
  ham/
    0001.1999-12-10.farmer.ham.txt
      0002.1999-12-13.farmer.ham.txt
      ......
      ......
    5172.2002-01-11.farmer.ham.txt
  spam/
    0006.2003-12-18.GP.spam.txt
      0008.2003-12-18.GP.spam.txt
      ......
      ......
    5171.2005-09-06.GP.spam.txt
  Summary.txt
```

Given a dataset for a classification problem, it is always good to keep in mind the number of samples per class and the proportion of samples from each class before applying any machine learning techniques. As written in the Summary.txt file, there are 3,672 ham (legitimate) emails and 1,500 spam emails so the spam: the legitimate-to-spam ratio is approximately 1:3 here. If such information was not given, you can also get the numbers by running the following commands:

```
ls -l enron1/ham/*.txt | wc -l
3672
ls -l enron1/spam/*.txt | wc -l
1500
```

 Class imbalance is critical to classification performance. Imagine if most samples are from one class—the classifier tends to only learn from the dominant class and neglect the minorities. Hence, paying extra attention to class imbalance is always recommended. If it does occur, we need to either downsample the majority class, or upsample the minor class, in order to mitigate the disproportion.

Let's have a look at a legitimate and a spam email by running the following scripts from the same path where the unzipped folder is located:

```
>>> file_path = 'enron1/ham/0007.1999-12-14.farmer.ham.txt'
>>> with open(file_path, 'r') as infile:
...     ham_sample = infile.read()
>>> print(ham_sample)
Subject: mcmullen gas for 11 / 99
jackie ,
since the inlet to 3 river plant is shut in on 10 / 19 / 99 ( the
last day of flow ) :
at what meter is the mcmullen gas being diverted to ?
at what meter is hpl buying the residue gas ? ( this is the gas
from teco ,vastar , vintage , tejones , and swift )
i still see active deals at meter 3405 in path manager for teco ,
vastar ,vintage , tejones , and swift
i also see gas scheduled in pops at meter 3404 and 3405 .
please advice . we need to resolve this as soon as possible so
settlement can send out payments .
thanks
```

Similarly, the spam sample is as follows:

```
>>> file_path = 'enron1/spam/0058.2003-12-21.GP.spam.txt'
>>> with open(file_path, 'r') as infile:
...     spam_sample = infile.read()
>>> print(spam_sample)
```

```
Subject: stacey automated system generating 8 k per week parallelogram
people are
getting rich using this system ! now it ' s your
turn !
we ' ve
cracked the code and will show you . . . .
this is the
only system that does everything for you , so you can make
money
. . . . . . . .
because your
success is . . . completely automated !
let me show
you how !
click
here
to opt out click here % random _ text
```

Next, we read all of the email text files and keep the ham/spam class information in the labels variable, where 1 represents spam emails, and 0 is for ham.

First, import the necessary modules, glob and os, in order to find all the .txt email files, and initialize the variables, keeping the text data and labels:

```
>>> import glob
>>> import os
>>> emails, labels = [], []
```

Then, to load the spam email files, run the following commands:

```
>>> file_path = 'enron1/spam/'
>>> for filename in glob.glob(os.path.join(file_path, '*.txt')):
...     with open(filename, 'r', encoding="ISO-8859-1") as infile:
...         emails.append(infile.read())
...         labels.append(1)
```

Load the legitimate email files by running the following commands:

```
>>> file_path = 'enron1/ham/'
>>> for filename in glob.glob(os.path.join(file_path, '*.txt')):
...     with open(filename, 'r', encoding="ISO-8859-1") as infile:
...         emails.append(infile.read())
...         labels.append(0)
>>> len(emails)
5172
>>> len(labels)
5172
```

The next step is to preprocess and clean the raw text data. To briefly recap, this includes the following:

- Number and punctuation removal
- Human name removal (optional)
- Stop-word removal
- Lemmatization

We herein reuse the code we developed in the previous two chapters:

```
>>> from nltk.corpus import names
>>> from nltk.stem import WordNetLemmatizer
>>> def is_letter_only(word):
...     return word.isalpha()
>>> all_names = set(names.words())
>>> lemmatizer = WordNetLemmatizer()
```

Put together a function performing text cleaning as follows:

```
>>> def clean_text(docs):
...     docs_cleaned = []
...     for doc in docs:
...         doc = doc.lower()
...         doc_cleaned = ' '.join(lemmatizer.lemmatize(word)
...                 for word in doc.split() if is_letter_only(word)
...                 and word not in all_names)
...         docs_cleaned.append(doc_cleaned)
...     return docs_cleaned
>>> emails_cleaned = clean_text(emails)
```

This leads to stop-word removal and term feature extraction, as follows:

```
>>> from sklearn.feature_extraction.text import CountVectorizer
>>> cv = CountVectorizer(stop_words="english", max_features=1000,
                                      max_df=0.5, min_df=2)
>>> docs_cv = cv.fit_transform(emails_cleaned)
```

The `max_features` parameter is set to `1000`, so it only considers the 1,000 most frequent terms, excluding those that are too common (50% `max_df`) and too rare (2 `min_df`). We can definitely tweak this parameter later on in order to achieve higher classification accuracy.

In case you forget what the resulting term vectors look like, let's take a peek:

```
>>> print(docs_cv[0])
  (0, 932)  1
  (0, 968)  1
  (0, 715)  1
```

```
(0, 151)  1
(0, 585)  1
(0, 864)  1
(0, 506)  1
(0, 691)  1
(0, 897)  1
(0, 476)  1
(0, 72)   1
(0, 86)   2
(0, 997)  1
(0, 103)  1
(0, 361)  2
(0, 229)  1
(0, 363)  2
(0, 482)  2
(0, 265)  2
```

The sparse vector is in the form of the following:

```
(row index, term index) term_frequency
```

We can also see what the corresponding terms are, as follows:

```
>>> terms = cv.get_feature_names()
>>> print(terms[932])
unsubscribe
>>> print(terms[968])
website
>>> print(terms[715])
read
```

With the `docs_cv` feature matrix just generated, we can now develop and train our Naïve Bayes model, from scratch as always.

Starting with the prior, we first group the data by label and record the index of samples:

```
>>> def get_label_index(labels):
...         from collections import defaultdict
...         label_index = defaultdict(list)
...         for index, label in enumerate(labels):
...             label_index[label].append(index)
...         return label_index
>>> label_index = get_label_index(labels)
```

The resulting `label_index` looks like `{0: [3000, 3001, 3002, 3003, ...... 6670, 6671], 1: [0, 1, 2, 3, ...., 2998, 2999]}`, where training sample indices are grouped by class. With this, we calculate `prior`:

```
>>> def get_prior(label_index):
...         """
...         Compute prior based on training samples
...         @param label_index: grouped sample indices by class
...         @return: dictionary, with class label as key, corresponding
                                                prior as the value
...         """
...         prior = {label: len(index) for label, index in
                                        label_index.items()}
...         total_count = sum(prior.values())
...         for label in prior:
...             prior[label] /= float(total_count)
...         return prior
>>> prior = get_prior(label_index)
>>> print('Prior:', prior)
Prior: {1: 0.2900232018561485, 0: 0.7099767981438515}
```

With `prior` calculated, we continue with `likelihood`:

```
>>> import numpy as np
>>> def get_likelihood(term_matrix, label_index, smoothing=0):
...         """
...         Compute likelihood based on training samples
...         @param term_matrix: sparse matrix of the term frequency features
...         @param label_index: grouped sample indices by class
...         @param smoothing: integer, additive Laplace smoothing parameter
...         @return: dictionary, with class as key, corresponding conditional
                    probability P(feature|class) vector as value
...         """
...         likelihood = {}
...         for label, index in label_index.items():
...             likelihood[label] = term_matrix[index, :].sum(axis=0) +
                                                smoothing
...             likelihood[label] = np.asarray(likelihood[label])[0]
...             total_count = likelihood[label].sum()
...             likelihood[label] = likelihood[label] /
                                                float(total_count)
...         return likelihood
```

We set the `smoothing` value to `1` here, which can also be `0` for no smoothing, and any other positive value, as long as high classification performance is achieved:

```
>>> smoothing = 1
>>> likelihood = get_likelihood(docs_cv, label_index, smoothing)
>>> len(likelihood[0])
1000
```

The `likelihood[0]` parameter is the conditional probability *P(feature | legitimate)* vector of length 1,000 (1,000 features) for the legitimate class. Probabilities *P(feature | legitimate)* for the first five features are as follows:

```
>>> likelihood[0][:5]
[0.00024653 0.00090705 0.00080007 0.00032096 0.00073495]
```

And you can probably guess that `likelihood[1]` would be for the spam class. Similarly, the first five conditional probabilities *P(feature | spam)* are:

```
>>> likelihood[1][:5]
[0.00063304 0.00078026 0.00101581 0.00022083 0.00326826]
```

If you ever find any of these confusing, feel free to check the following toy example to refresh (14 comes from 2 + 1 + 1 + 1 + 1 + 1 + 1 + smoothing 1 * 5, 16 comes from 1 + 1 + 2 + 1 + 3 + 2 + 1 + smoothing 1 * 5):

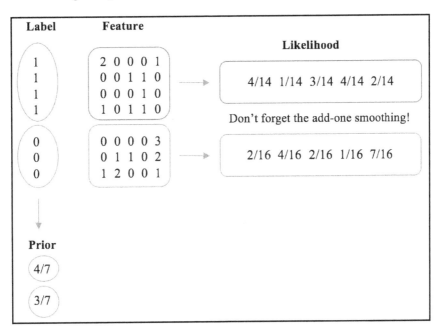

With prior and likelihood ready, we can now compute the posterior for the testing/new samples. There is a trick we use: instead of calculating the multiplication of hundreds of thousands of small value conditional probabilities of *P(feature | class)* (for example, `0.00024653`, as we just saw), which may cause overflow error, we instead calculate the summation of their natural logarithms, then convert it back to its natural exponential value:

```
>>> def get_posterior(term_matrix, prior, likelihood):
...     """
...     Compute posterior of testing samples, based on prior and likelihood
...     @param term_matrix: sparse matrix of the term frequency features
...     @param prior: dictionary, with class label as key,
...                             corresponding prior as the value
...     @param likelihood: dictionary, with class label as key,
...                     corresponding conditional probability vector as value
...     @return: dictionary, with class label as key, corresponding
...                                             posterior as value
...     """
...     num_docs = term_matrix.shape[0]
...     posteriors = []
...     for i in range(num_docs):
...         # posterior is proportional to prior * likelihood
...         # = exp(log(prior * likelihood))
...         # = exp(log(prior) + log(likelihood))
...         posterior = {key: np.log(prior_label) for key,
...                                 prior_label in prior.items()}
...         for label, likelihood_label in likelihood.items():
...             term_document_vector = term_matrix.getrow(i)
...             counts = term_document_vector.data
...             indices = term_document_vector.indices
...             for count, index in zip(counts, indices):
...                 posterior[label] +=
...                     np.log(likelihood_label[index]) * count
...         # exp(-1000):exp(-999) will cause zero division error,
...         # however it equates to exp(0):exp(1)
...         min_log_posterior = min(posterior.values())
...         for label in posterior:
...             try:
...                 posterior[label] = np.exp(
...                             posterior[label] - min_log_posterior)
...             except:
...                 posterior[label] = float('inf')
...         # normalize so that all sums up to 1
...         sum_posterior = sum(posterior.values())
...         for label in posterior:
...             if posterior[label] == float('inf'):
...                 posterior[label] = 1.0
```

```
...                      else:
...                          posterior[label] /= sum_posterior
...                  posteriors.append(posterior.copy())
...          return posteriors
```

The prediction function is finished. Let's take one ham and one spam sample from another Enron email dataset to quickly verify our algorithm:

```
>>> emails_test = [
...         '''Subject: flat screens
...         hello ,
...         please call or contact regarding the other flat screens
...         requested .
...         trisha tlapek - eb 3132 b
...         michael sergeev - eb 3132 a
...         also the sun blocker that was taken away from eb 3131 a .
...         trisha should two monitors also michael .
...         thanks
...         kevin moore''',
...         '''Subject: let ' s stop the mlm insanity !
...         still believe you can earn $ 100 , 000 fast in mlm ? get real !
...         get emm , a brand new system that replaces mlm with something that
works !
...         start earning 1 , 000 ' s now ! up to $ 10 , 000 per week doing
simple
...         online tasks .
...         free info - breakfree @ luxmail . com - type " send emm info " in
the
...         subject box .
...         this message is sent in compliance of the proposed bill section 301
. per
...         section 301 , paragraph ( a ) ( 2 ) ( c ) of s . 1618 . further
transmission
...         to you by the sender of this e - mail may be stopped at no cost to
you by
...         sending a reply to : " email address " with the word remove in the
subject
...         line .''',
... ]
```

Go through the same cleaning and preprocessing steps as in training stage:

```
>>> emails_cleaned_test = clean_text(emails_test)
>>> term_docs_test = cv.transform(emails_cleaned_test)
>>> posterior = get_posterior(term_docs_test, prior, likelihood)
>>> print(posterior)
[{1: 5.958269329017321e-08, 0: 0.9999999404173067},
 {1: 0.999999999999948, 0: 5.21386259888798 95e-15}]
```

For the first email, 99.5% legitimate; the second email nearly 100% spam. Both are predicted correctly.

Further, to comprehensively evaluate our classifier's performance, we can randomly split the original dataset into two sets, the training and testing sets, which simulate learning data and prediction data respectively. Generally, the proportion of the original dataset to include in the testing split can be 25%, 33.3%, or 40%. We use the `train_test_split` function from scikit-learn to do the random splitting and to preserve the percentage of samples for each class:

```
>>> from sklearn.model_selection import train_test_split
>>> X_train, X_test, Y_train, Y_test =
            train_test_split(emails_cleaned, labels, test_size=0.33,
            random_state=42)
```

 It is a good practice to assign a fixed `random_state` (for example, `42`) during experiments and exploration in order to guarantee that the same training and testing sets are generated every time the program runs. This allows us to make sure that the classifier functions and performs well on a fixed dataset before we incorporate randomness and proceed further.

Check the training size and testing size as follows:

```
>>> len(X_train), len(Y_train)
(3465, 3465)
>>> len(X_test), len(Y_test)
(1707, 1707)
```

Retrain the term frequency `CountVectorizer` based on the training set and recompute `prior` and `likelihood` accordingly:

```
>>> term_docs_train = cv.fit_transform(X_train)
>>> label_index = get_label_index(Y_train)
>>> prior = get_prior(label_index)
>>> likelihood = get_likelihood(term_docs_train, label_index, smoothing)
```

We then convert the testing documents into term matrix as follows:

```
>>> term_docs_test = cv.transform(X_test)
```

 It is noted that we can't train `CountVectorizer` using both the training and testing sets. Otherwise, it will cause data leakage, as the testing set is supposed to be unknown beforehand to all feature extractors. Hence, the term pool and the term counter should be built solely on the training set.

Now, predict the posterior of the testing/new dataset as follows:

```
>>> posterior = get_posterior(term_docs_test, prior, likelihood)
```

Finally, we evaluate the model's performance with classification accuracy, which is the proportion of correct prediction:

```
>>> correct = 0.0
>>> for pred, actual in zip(posterior, Y_test):
...        if actual == 1:
...            if pred[1] >= 0.5:
...                correct += 1
...        elif pred[0] > 0.5:
...            correct += 1
>>> print('The accuracy on {0} testing samples is:
          {1:.1f}%'.format(len(Y_test), correct/len(Y_test)*100))
The accuracy on 1707 testing samples is: 93.0%
```

The Naïve Bayes classifier we just developed line by line correctly classifies 93% emails!

Implementing Naïve Bayes with scikit-learn

Coding from scratch and implementing on your own solutions is the best way to learn about machine learning model. Of course, we can take a shortcut by directly using the `MultinomialNB` class from the scikit-learn API:

```
>>> from sklearn.naive_bayes import MultinomialNB
```

Let's initialize a model with a smoothing factor (specified as `alpha` in `scikit-learn`) of `1.0`, and `prior` learned from the training set (specified as `fit_prior` in scikit-learn):

```
>>> clf = MultinomialNB(alpha=1.0, fit_prior=True)
```

To train the Naïve Bayes classifier with the `fit` method, use the following command:

```
>>> clf.fit(term_docs_train, Y_train)
```

And to obtain the prediction results with the `predict_proba` method, use the following commands:

```
>>> prediction_prob = clf.predict_proba(term_docs_test)
>>> prediction_prob[0:10]
[[1.00000000e+00 3.96500362e-13]
[1.00000000e+00 2.15303766e-81]
[6.59774100e-01 3.40225900e-01]
[1.00000000e+00 2.28043493e-15]
```

```
[1.00000000e+00 1.77156705e-15]
[5.53261316e-05 9.99944674e-01]
[0.00000000e+00 1.00000000e+00]
[1.00000000e+00 3.49697719e-28]
[1.00000000e+00 4.43498548e-14]
[3.39263684e-01 6.60736316e-01]]
```

Do the following to directly acquire the predicted class values with the predict method (0.5 is the default threshold; if the predicted probability of class 1 is great than 0.5, class 1 is assigned, otherwise, 0 is used):

```
>>> prediction = clf.predict(term_docs_test)
>>> prediction[:10]
[0 0 0 0 0 1 1 0 0 1]
```

Finally, we measure the accuracy performance by calling the score method:

```
>>> accuracy = clf.score(term_docs_test, Y_test)
>>> print('The accuracy using MultinomialNB is:
                        {0:.1f}%'.format(accuracy*100))
The accuracy using MultinomialNB is: 93.0%
```

Classification performance evaluation

So far, we have covered in depth the first machine learning classifier and evaluated its performance by prediction **accuracy**. Beyond accuracy, there are several measurements that give us more insight and allow us to avoid class imbalance effects. They are as follows:

- Confusion matrix
- Precision
- recall
- F1 score
- AUC

A **confusion matrix** summarizes testing instances by their predicted values and true values, presented as a contingency table:

		Predicted	
		Negative	Positive
Actual	Negative	TN	FP
	Positive	FN	TP

TN = True Negative
FP = False Positive
FN = False Negative
TP = True Positive

To illustrate this, we compute the confusion matrix of our Naïve Bayes classifier. Herein, the `confusion_matrix` function of scikit-learn is used, but it is very easy to code it ourselves:

```
>>> from sklearn.metrics import confusion_matrix
>>> confusion_matrix(Y_test, prediction, labels=[0, 1])
[[1102   89]
 [  31 485]]
```

Note that we consider 1, the spam class, to be positive. From the confusion matrix, for example, there are 93 false-positive cases (where it misinterprets a legitimate email as a spam one), and 43 false-negative cases (where it fails to detect a spam email). So, classification accuracy is just the proportion of all true cases:

$$\frac{TN + TP}{TN + TP + FP + FN} = \frac{1098 + 473}{1707} = 92.0\%$$

Precision measures the fraction of positive calls that are correct, which is $\frac{TP}{TP + FP}$ and $\frac{473}{473 + 93} = 0.836$ in our case.

Recall, on the other hand, measures the fraction of true positives that are correctly identified, which is $\frac{TP}{TP + FN}$ and $\frac{473}{473 + 43} = 0.917$ in our case. Recall is also called **true positive rate**.

The **f1 score** comprehensively includes both the *precision* and the *recall*, and equates to their harmonic mean: $f1 = 2 * \frac{precision * recall}{precision + recall}$. We tend to value the f1 score above precision or recall alone.

Let's compute these three measurements using corresponding functions from scikit-learn, as follows:

```
>>> from sklearn.metrics import precision_score, recall_score, f1_score
>>> precision_score(Y_test, prediction, pos_label=1)
0.8449477351916377
>>> recall_score(Y_test, prediction, pos_label=1)
0.939922480620155
>>> f1_score(Y_test, prediction, pos_label=1)
0.889908256880734
```

0, the legitimate class, can also be viewed as positive, depending on the context. For example, assign the 0 class as `pos_label`:

```
>>> f1_score(Y_test, prediction, pos_label=0)
0.9483648881239244
```

To obtain the precision, recall, and f1 score for each class, instead of exhausting all class labels in the three function calls above, a quicker way is to call the `classification_report` function:

```
>>> from sklearn.metrics import classification_report
>>> report = classification_report(Y_test, prediction)
>>> print(report)
              precision    recall  f1-score   support
           0       0.97      0.93      0.95      1191
           1       0.84      0.94      0.89       516

   micro avg       0.93      0.93      0.93      1707
   macro avg       0.91      0.93      0.92      1707
weighted avg       0.93      0.93      0.93      1707
```

Here, `avg` is the weighted average according to the proportions of the class.

The measurement report provides a comprehensive view on how the classifier performs on each class. It is, as a result, useful in imbalanced classification, where we can easily obtain a high accuracy by simply classifying every sample as the dominant class, while the precision, recall, and f1 score measurements for the minority class however will be significantly low.

Precision, recall, and f1 score are also applicable to the **multiclass** classification, where we can simply treat a class we are interested in as a positive case, and any other classes as negative cases.

During the process of tweaking a binary classifier (that is, trying out different combinations of hyperparameters, for example, term feature dimension, a smoothing factor in our spam email classifier), it would be perfect if there was a set of parameters in which the highest averaged and class individual f1 scores achieve at the same time. It is, however, usually not the case. Sometimes, a model has a higher average f1 score than another model, but a significantly low f1 score for a particular class; sometimes, two models have the same average f1 scores, but one has a higher f1 score for one class and lower score for another class. In situations like these, how can we judge which model works better? **Area under the curve (AUC)** of the **receiver operating characteristic (ROC)** is a united measurement frequently used in binary classification.

The ROC curve is a plot of the true positive rate versus the false positive rate at various probability thresholds, ranging from 0 to 1. For a testing sample, if the probability of a positive class is greater than the threshold, then a positive class is assigned; otherwise, we use negative. To recap, the true positive rate is equivalent to recall, and the false positive rate is the fraction of negatives that are incorrectly identified as positive. Let's code and exhibit the ROC curve (under thresholds of 0.0, 0.1, 0.2, ..., 1.0) of our model:

```
>>> pos_prob = prediction_prob[:, 1]
>>> thresholds = np.arange(0.0, 1.2, 0.1)
>>> true_pos, false_pos = [0]*len(thresholds), [0]*len(thresholds)
>>> for pred, y in zip(pos_prob, Y_test):
...     for i, threshold in enumerate(thresholds):
...         if pred >= threshold:
                # if truth and prediction are both 1
...             if y == 1:
...                 true_pos[i] += 1
                # if truth is 0 while prediction is 1
...             else:
...                 false_pos[i] += 1
...         else:
...             break
```

Then calculate the true and false positive rates for all threshold settings (remember, there are `516.0` positive testing samples and `1191` negative ones):

```
>>> true_pos_rate = [tp / 516.0 for tp in true_pos]
>>> false_pos_rate = [fp / 1191.0 for fp in false_pos]
```

Now we can plot the ROC curve with `matplotlib`:

```
>>> import matplotlib.pyplot as plt
>>> plt.figure()
>>> lw = 2
>>> plt.plot(false_pos_rate, true_pos_rate, color='darkorange', lw=lw)
>>> plt.plot([0, 1], [0, 1], color='navy', lw=lw, linestyle='--')
```

```
>>> plt.xlim([0.0, 1.0])
>>> plt.ylim([0.0, 1.05])
>>> plt.xlabel('False Positive Rate')
>>> plt.ylabel('True Positive Rate')
>>> plt.title('Receiver Operating Characteristic')
>>> plt.legend(loc="lower right")
>>> plt.show()
```

Refer to the following screenshot for the resulting ROC curve:

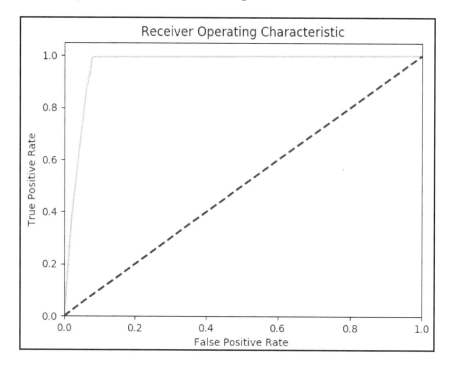

In the graph, the dashed line is the baseline representing random guessing where the true positive rate increases linearly with the false positive rate. Its AUC is 0.5; the orange line is the ROC plot of our model, and its AUC is somewhat less than 1. In a perfect case, the true positive samples have a probability of 1, so that the ROC starts at the point with 100% true positive and 0 false positive. The AUC of such a perfect curve is 1. To compute the exact AUC of our model, we can resort to the roc_auc_score function of scikit-learn:

```
>>> from sklearn.metrics import roc_auc_score
>>> roc_auc_score(Y_test, pos_prob)
0.965361984912685
```

Model tuning and cross-validation

Having learned what metrics to use to measure a classification model, we'll now study how to measure it properly. We simply can avoid adopting the classification results from one fixed testing set, which we did in experiments previously. Instead, we usually apply the **k-fold cross-validation** technique to assess how a model will generally perform in practice.

In the k-fold cross-validation setting, the original data is first randomly divided into the *k* equal-sized subsets, in which class proportion is often preserved. Each of these *k* subsets is then successively retained as the testing set for evaluating the model. During each trial, the rest k -1 subsets (excluding the one-fold holdout) form the training set for driving the model. Finally, the average performance across all *k* trials is calculated to generate an overall result:

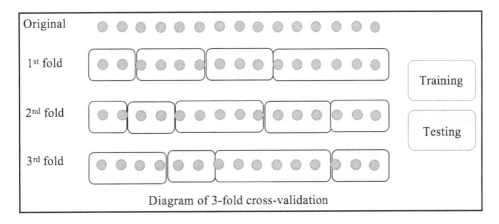

Diagram of 3-fold cross-validation

Statistically, the averaged performance of k-fold cross-validation is an accurate estimate of how a model performs in general. Given different sets of parameters pertaining to a machine learning model and/or data preprocessing algorithms, or even two or more different models, the goal of model tuning and/or model selection is to pick a set of parameters of a classifier so that the best averaged performance is achieved. With these concepts in mind, we can now start to tweak our Naïve Bayes classifier, incorporating cross-validation and AUC of ROC measurement.

In k-fold cross-validation, k is usually set *3*, *5*, or *10*. If the training size is small, a large k (*5* or *10*) is recommended to ensure enough training samples in each fold. If the training size is large, a small value (such *3* or *4*) works fine since a higher k will lead to even higher computational cost of training on large dataset.

We herein use the `split()` method from the `StratifiedKFold` class of scikit-learn to divide the data into chunks with preserved class fractions:

```
>>> from sklearn.model_selection import StratifiedKFold
>>> k = 10
>>> k_fold = StratifiedKFold(n_splits=k, random_state=42)
>>> cleaned_emails_np = np.array(cleaned_emails)
>>> labels_np = np.array(labels)
```

After initializing a 10-fold generator, we choose to explore the following values for the following parameters:

- `max_features`: This represents the n most frequent terms used as feature space
- `alpha`: This represents the smoothing factor, the initial count for a term
- `fit_prior`: This represents whether or not to use `prior` tailored to the training data

We start with the following options:

```
>>> max_features_option = [2000, 8000, None]
>>> smoothing_factor_option = [0.5, 1.0, 2.0, 4.0]
>>> fit_prior_option = [True, False]
>>> auc_record = {}
```

Then, for each fold generated by the `split()` method of the `k_fold` object, repeat the process of term count feature extraction, classifier training, and prediction with one of the aforementioned combinations of parameters, and record the resulting AUCs:

```
>>> for train_indices, test_indices in k_fold.split(emails_cleaned,
                                                    labels):
...     X_train, X_test = cleaned_emails_np[train_indices],
                          cleaned_emails_np[test_indices]
...     Y_train, Y_test = labels_np[train_indices],
                          labels_np[test_indices]
...     for max_features in max_features_option:
...         if max_features not in auc_record:
...             auc_record[max_features] = {}
...         cv = CountVectorizer(stop_words="english",
                max_features=max_features, max_df=0.5, min_df=2)
...         term_docs_train = cv.fit_transform(X_train)
...         term_docs_test = cv.transform(X_test)
...         for alpha in smoothing_factor_option:
...             if alpha not in auc_record[max_features]:
...                 auc_record[max_features][alpha] = {}
...             for fit_prior in fit_prior_option:
...                 clf = MultinomialNB(alpha=alpha, fit_prior=fit_prior)
```

```
...          clf.fit(term_docs_train, Y_train)
...          prediction_prob = clf.predict_proba(term_docs_test)
...          pos_prob = prediction_prob[:, 1]
...          auc = roc_auc_score(Y_test, pos_prob)
...          auc_record[max_features][alpha][fit_prior] =
                   auc+ auc_record[max_features][alpha].get(
                   fit_prior, 0.0)
```

Finally, we present the results as follows:

```
>>> print('max features   smoothing fit prior auc')
>>> for max_features, max_feature_record in auc_record.items():
...      for smoothing, smoothing_record in max_feature_record.items():
...          for fit_prior, auc in smoothing_record.items():
...              print(' {0}       {1}    {2}
                 {3:.5f}'.format(
                 max_features, smoothing, fit_prior, auc/k))
```

max features	smoothing	fit prior	auc
2000	0.5	False	0.97421
2000	1.0	True	0.97237
2000	1.0	False	0.97238
2000	2.0 .	True	0.97043
2000	2.0	False	0.97057
2000	4.0	True	0.96853
2000	4.0	False	0.96843
8000	0.5	True	0.98533
8000	0.5	False	0.98530
8000	1.0	True	0.98428
8000	1.0	False	0.98430
8000	2.0	True	0.98338
8000	2.0	False	0.98337
8000	4.0	True	0.98291
8000	4.0	False	0.98296
None	0.5	True	0.98890
None	0.5	False	0.98884
None	1.0	True	0.98899
None	1.0	False	0.98904
None	2.0	True	0.98906
None	2.0	False	0.98915
None	4.0	True	0.98965
None	4.0	False	0.98969

The (None, 4.0, False) set enables the best AUC, at 0.98969. In fact, not limiting the maximal number of features outperforms doing so, as 4.0, the highest smoothing factor, always beats other values. Hence, we conduct a second tweak, with the following options for greater values of smoothing factor:

```
>>> max_features_option = [None]
>>> smoothing_factor_option = [4.0, 10, 16, 20, 32]
>>> fit_prior_option = [True, False]
```

Repeat the cross-validation process and we get the following results:

max features	smoothing	fit prior	auc
None	4.0	True	0.98965
None	4.0	False	0.98969
None	10	True	0.99208
None	10	False	0.99211
None	16	True	0.99329
None	16	False	0.99329
None	20	True	0.99362
None	20	False	0.99362
None	32	True	0.99307
None	32	False	0.99307

The (None, 20, False) set enables the best AUC, at 0.99362!

Summary

In this chapter, we acquired the fundamental and important concepts of machine learning classification, including types of classification, classification performance evaluation, cross-validation, and model tuning, as well as learning about the simple yet powerful classifier, Naïve Bayes. We went in depth through the mechanics and implementations of Naïve Bayes with couple of examples and the most important one, the spam email detection project. In the end, we developed a high-performing spam detector with AUC score close to 1.

Binary classification is our main talking point of this chapter, and as you can imagine, multiclass classification will be that of the next chapter. Specifically, we will talk about support vector machines (SVMs) for classification.

Exercise

1. Can you also tweak other hyperparameters, such as the `max_df` and `min_df` parameters in `CountVectorizer`? What are their optimal values?

2. Practice makes perfect—another great project to deepen your understanding could be sentiment (positive/negative) classification for movie review data, which can be downloaded directly at `http://www.cs.cornell.edu/people/pabo/movie-review-data/review_polarity.tar.gz`, or from the page at `http://www.cs.cornell.edu/people/pabo/movie-review-data/`.

5
Classifying Newsgroup Topics with Support Vector Machines

In the previous chapter, we built a spam email detector with Naïve Bayes. This chapter continues our journey of supervised learning and classification. Specifically, we will be focusing on multiclass classification and support vector machine classifiers. The support vector machine has been one of the most popular algorithms when it comes to text classification. The goal of the algorithm is to search for a decision boundary in order to separate data from different classes. We will be discussing in detail how that works. Also, we will be implementing the algorithm with scikit-learn and TensorFlow, and applying it to solve various real-life problems, including newsgroup topic classification, fetal state categorization on cardiotocography, as well as breast cancer prediction.

We will go into detail as regards the topics mentioned:

- What is support vector machine?
- The mechanics of SVM through three cases
- The implementations of SVM with scikit-learn
- Multiclass classification strategies
- The kernel method
- SVM with non-linear kernels
- How to choose between linear and Gaussian kernels
- Overfitting and reducing overfitting in SVM
- Newsgroup topic classification with SVM
- Tuning with grid search and cross-validation
- Fetal state categorization using SVM with non-linear kernel
- Breast cancer prediction with TensorFlow

Finding separating boundary with support vector machines

After introducing a powerful, yet simple classifier Naïve Bayes, we will continue with another great classifier that is popular for text classification, the **support vector machine** (**SVM**).

In machine learning classification, SVM finds an optimal hyperplane that best segregates observations from different classes. A **hyperplane** is a plane of n -1 dimension that separates the n dimensional feature space of the observations into two spaces. For example, the hyperplane in a two-dimensional feature space is a line, and a surface in a three-dimensional feature space. The optimal hyperplane is picked so that the distance from its nearest points in each space to itself is maximized. And these nearest points are the so-called **support vectors**. The following toy example demonstrates what support vector and a separating hyperplane (along with the distance margin which we will explain later) look like in a binary classification case:

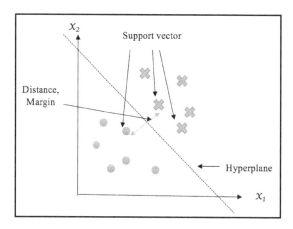

Understanding how SVM works through different use cases

Based on the preceding stated definition of SVM, there can be an infinite number of feasible hyperplanes. How can we identify the optimal one? Let's discuss the logic behind SVM in further detail through a few cases.

Case 1 – identifying a separating hyperplane

First, we need to understand what qualifies for a separating hyperplane. In the following example, hyperplane **C** is the only correct one, as it successfully segregates observations by their labels, while hyperplanes **A** and **B** fail:

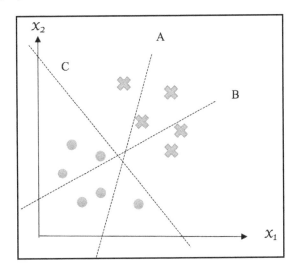

This is an easy observation. Let's express a separating hyperplane in a formal or mathematical way.

In a two-dimensional space, a line can be defined by a slope vector w (represented as a two-dimensional vector), and an intercept b. Similarly, in a space of n dimensions, a hyperplane can be defined by an n-dimensional vector w, and an intercept b. Any data point x on the hyperplane satisfies $wx + b = 0$. A hyperplane is a separating hyperplane if the following conditions are satisfied:

- For any data point x from one class, it satisfies $wx + b > 0$
- For any data point x from another class, it satisfies $wx + b < 0$

However, there can be countless possible solutions for w and b. You can move or rotate hyperplane **C** to certain extents and it still remains a separating hyperplane. So next, we will learn how to identify the best hyperplane among possible separating hyperplanes.

Case 2 – determining the optimal hyperplane

Look at the following example, hyperplane **C** is the preferred one as it enables the maximum sum of the distance between the nearest data point in the positive side to itself and the distance between the nearest data point in the negative side to itself:

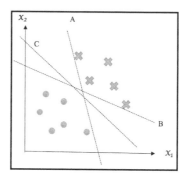

The nearest point(s) in the positive side can constitute a hyperplane parallel to the decision hyperplane, which we call a **Positive hyperplane**; on the other hand, the nearest point(s) in the negative side constitute the **Negative hyperplane**. The perpendicular distance between the positive and negative hyperplanes is called the **Margin**, whose value equates to the sum of the two aforementioned distances. A **Decision** hyperplane is deemed **optimal** if the margin is maximized.

The optimal (also called maximum-margin) hyperplane and distance margins for a trained SVM model are illustrated in the following diagram. Again, samples on the margin (two from one class, and one from another class, as shown) are the so-called support vectors:

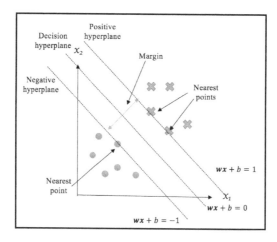

We can interpret it in a mathematical way by first describing the positive and negative hyperplanes as follows:

$$wx^{(p)} + b = 1$$
$$wx^{(n)} + b = -1$$

Here, $x^{(p)}$ is a data point on the positive hyperplane, and $x^{(n)}$ a data point on the negative hyperplane, respectively.

The distance between a point $x^{(p)}$ to the decision hyperplane can be calculated as follows:

$$\frac{\left|wx^{(p)} + b\right|}{\|w\|} = \frac{1}{\|w\|}$$

Similarly, the distance between a point $x^{(n)}$ to the decision hyperplane is as follows:

$$\frac{\left|wx^{(n)} + b\right|}{\|w\|} = \frac{1}{\|w\|}$$

So the margin becomes $\frac{2}{|w|}$. As a result, we need to minimize $|w|$ in order to maximize the margin. Importantly, to comply with the fact that the support vectors on the positive and negative hyperplanes are the nearest data points to the decision hyperplane, we add a condition that no data point falls between the positive and negative hyperplanes:

$$wx^{(i)} + b \geq 1 \; if \; y^{(i)} = 1$$
$$wx^{(i)} + b \leq 1 \; if \; y^{(i)} = -1$$

Here, $\left(x^{(i)}, y^{(i)}\right)$ is an observation. And this can be combined further into the following:

$$y^{(i)} \left(wx^{(i)} + b\right) \geq 1$$

To summarize, w and b, which determine the SVM decision hyperplane, are trained and solved by the following optimization problem:

- Minimizing $|w|$
- Subject to $y^{(i)}(wx^{(i)} + b \geq 1)$, for a training set of $(x^{(1)}, y^{(1)})$, $(x^{(2)}, y^{(2)})$,... $(x^{(i)}, y^{(i)})$..., $(x^{(m)}, y^{(m)})$

To solve this optimization problem, we need to resort to quadratic programming techniques, which are beyond the scope of our learning journey. Therefore, we will not cover the computation methods in detail and will implement the classifier using the SVC and LinearSVC modules from scikit-learn, which are realized respectively based on libsvm (https://www.csie.ntu.edu.tw/~cjlin/libsvm/) and liblinear (https://www.csie.ntu.edu.tw/~cjlin/liblinear/) as two popular open source SVM machine learning libraries. But it is always encouraging to understand the concepts of computing SVM.

Shai Shalev-Shwartz et al. "Pegasos: Primal estimated sub-gradient solver for SVM" (Mathematical Programming, March 2011, volume 127, issue 1, pp. 3-30), and Cho-Jui Hsieh et al. "A dual coordinate descent method for large-scale linear SVM" (Proceedings of the 25th international conference on machine learning, pp 408-415) would be great learning materials. They cover two modern approaches, sub-gradient descent and coordinate descent, accordingly.

The learned model parameters w and b are then used to classify a new sample x', based on the following conditions:

$$y' = \begin{cases} 1, if\ wx' + b > 0 \\ -1, if\ wx' + b < 0 \end{cases}$$

Moreover, $|wx'+b|$ can be portrayed as the distance from the data point x' to the decision hyperplane, and also interpreted as the confidence of prediction: the higher the value, the further away from the decision boundary, hence the higher prediction certainty.

Although you might be eager to implement the SVM algorithm, let's take a step back and look at a common scenario where data points are not linearly separable, in a strict way. Try to find a separating hyperplane in the following example:

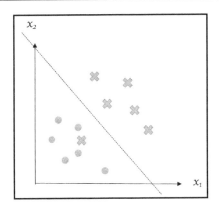

Case 3 – handling outliers

How can we deal with cases where it is unable to linearly segregate a set of observations containing outliers? We can actually allow misclassification of such outliers and try to minimize the error introduced. The misclassification error $\zeta^{(i)}$ (also called **hinge loss**) for a sample $x^{(i)}$ can be expressed as follows:

$$\zeta^{(i)} = \begin{cases} 1 - y^{(i)}\left(wx^{(i)} + b\right), if\ misclassified \\ \qquad\quad 0 \qquad\qquad ,otherwise \end{cases}$$

Together with the ultimate term $\|w\|$ to reduce, the final objective value we want to minimize becomes the following:

$$\|w\| + C\frac{\sum_{i=1}^{m}\zeta^{(i)}}{m}$$

As regards a training set of m samples $\left(x^{(1)}, y^{(1)}\right)$, $\left(x^{(2)}, y^{(2)}\right)$,... $\left(x^{(i)}, y^{(i)}\right)$..., $\left(x^{(m)}, y^{(m)}\right)$, where the hyperparameter **C** controls the trade-off between two terms:

- If a large value of **C** is chosen, the penalty for misclassification becomes relatively high. It means the thumb rule of data segregation becomes stricter and the model might be prone to overfit, since few mistakes are allowed during training. An SVM model with a large **C** has a low bias, but it might suffer high variance.

- Conversely, if the value of **C** is sufficiently small, the influence of misclassification becomes fairly low. The model allows more misclassified data points than the model with large **C** does. Thus, data separation becomes less strict. Such a model has a low variance, but it might be compromised by a high bias.

A comparison between a large and small **C** is shown in the following diagram:

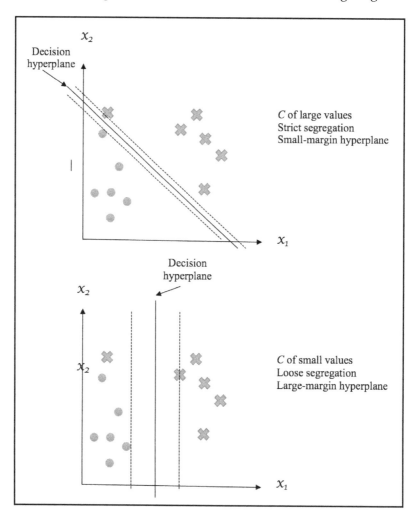

The parameter **C** determines the balance between bias and variance. It can be fine-tuned with cross-validation, which we will practice shortly.

Implementing SVM

We have largely covered the fundamentals of the SVM classifier. Now, let's apply it right away to newsgroup topic classification. We start with a binary case classifying two topics – comp.graphics and sci.space:

Let's take a look at the following steps:

1. First, we load the training and testing subset of the computer graphics and science space newsgroup data respectively:

   ```
   >>> from sklearn.datasets import fetch_20newsgroups
   >>> categories = ['comp.graphics', 'sci.space']
   >>> data_train = fetch_20newsgroups(subset='train',
                             categories=categories, random_state=42)
   >>> data_test = fetch_20newsgroups(subset='test',
                             categories=categories, random_state=42)
   ```

   Don't forget to specify a random state in order to reproduce experiments.

2. Clean the text data using the clean_text function we developed in previous chapters and retrieve the label information:

   ```
   >>> cleaned_train = clean_text(data_train.data)
   >>> label_train = data_train.target
   >>> cleaned_test = clean_text(data_test.data)
   >>> label_test = data_test.target
   >>> len(label_train), len(label_test)
   (1177, 783)
   ```

   There are 1,177 training samples and 783 testing ones.

3. By way of good practice, check whether the two classes are imbalanced:

   ```
   >>> from collections import Counter
   >>> Counter(label_train)
   Counter({1: 593, 0: 584})
   >>> Counter(label_test)
   Counter({1: 394, 0: 389})
   ```

   They are quite balanced.

4. Next, we extract the tf-idf features from the cleaned text data:

```
>>> from sklearn.feature_extraction.text import TfidfVectorizer
>>> tfidf_vectorizer = TfidfVectorizer(stop_words='english',
max_features=None)
>>> term_docs_train = tfidf_vectorizer.fit_transform(cleaned_train)
>>> term_docs_test = tfidf_vectorizer.transform(cleaned_test)
```

5. We can now apply the SVM classifier to the data. We first initialize an `SVC` model with the `kernel` parameter set to `linear` (we will explain what kernel means in the next section) and the penalty hyperparameter `C` set to the default value, `1.0`:

```
>>> from sklearn.svm import SVC
>>> svm = SVC(kernel='linear', C=1.0, random_state=42)
```

6. We then fit our model on the training set as follows:

```
>>> svm.fit(term_docs_train, label_train)
SVC(C=1.0, cache_size=200, class_weight=None, coef0=0.0,
  decision_function_shape=None, degree=3, gamma='auto',
  kernel='linear',max_iter=-1, probability=False, random_state=42,
  shrinking=True, tol=0.001, verbose=False)
```

7. And we predict on the testing set with the trained model and obtain the prediction accuracy directly:

```
>>> accuracy = svm.score(term_docs_test, label_test)
>>> print('The accuracy of binary classification is:
{0:.1f}%'.format(accuracy*100))
The accuracy of binary classification is: 96.4%
```

Our first SVM model works just great, achieving an accuracy of `96.4%`. How about more than two topics? How does SVM handle multiclass classification?

Case 4 – dealing with more than two classes

SVM and many other classifiers can be applied to cases with more than two classes. There are two typical approaches we can take, **one-vs-rest** (also called one-versus-all), and **one-vs-one**.

In the one-vs-rest setting, for a K-class problem, it constructs K different binary SVM classifiers. For the kth classifier, it treats the kth class as the positive case and the remaining K-1 classes as the negative case as a whole; the hyperplane denoted as (w_k, b_k) is trained to separate these two cases. To predict the class of a new sample, x', it compares the resulting predictions $w_k x' + b_k$ from K individual classifiers from 1 to k. As we discussed in the previous section, the larger value of $wx' + b$ means higher confidence that x' belongs to the positive case. Therefore, it assigns x' to the class i where $w_i x' + b_i$ has the largest value among all prediction results:

$$y' = (w_i x' + b_i)$$

The following diagram presents how the one-vs-rest strategy works in a three-class case:

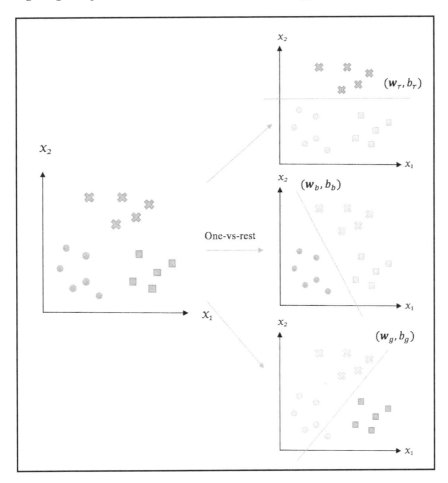

For instance, if we have the following (r, b, and g denote the red, blue, and green classes respectively):

$$w_r x' + b_r = 0.78$$
$$w_b x' + b_b = 0.35$$
$$w_g x' + b_g = -0.64$$

We can say x' belongs to the red class since *0.78 > 0.35 > -0.64*. If we have the following:

$$w_r x' + b_r = -0.78$$
$$w_b x' + b_b = -0.35$$
$$w_g x' + b_g = -0.64$$

Then, we can determine that x' belongs to the blue class regardless of the sign since -0.35 > -0.64 > -0.78.

In the one-vs-one strategy, it conducts pairwise comparison by building a set of SVM classifiers distinguishing data points from each pair of classes. This will result in $\frac{K(K-1)}{2}$ different classifiers.

For a classifier associated with classes i and j, the hyperplane denoted as (w_{ij}, b_{ij}) is trained only on the basis of observations from i (can be viewed as a positive case) and j (can be viewed as a negative case); it then assigns the class, either i or j, to a new sample, x', based on the sign of $w_{ij} x' + b_{ij}$. Finally, the class with the highest number of assignments is considered the predicting result of x'. The winner is the one that gets the most votes.

The following diagram presents how the one-vs-one strategy works in a three-class case:

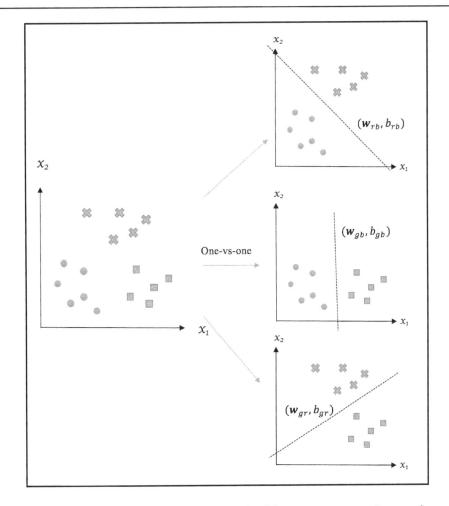

In general, an SVM classifier with one-vs-rest and with one-vs-one setting perform comparably in terms of accuracy. The choice between these two strategies is largely computational. Although one-vs-one requires more classifiers $\left(\frac{K(K-1)}{2}\right)$ than one-vs-rest (K), each pairwise classifier only needs to learn on a small subset of data, as opposed to the entire set in the one-vs-rest setting. As a result, training an SVM model in the one-vs-one setting is generally more memory-efficient and less computationally expensive, and hence more preferable for practical use, as argued in *Chih-Wei Hsu* and *Chih-Jen Lin's A comparison of methods for multiclass support vector machines (IEEE Transactions on Neural Networks, March 2002, Volume 13, pp. 415-425)*.

In `scikit-learn`, classifiers handle multiclass cases internally, and we do not need to explicitly write any additional codes to enable it. We can see how simple it is in the following example of classifying five topics - `comp.graphics`, `sci.space`, `alt.atheism`, `talk.religion.misc`, and `rec.sport.hockey`:

```
>>> categories = [
...        'alt.atheism',
...        'talk.religion.misc',
...        'comp.graphics',
...        'sci.space',
...        'rec.sport.hockey'
... ]
>>> data_train = fetch_20newsgroups(subset='train',
                         categories=categories, random_state=42)
>>> data_test = fetch_20newsgroups(subset='test',
                         categories=categories, random_state=42)
>>> cleaned_train = clean_text(data_train.data)
>>> label_train = data_train.target
>>> cleaned_test = clean_text(data_test.data)
>>> label_test = data_test.target
>>> term_docs_train = tfidf_vectorizer.fit_transform(cleaned_train)
>>> term_docs_test = tfidf_vectorizer.transform(cleaned_test)
```

In an `SVC` model, multiclass support is implicitly handled according to the one-vs-one scheme:

```
>>> svm = SVC(kernel='linear', C=1.0, random_state=42)
>>> svm.fit(term_docs_train, label_train)
>>> accuracy = svm.score(term_docs_test, label_test)
>>> print('The accuracy of 5-class classification is:
                         {0:.1f}%'.format(accuracy*100))
The accuracy on testing set is: 88.6%
```

We also check how it performs for individual classes:

```
>>> from sklearn.metrics import classification_report
>>> prediction = svm.predict(term_docs_test)
>>> report = classification_report(label_test, prediction)
>>> print(report)
            precision recall  f1-score support

         0  0.79        0.77 0.78     319
         1  0.92        0.96 0.94     389
         2  0.98        0.96 0.97     399
         3  0.93        0.94 0.93     394
         4  0.74        0.73 0.73     251
```

micro avg	0.89 0.89	0.89	1752
macro avg	0.87 0.87	0.87	1752
weighted avg	0.89 0.89	0.89	1752

Not bad! Also, we could further tweak the values of the hyperparameters `kernel` and `C`. As discussed, the factor `C` controls the strictness of separation, and it can be tuned to achieve the best trade-off between bias and variance. How about the kernel? What does it mean and what are the alternatives to a `linear` kernel?

The kernels of SVM

In this section, we will answer those two questions we raised in the preceding case as a result of the fifth case. You will see how the kernel trick makes SVM so powerful.

Case 5 – solving linearly non-separable problems

The hyperplanes we have found up till now are linear, for instance, a line in a two-dimensional feature space, or a surface in a three-dimensional one. However, in the following example, we are not able to find any linear hyperplane that can separate two classes:

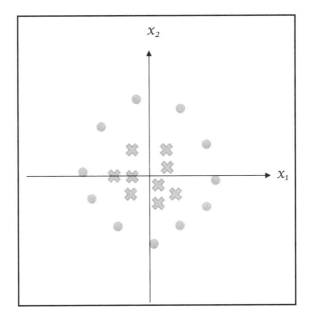

Intuitively, we observe that data points from one class are closer to the origin than those from another class. The distance to the origin provides distinguishable information. So we add a new feature, $z = (x_1^2 + x_2^2)^2$, and transform the original two-dimensional space into a three-dimensional one. In the new space, as displayed in the following, we can find a surface hyperplane separating the data, or a line in the two-dimension view. With the additional feature, the dataset becomes linearly separable in the higher dimensional space, (x_1, x_2, z):

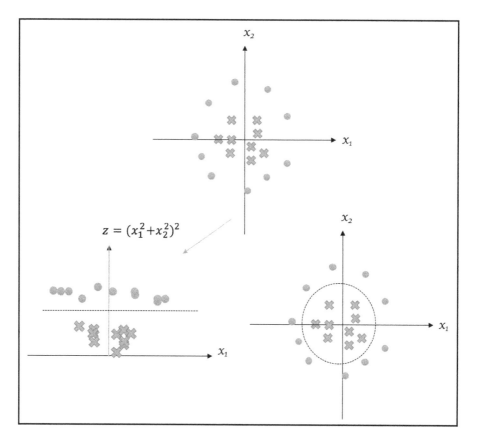

Based upon similar logics, **SVMs with kernels** are invented to solve non-linear classification problems by converting the original feature space, $x^{(i)}$, to a higher dimensional feature space with a transformation function, ϕ, such that the transformed dataset $\phi(x^{(i)})$ is linearly separable. A linear hyperplane (w_ϕ, b_ϕ) is then learned using observations $(\phi(x^{(i)}), y^{(i)})$. For an unknown sample x', it is first transformed into $\phi(x')$; the predicted class is determined by $w_\phi x' + b_\phi$.

An SVM with kernels enables non-linear separation. But it does not explicitly map each original data point to the high-dimensional space and then perform expensive computation in the new space. Instead, it approaches this in a **tricky** way:

During the course of solving the SVM quadratic optimization problems, feature vectors $x^{(1)}, x^{(2)}, \ldots, x^{(m)}$ are involved only in the form of a pairwise dot product $x^{(i)} \cdot x^{(j)}$, although we will not expand this mathematically in this book. With kernels, the new feature vectors are $\phi(x^{(1)}), \phi(x^{(2)}), \ldots, \phi(x^{(m)})$ and their pairwise dot products can be expressed as $\phi(x^{(i)}) \cdot \phi(x^{(j)})$. It would be computationally efficient if we can first implicitly conduct pairwise operation on two low-dimensional vectors and later map the result to the high-dimensional space. In fact, a function K that satisfies this does exist:

$$K(x^{(i)}, x^{(i)}) = \phi(x^{(i)}) \cdot \phi(x^{(j)})$$

The function K is the so-called **kernel function**. With this trick, the transformation ϕ becomes implicit, and the non-linear decision boundary can be efficiently learned by simply replacing the term $\phi(x^{(i)}) \cdot \phi(x^{(j)})$ with $K(x^{(i)}, x^{(j)})$.

The most popular kernel function is probably the **radial basis function** (RBF) kernel (also called the **Gaussian** kernel), which is defined as follows:

$$K(x^{(i)}, x^{(j)}) = exp\left(-\frac{\|x^{(i)} - x^{(j)}\|^2}{2\sigma^2} \right) = exp\left(-\gamma \|x^{(i)} - x^{(j)}\|^2 \right)$$

Here, $\gamma = \frac{1}{2\sigma^2}$. In the Gaussian function, the standard deviation σ controls the amount of variation or dispersion allowed: the higher σ (or lower γ), the larger width of the bell, the wider range of data points allowed to spread out over. Therefore, γ as the **kernel coefficient** determines how particularly or generally the kernel function fits the observations. A large γ implies a small variance allowed and a relatively exact fit on the training samples, which might lead to overfitting. On the other hand, a small γ implies a high variance allowed and a loose fit on the training samples, which might cause underfitting. To illustrate this trade-off, let's apply the RBF kernel with different values to a toy dataset:

```
>>> import numpy as np
>>> import matplotlib.pyplot as plt
>>> X = np.c_[# negative class
...          (.3, -.8),
...          (-1.5, -1),
```

```
...                   (-1.3, -.8),
...                   (-1.1, -1.3),
...                   (-1.2, -.3),
...                   (-1.3, -.5),
...                   (-.6, 1.1),
...                   (-1.4, 2.2),
...                   (1, 1),
...                   # positive class
...                   (1.3, .8),
...                   (1.2, .5),
...                   (.2, -2),
...                   (.5, -2.4),
...                   (.2, -2.3),
...                   (0, -2.7),
...                   (1.3, 2.1)].T
>>> Y = [-1] * 8 + [1] * 8
```

Eight data points are from one class, and eight from another. We take three values, 1, 2, and 4, for kernel coefficient as an example:

```
>>> gamma_option = [1, 2, 4]
```

Under each kernel coefficient, we fit an individual SVM classifier and visualize the trained decision boundary:

```
>>> import matplotlib.pyplot as plt
>>> gamma_option = [1, 2, 4]
>>> for i, gamma in enumerate(gamma_option, 1):
...     svm = SVC(kernel='rbf', gamma=gamma)
...     svm.fit(X, Y)
...     plt.scatter(X[:, 0], X[:, 1], c=['b']*8+['r']*8, zorder=10,
cmap=plt.cm.Paired)
...     plt.axis('tight')
...     XX, YY = np.mgrid[-3:3:200j, -3:3:200j]
...     Z = svm.decision_function(np.c_[XX.ravel(), YY.ravel()])
...     Z = Z.reshape(XX.shape)
...     plt.pcolormesh(XX, YY, Z > 0, cmap=plt.cm.Paired)
...     plt.contour(XX, YY, Z, colors=['k', 'k', 'k'],
                    linestyles=['--', '-', '--'], levels=[-.5, 0, .5])
...     plt.title('gamma = %d' % gamma)
...     plt.show()
```

Refer to the following screenshot for the end results:

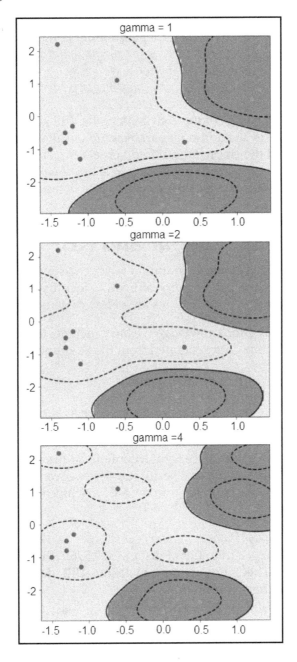

We can observe that a larger γ results in a stricter fit on the dataset. Of course, γ can be fine-tuned through cross-validation to obtain the best performance.

Some other common kernel functions include **polynomial** kernel and **sigmoid** kernel:

$$K(x^{(i)}, x^{(j)}) = (x^{(i)} \cdot x^{(j)} + \gamma)^d$$
$$K(x^{(i)}, x^{(j)}) = tanh(x^{(i)} \cdot x^{(j)} + \gamma)$$

In the absence of prior knowledge of the distribution, the RBF kernel is usually preferable in practical usage, as there is an additional parameter to tweak in the polynomial kernel (polynomial degree d) and the empirical sigmoid kernel can perform approximately on a par with the RBF, but only under certain parameters. Hence, we come to a debate between linear (also considered no kernel) and RBF kernel given a dataset.

Choosing between linear and RBF kernels

Of course, linear separability is the rule of thumb when choosing the right kernel to start with. However, most of the time, this is very difficult to identify, unless you have sufficient prior knowledge of the dataset, or its features are of low dimensions (1 to 3).

 Some general prior knowledge we have include: text data is often linearly separable, while data generated from the XOR function is not.

Now, let's look at the following three scenarios where linear kernel is favored over RBF:

Scenario 1: Both the numbers of features and instances are large (more than 10^4 or 10^5). Since the dimension of the feature space is high enough, additional features as a result of RBF transformation will not provide any performance improvement, but will increase computational expense. Some examples from the UCI machine learning repository are of this type:

- *URL Reputation Dataset*: `https://archive.ics.uci.edu/ml/datasets/URL+Reputation` (number of instances: 2,396,130; number of features: 3,231,961). This is designed for malicious URL detection based on their lexical and host information.
- *YouTube Multiview Video Games Dataset*: `https://archive.ics.uci.edu/ml/datasets/YouTube+Multiview+Video+Games+Dataset` (number of instances: 120,000; number of features: 1,000,000). This is designed for topic classification.

Scenario 2: The number of features is noticeably large compared to the number of training samples. Apart from the reasons stated in *scenario 1*, the RBF kernel is significantly more prone to overfitting. Such a scenario occurs, for example, in the following referral links:

- *Dorothea Dataset*: `https://archive.ics.uci.edu/ml/datasets/Dorothea` (number of instances: 1,950; number of features: 100,000). This is designed for drug discovery that classifies chemical compounds as active or inactive according to their structural molecular features.
- *Arcene Dataset*: `https://archive.ics.uci.edu/ml/datasets/Arcene` (number of instances: 900; number of features: 10,000). This represents a mass-spectrometry dataset for cancer detection.

Scenario 3: The number of instances is significantly large compared to the number of features. For a dataset of low dimension, the RBF kernel will, in general, boost the performance by mapping it to a higher-dimensional space. However, due to the training complexity, it usually becomes no longer efficient on a training set with more than 10^6 or 10^7 samples. Example datasets include the following:

- *Heterogeneity Activity Recognition Dataset*: `https://archive.ics.uci.edu/ml/datasets/Heterogeneity+Activity+Recognition` (number of instances: 43,930,257; number of features: 16). This is designed for human activity recognition.
- *HIGGS Dataset*: `https://archive.ics.uci.edu/ml/datasets/HIGGS` (number of instances: 11,000,000; number of features: 28). This is designed to distinguish between a signal process producing Higgs bosons or a background process

Aside from these three scenarios, RBF is ordinarily the first choice.

The rules for choosing between linear and RBF kernel can be summarized as follows:

Scenario	Linear	RBF
Prior knowledge	If linearly separable	If nonlinearly separable
Visualizable data of 1 to 3 dimension(s)	If linearly separable	If nonlinearly separable
Both numbers of features and instances are large	First choice	
Features ≫ Instances	First choice	
Instances ≫ Features	First choice	
Others		First choice

Once again, **first choice** means what we can **begin with** this option; it does not mean that this is the only option moving forward.

Classifying newsgroup topics with SVMs

Finally, it is time to build our state-of-the-art SVM-based newsgroup topic classifier using everything we just learned.

First we load and clean the dataset with the entire 20 groups as follows:

```
>>> categories = None
>>> data_train = fetch_20newsgroups(subset='train',
                        categories=categories, random_state=42)
>>> data_test = fetch_20newsgroups(subset='test',
                        categories=categories, random_state=42)
>>> cleaned_train = clean_text(data_train.data)
>>> label_train = data_train.target
>>> cleaned_test = clean_text(data_test.data)
>>> label_test = data_test.target
>>> term_docs_train = tfidf_vectorizer.fit_transform(cleaned_train)
>>> term_docs_test = tfidf_vectorizer.transform(cleaned_test)
```

As we have seen that the linear kernel is good at classifying text data, we will continue using `linear` as the value of the `kernel` hyperparameter so we only need to tune the penalty `C`, through cross-validation:

```
>>> svc_libsvm = SVC(kernel='linear')
```

The way we have conducted cross-validation so far is to explicitly split data into folds and repetitively write a `for` loop to consecutively examine each hyperparameter. To make this less redundant, we introduce a more elegant approach utilizing the `GridSearchCV` module from scikit-learn. `GridSearchCV` handles the entire process implicitly, including data splitting, fold generation, cross training and validation, and finally, an exhaustive search over the best set of parameters. What is left for us is just to specify the hyperparameter(s) to tune and the values to explore for each individual hyperparameter:

```
>>> parameters = {'C': (0.1, 1, 10, 100)}
>>> from sklearn.model_selection import GridSearchCV
>>> grid_search = GridSearchCV(svc_libsvm, parameters, n_jobs=-1, cv=5)
```

The `GridSearchCV` model we just initialized will conduct five-fold cross-validation (`cv=5`) and will run in parallel on all available cores (`n_jobs=-1`). We then perform hyperparameter tuning by simply applying the `fit` method, and record the running time:

```
>>> import timeit
>>> start_time = timeit.default_timer()
>>> grid_search.fit(term_docs_train, label_train)
>>> print("--- %0.3fs seconds ---" % (timeit.default_timer() - start_time))
--- 525.728s seconds ---
```

We can obtain the optimal set of parameters (the optimal `C` in this case) using the following code:

```
>>> grid_search.best_params_
{'C': 10}
```

And the best five-fold averaged performance under the optimal set of parameters by using the following code:

```
>>> grid_search.best_score_
0.8888987095633728
```

We then retrieve the SVM model with the optimal hyperparameter and apply it to the testing set:

```
>>> svc_libsvm_best = grid_search.best_estimator_
>>> accuracy = svc_libsvm_best.score(term_docs_test, label_test)
>>> print('The accuracy of 20-class classification is:
                                {0:.1f}%'.format(accuracy*100))
The accuracy of 20-class classification is: 78.7%
```

It should be noted that we tune the model based on the original training set, which is divided into folds for cross training and validation, and that we adopt the optimal model to the original testing set. We examine the classification performance in this manner in order to measure how well generalized the model is to make correct predictions on a completely new dataset. An accuracy of 78.7% is achieved with our first SVC model.

There is another SVM classifier, `LinearSVC`, from `scikit-learn`. How will we perform this? `LinearSVC` is similar to `SVC` with linear kernels, but it is implemented based on the `liblinear` library, which is better optimized than `libsvm` with linear kernel. We then repeat the same preceding process with `LinearSVC` as follows:

```
>>> from sklearn.svm import LinearSVC
>>> svc_linear = LinearSVC()
>>> grid_search = GridSearchCV(svc_linear, parameters,
                                n_jobs=-1, cv=5))
```

```
>>> start_time = timeit.default_timer()
>>> grid_search.fit(term_docs_train, label_train)
>>> print("--- %0.3fs seconds ---" %
                        (timeit.default_timer() - start_time))
--- 19.915s seconds ---
>>> grid_search.best_params_
{'C': 1}
>>> grid_search.best_score_
0.894643804136468
>>> svc_linear_best = grid_search.best_estimator_
>>> accuracy = svc_linear_best.score(term_docs_test, label_test)
>>> print('The accuracy of 20-class classification is:
                        {0:.1f}%'.format(accuracy*100))
The accuracy on testing set is: 79.9%
```

The `LinearSVC` model outperforms `SVC`, and its training is more than 26 times faster. This is because the `liblinear` library with high scalability is designed for large datasets, while the `libsvm` library with more than quadratic computation complexity is not able to scale well with more than 10^5 training instances.

We can also tweak the feature extractor, the `TfidfVectorizer` model, to further improve the performance. Feature extraction and classification as two consecutive steps should be cross-validated collectively. We utilize the `pipeline` API from scikit-learn to facilitate this.

The `tfidf` feature extractor and linear SVM classifier are first assembled in the pipeline:

```
>>> from sklearn.pipeline import Pipeline
>>> pipeline = Pipeline([
...     ('tfidf', TfidfVectorizer(stop_words='english')),
...     ('svc', LinearSVC()),
... ])
```

The hyperparameters to tune are defined as follows, with a pipeline step name joined with a parameter name by a __ as the key, and a tuple of corresponding options as the value:

```
>>> parameters_pipeline = {
...     'tfidf__max_df': (0.25, 0.5, 1.0),
...     'tfidf__max_features': (10000, None),
...     'tfidf__sublinear_tf': (True, False),
...     'tfidf__smooth_idf': (True, False),
...     'svc__C': (0.3, 1, 3),
... }
```

Besides the penalty C, for the SVM classifier, we tune the tfidf feature extractor in terms of the following:

- max_df: The maximum document frequency of a term to be allowed, in order to avoid common terms generally occurring in documents
- max_features: The number of top features to consider
- sublinear_tf: Whether scaling term frequency with the logarithm function or not
- smooth_idf: Adding an initial 1 to the document frequency or not, similar to smoothing factor for the term frequency

The grid search model searches for the optimal set of parameters throughout the entire pipeline:

```
>>> grid_search = GridSearchCV(pipeline, parameters_pipeline,
                                         n_jobs=-1, cv=5)
>>> start_time = timeit.default_timer()
>>> grid_search.fit(cleaned_train, label_train)
>>> print("--- %0.3fs seconds ---" %
                         (timeit.default_timer() - start_time))
--- 333.761s seconds ---
>>> grid_search.best_params_
{'svc__C': 1, 'tfidf__max_df': 0.5, 'tfidf__max_features': None,
'tfidf__smooth_idf': False, 'tfidf__sublinear_tf': True}
>>> grid_search.best_score_
0.9018914619056037
>>> pipeline_best = grid_search.best_estimator_
```

Finally, the optimal model is applied to the testing set as follows:

```
>>> accuracy = pipeline_best.score(cleaned_test, label_test)
>>> print('The accuracy of 20-class classification is:
                         {0:.1f}%'.format(accuracy*100))
The accuracy of 20-class classification is: 81.0%
```

The set of hyperparameters, {max_df: 0.5, smooth_idf: False, max_features: 40000, sublinear_tf: True, C: 1}, facilitates the best classification accuracy, 81.0%, on the entire 20 groups of text data.

More example – fetal state classification on cardiotocography

After a successful application of SVM with linear kernel, we will look at one more example of an SVM with RBF kernel to start with.

We are going to build a classifier that helps obstetricians categorize cardiotocograms (CTGs) into one of the three fetal states (normal, suspect, and pathologic). The cardiotocography dataset we use is from `https://archive.ics.uci.edu/ml/datasets/Cardiotocography` under the UCI Machine Learning Repository and it can be directly downloaded from `https://archive.ics.uci.edu/ml/machine-learning-databases/00193/CTG.xls` as an `.xls` Excel file. The dataset consists of measurements of fetal heart rate and uterine contraction as features, and the fetal state class code (1=normal, 2=suspect, 3=pathologic) as a label. There are in total 2,126 samples with 23 features. Based on the numbers of instances and features (2,126 is not far more than 23), the RBF kernel is the first choice.

We work with the Excel file using pandas, which is suitable for table data. It might request an additional installation of the `xlrd` package when you run the following lines of codes, since its Excel module is built based on `xlrd`. If so, just run `pip install xlrd` in the terminal to install `xlrd`.

We first read the data located in the sheet named `Raw Data`:

```
>>> import pandas as pd
>>> df = pd.read_excel('CTG.xls', "Raw Data")
```

Then, we take these 2,126 data samples, and assign the feature set (from columns `D` to `AL` in the spreadsheet), and label set (column `AN`) respectively:

```
>>> X = df.ix[1:2126, 3:-2].values
>>> Y = df.ix[1:2126, -1].values
```

Don't forget to check the class proportions:

```
>>> Counter(Y)
Counter({1.0: 1655, 2.0: 295, 3.0: 176})
```

We set aside 20% of the original data for final testing:

```
>>> from sklearn.model_selection import train_test_split
>>> X_train, X_test, Y_train, Y_test = train_test_split(X, Y,
                                                test_size=0.2,
random_state=42)
```

Now, we tune the RBF-based SVM model in terms of the penalty C, and the `kernel` coefficient γ:

```
>>> svc = SVC(kernel='rbf')
>>> parameters = {'C': (100, 1e3, 1e4, 1e5),
...               'gamma': (1e-08, 1e-7, 1e-6, 1e-5)}
>>> grid_search = GridSearchCV(svc, parameters, n_jobs=-1, cv=5)
>>> start_time = timeit.default_timer()
>>> grid_search.fit(X_train, Y_train)
>>> print("--- %0.3fs seconds ---" %
                    (timeit.default_timer() - start_time))
--- 11.751s seconds ---
>>> grid_search.best_params_
{'C': 100000.0, 'gamma': 1e-07}
>>> grid_search.best_score_
0.9547058823529412
>>> svc_best = grid_search.best_estimator_
```

Finally, we apply the optimal model to the testing set:

```
>>> accuracy = svc_best.score(X_test, Y_test)
>>> print('The accuracy on testing set is:
                    {0:.1f}%'.format(accuracy*100))
The accuracy on testing set is: 96.5%
```

Also, we have to check the performance for individual classes since the data is not quite balanced:

```
>>> prediction = svc_best.predict(X_test)
>>> report = classification_report(Y_test, prediction)
>>> print(report)
              precision recall f1-score  support

         1.0      0.98   0.98     0.98      333
         2.0      0.89   0.91     0.90       64
         3.0      0.96   0.93     0.95       29

   micro avg      0.96   0.96     0.96      426
   macro avg      0.95   0.94     0.94      426
weighted avg      0.96   0.96     0.96      426
```

A further example – breast cancer classification using SVM with TensorFlow

So far, we have been using scikit-learn to implement SVMs. Let's now look at how to do so with TensorFlow. Note that, up until now (the end of 2018), the only SVM API provided in TensorFlow is with linear kernel for binary classification.

We are using the breast cancer dataset (https://archive.ics.uci.edu/ml/datasets/ Breast+Cancer+Wisconsin+(Diagnostic)) as an example. Its feature space is 30-dimensional, and its target variable is binary. Let's see how it's done by performing the following steps:

1. First, import the requisite modules and load the dataset as well as check its class distribution:

```
>>> import tensorflow as tf
>>> from sklearn import datasets
>>> cancer_data = datasets.load_breast_cancer()
>>> X = cancer_data.data
>>> Y = cancer_data.target
>>> print(Counter(Y))
Counter({1: 357, 0: 212})
```

2. Split the data into training and testing sets as follows:

```
>>> np.random.seed(42)
>>> train_indices = np.random.choice(len(Y), round(len(Y) * 0.8),
replace=False)
>>> test_indices = np.array(list(set(range(len(Y))) -
set(train_indices)))
>>> X_train = X[train_indices]
>>> X_test = X[test_indices]
>>> Y_train = Y[train_indices]
>>> Y_test = Y[test_indices]
```

3. Now, initialize the SVM classifier as follows:

```
>>> svm_tf = tf.contrib.learn.SVM(
feature_columns=(tf.contrib.layers.real_valued_column(column_name='
x'),),
example_id_column='example_id')
```

4. Then, we construct the input function for training data, before calling the fit method:

```
>>> input_fn_train = tf.estimator.inputs.numpy_input_fn(
...        x={'x': X_train,
               'example_id': np.array(['%d' % i for i in
range(len(Y_train))])},
...        y=Y_train,
...        num_epochs=None,
...        batch_size=100,
...        shuffle=True)
```

The example_id is something different to scikit-learn. It is basically a placeholder for the id of samples.

5. Fit the model on the training set as follows:

```
>>> svm_tf.fit(input_fn=input_fn_train, max_steps=100)
```

6. Evaluate the classification accuracy on the training set as follows:

```
>>> metrics = svm_tf.evaluate(input_fn=input_fn_train, steps=1)
>>> print('The training accuracy is:
                        {0:.1f}%'.format(metrics['accuracy']*100))
The training accuracy is: 94.0%
```

7. To predict on the testing set, we construct the input function for testing data in a similar way:

```
>>> input_fn_test = tf.estimator.inputs.numpy_input_fn(
...        x={'x': X_test,
               'example_id': np.array(
                        ['%d' % (i + len(Y_train)) for i in
range(len(X_test))])},
...        y=Y_test,
...        num_epochs=None,
...        shuffle=False)
```

8. Finally, evaluate its classification accuracy as follows:

```
>>> metrics = svm_tf.evaluate(input_fn=input_fn_test, steps=1)
>>> print('The testing accuracy is:
                        {0:.1f}%'.format(metrics['accuracy']*100))
The testing accuracy is: 90.6%
```

Note, you will get different results every time you run the codes. This is because, for the underlying optimization of the `tf.contrib.learn.SVM` module, the **Stochastic Dual Coordinate Ascent** (**SDCA**) method is used, which incorporates inevitable randomness.

Summary

In this chapter, we continued our journey of classifying news data with the SVM classifier, where we acquired the mechanics of an SVM, kernel techniques and implementations of SVM, and other important concepts of machine learning classification, including multiclass classification strategies and grid search, as well as useful tips for using an SVM (for example, choosing between kernels and tuning parameters). Then, we finally put into practice what we had learned in the form of two use cases: news topic classification and fetal state classification.

We have learned and adopted two classification algorithms so far, Naïve Bayes and SVM. Naïve Bayes is a simple algorithm (as its name implies). For a dataset with independent, or close to independent, features, Naïve Bayes will usually perform well. SVM is versatile and adaptive to the linear separability of data. In general, high accuracy can be achieved by SVM with the right kernel and parameters. However, this might be at the expense of intense computation and high memory consumption. When it comes to text classification, since text data is, in general, linearly separable, an SVM with linear kernels and Naïve Bayes often end up performing in a comparable way. In practice, we can simply try both and select the better one with optimal parameters.

In the next chapter, we will look at online advertising and predict whether a user will click through an ad. This will be accomplished by means of tree-based algorithms, including **decision tree** and **random forest**.

Exercise

- Can you also tweak the `kernel` hyperparameter in the newsgroup topic classifier? For example, if you go with RBF kernels, you will also need to tune gamma. Can you achieve higher accuracy?
- Can you classify the 20 newsgroup dataset using Naïve Bayes? What is the best accuracy you can achieve using grid search and cross-validation?

6
Predicting Online Ad Click-Through with Tree-Based Algorithms

In this chapter and the next, we will be solving one of the most data-driven problems in digital advertising: ad click-through prediction - given a user and the page he/she is visiting, this predicts how likely it is that they will click on a given ad. We will be focusing on learning tree-based algorithms (decision tree and random forest) and utilizing them to tackle this billion-dollar problem. We will be exploring decision trees from the root to the leaves, as well as the aggregated version, a forest of trees. This won't be a bland chapter, as there are a lot of hand-calculations and implementations of tree models from scratch, and using scikit-learn and TensorFlow.

We will cover the following topics in this chapter:

- Introduction to online advertising click-through
- Two types of feature: numerical and categorical
- What is decision tree
- The mechanics of a decision tree classifier
- The construction of decision tree
- The implementation of decision tree from scratch
- The implementation of decision tree using scikit-learn
- Click-through predictions with decision tree
- The ensemble method and bagging technique

- What is random forest?
- The mechanics of random forest
- Click-through predictions with random forest
- Tuning a tree model using grid search and cross-validation
- The implementation of random forest using TensorFlow

Brief overview of advertising click-through prediction

Display online advertising is a multibillion-dollar industry. It comes in different formats, including banner ads composed of text, images, flash, and rich media such as audio and video. Advertisers or their agencies place advertisements on a variety of websites, even mobile apps, across the internet to reach potential customers and deliver an advertising message.

Display online advertising has served as one of the greatest examples of machine learning utilization. Obviously, advertisers and consumers are keenly interested in well-targeted ads. The industry has relied heavily on the ability of machine learning models to predict the effectiveness of ad targeting: how likely it is that an audience in a certain age group will be interested in this product, customers with a certain household income will purchase this product after seeing the ad, frequent sports site visitors will spend more time reading this ad, and so on. The most common measurement of effectiveness is the **click-through rate** (**CTR**), which is the ratio of clicks on a specific ad to its total number of views. The higher the CTR in general, the better targeted an ad is, and the more successful an online advertising campaign is.

Click-through prediction entails both promise and challenges for machine learning. It mainly involves binary classification of whether a given ad on a given page (or app) will be clicked by a given user, with predictive features from the following three aspects:

- Ad content and information (category, position, text, format, and so on)
- Page content and publisher information (category, context, domain, and so on)
- User information (age, gender, location, income, interests, search history, browsing history, device, and so on)

Suppose we as an agency are operating ads on behalf of several advertisers, and our job is to place the right ads for the right audience. With an existing dataset in hand (the following small chunk is an example; the number of predictive features can easily go into the thousands in reality) taken from millions records of campaigns running a month ago (let's say), we need to develop a classification model to learn and predict future ad placement outcomes:

Ad category	Site category	Site domain	User age	User gender	User occupation	Interested in sports	Interested in tech	Click
Auto	News	cnn.com	25-34	M	Professional	True	True	1
Fashion	News	bbc.com	35-54	F	Professional	False	False	0
Auto	Edu	onlinestudy.com	17-24	F	Student	True	True	0
Food	Entertainment	movie.com	25-34	M	Clerk	True	False	1
Fashion	Sports	football.com	55+	M	Retired	True	False	0
...	...	...	...	...	...	...	...	...
...	...	...	...	...	...	...	...	...
Food	News	abc.com	17-24	M	Student	True	True	?
Auto	Entertainment	movie.com	35-54	F	Professional	True	False	?

Getting started with two types of data – numerical and categorical

At first glance, the features in the preceding dataset are **categorical**, for example, male or female, one of four age groups, one of the predefined site categories, and whether or not the user is interested in sports. Such data is different from the **numerical** feature data we have worked with till now.

Categorical (also called **qualitative**) features represent characteristics, distinct groups, and a countable number of options. Categorical features may or may not have logical order. For example, household income from low, median, to high is an **ordinal** feature, while the category of an ad is not ordinal. Numerical (also called **quantitative**) features, on the other hand, have mathematical meaning as a measurement and, of course, are ordered. For instance, term frequency and the tf-idf variant are discrete and continuous numerical features respectively; the cardiotocography dataset contains both discrete (such as number of accelerations per second and number of fetal movements per second) and continuous (such as the mean value of long-term variability) numerical features.

Categorical features can also take on numerical values. For example, 1 to 12 can represent months of the year, and 1 and 0 can indicate male and female. Still, these values do not have mathematical implications.

Of the two classification algorithms we learned previously, Naïve Bayes and SVM, the Naïve Bayes classifier works for both numerical and categorical features as likelihoods $P(x|y)$ or $P(feature|class)$ are calculated in the same way, while SVM requires features to be numerical in order to compute and maximize distance margins.

Now, we are thinking of predicting click-through using Naïve Bayes, and trying to explain the model to our advertising clients. However, our clients may find it difficult to understand the prior and the likelihood of individual attributes, and their multiplication. Is there a classifier that is easy to interpret and explain to clients, and is also able to directly handle categorical data? Decision trees are the answer!

Exploring decision tree from root to leaves

A decision tree is a tree-like graph, a sequential diagram illustrating all of the possible decision alternatives and the corresponding outcomes. Starting from the **root** of a tree, every internal **node** represents the basis on which a decision is made; each branch of a node represents how a choice may lead to the next nodes; and finally, each **terminal node**, the **leaf**, represents the outcome produced.

For example, we have just made a couple of decisions that brought us to the point of using a decision tree to solve our advertising problem:

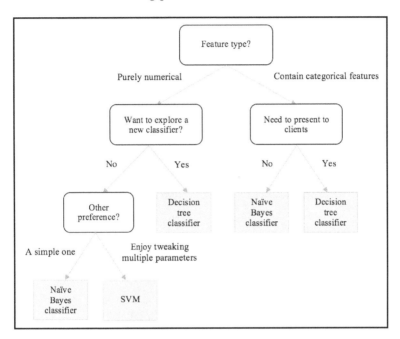

The first condition, or the root is whether the feature type is numerical or categorical. Ad click stream data contain mostly categorical features, so it goes to the right branch. In the next node, our work needs to be interpretable by non-technical clients. So, it goes to the right branch and reaches the leaf of choosing the decision tree classifier. You can also look at paths and see what kinds of problems they can fit in.

Decision tree classifier operates in a form of a decision tree, which maps observations to class assignments (symbolized as leaf nodes) through a series of tests (represented as internal nodes) based on feature values and corresponding conditions (represented as branches). In each node, a question regarding the values and characteristics of a feature is asked; depending on the answer to the question, observations are split into subsets. Sequential tests are conducted until a conclusion about the observations' target label is reached. The paths from root to end leaves represent the decision-making process, the classification rules.

In a much simplified scenario, shown in the following diagram, where we want to predict Click or No click on a self-driven car ad, we manually construct a decision tree classifier that works for an available dataset. For example, if a user is interested in technology and has a car, they will tend to click on the ad; for a person outside of this subset, if the person is a high-income woman, then she is unlikely to click on the ad. We then use the trained tree to predict two new inputs, whose results are Click and No click respectively:

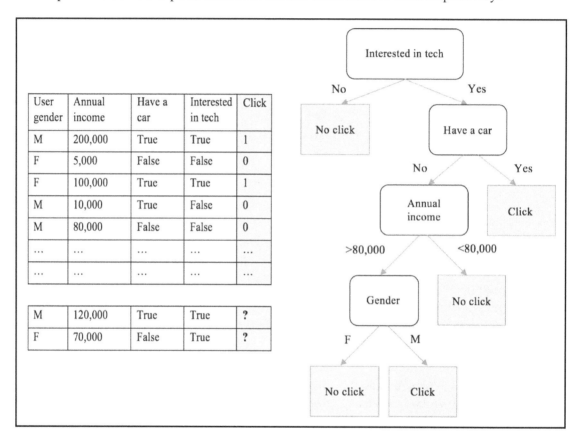

After a decision tree has been constructed, classifying a new sample is straightforward, as we just saw: starting from the root, apply the test condition and follow the branch accordingly until a leaf node is reached, and the class label associated will be assigned to the new sample.

So, how can we build an appropriate decision tree?

Constructing a decision tree

A decision tree is constructed by partitioning the training samples into successive subsets. The partitioning process is repeated in a recursive fashion on each subset. For each partitioning at a node, a condition test is conducted based on the value of a feature of the subset. When the subset shares the same class label, or no further splitting can improve the class purity of this subset, recursive partitioning on this node is finished.

Theoretically, for a partitioning on a feature (numerical or categorical) with n different values, there are n different ways of binary splitting (yes or no to the condition test), not to mention other ways of splitting. Without considering the order of features partitioning is taking place on, there are already n^m possible trees for an m-dimension dataset:

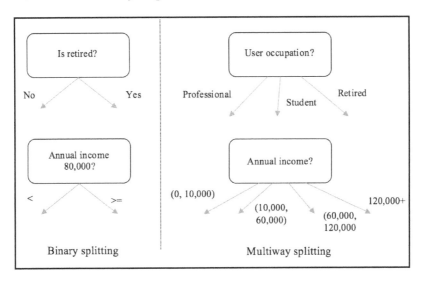

Many algorithms have been developed to efficiently construct an accurate decision tree. Popular ones include the following:

- **Iterative Dichotomiser 3 (ID3)**: This algorithm uses a greedy search in a top-down manner by selecting the best attribute to split the dataset on each iteration without backtracking.
- **C4.5**: An improved version on ID3 that introduces backtracking; it traverses the constructed tree and replaces branches with leaf nodes if purity is improved this way.
- **Classification and Regression Tree (CART)**: It constructs the tree using binary splitting, which we will discuss in detail shortly.

- **CHi-squared Automatic Interaction Detector (CHAID)**: This algorithm is often used in direct marketing. It involves complicated statistical concepts, but basically determines the optimal way of merging predictive variables in order to best explain the outcome.

The basic idea of these algorithms is to grow the tree greedily by making a series of local optimizations on choosing the most significant feature to use to partition the data. The dataset is then split based on the optimal value of that feature. We will discuss the measurement of a significant feature and the optimal splitting value of a feature in the next section.

We now study the CART algorithm in detail and will implement it as the most notable decision tree algorithm after. It constructs the tree using binary splitting and growing each node into left and right children. In each partition, it greedily searches for the most significant combination of a feature and its value; all different possible combinations are tried and tested using a measurement function. With the selected feature and value as a splitting point, it then divides the dataset as follows:

- Samples with the feature of this value (for a categorical feature) or a greater value (for a numerical feature) become the right child
- The remainder becomes the left child

This partitioning process repeats and recursively divides up the input samples into two subgroups. When the dataset becomes unmixed, a splitting process stops at a subgroup where either of the following two criteria are met:

- **The minimum number of samples for a new node**: When the number of samples is not greater than the minimum number of samples required for a further split, the partitioning stops in order to prevent the tree from excessively tailoring to the training set and, as a result, overfitting.
- **The maximum depth of the tree**: A node stops growing when its depth, which is defined as the number of partitioning taking place from the top down, starting from the root node ending in a terminal node, is not less than the maximum tree depth. Deeper trees are more specific to the training set and lead to overfitting.

A node with no branches becomes a leaf, and the dominant class of samples at this node is the prediction. Once all splitting processes finish, the tree is constructed and is portrayed with the assigned labels at the terminal nodes and the splitting points (feature + value) at all the internal nodes above.

We will implement the CART decision tree algorithm from scratch after studying the metrics of selecting the optimal splitting feature and value, as promised.

The metrics for measuring a split

When selecting the best combination of feature and value as the splitting point, two criteria such as **Gini Impurity** and **Information Gain** can be used to measure the quality of separation.

Gini Impurity, as its name implies, measures the impurity rate of the class distribution of data points, or the class mixture rate. For a dataset with K classes, suppose data from class $k(1 \leq k \leq K)$ take up a fraction $f_k(0 \leq f_k \leq 1)$ of the entire dataset, the *Gini Impurity* of this dataset is written as follows:

$$GiniImpurity = 1 - \sum_{k=1}^{K} f_k^2$$

Lower Gini Impurity indicates a purer dataset. For example, when the dataset contains only one class, say the fraction of this class is **1** and that of others is **0**, its Gini Impurity becomes $1 - (1^2 + 0^2) = 0$. In another example, a dataset records a large number of coin flips, and heads and tails each take up half of the samples. The Gini Impurity is $1 - (0.5^2 + 0.5^2) = 0.5$. In binary cases, Gini Impurity under different values of the positive class' fraction can be visualized by the following code blocks:

```
>>> import matplotlib.pyplot as plt
>>> import numpy as np
```

The fraction of the positive class varies from 0 to 1:

```
>>> pos_fraction = np.linspace(0.00, 1.00, 1000)
```

Gini Impurity is calculated accordingly, followed by the plot of Gini Impurity versus Positive fraction:

```
>>> gini = 1 - pos_fraction**2 - (1-pos_fraction)**2
>>> plt.plot(pos_fraction, gini)
>>> plt.ylim(0, 1)
>>> plt.xlabel('Positive fraction')
>>> plt.ylabel('Gini Impurity')
>>> plt.show()
```

Refer to the following screenshot for the end result:

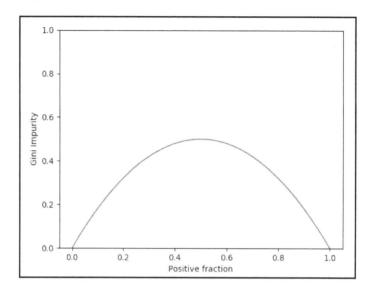

Given the labels of a dataset, we can implement the `Gini Impurity` calculation function as follows:

```
>>> def gini_impurity(labels):
...      # When the set is empty, it is also pure
...      if not labels:
...          return 0
...      # Count the occurrences of each label
...      counts = np.unique(labels, return_counts=True)[1]
...      fractions = counts / float(len(labels))
...      return 1 - np.sum(fractions ** 2)
```

Test it out with some examples:

```
>>> print('{0:.4f}'.format(gini_impurity([1, 1, 0, 1, 0])))
0.4800
>>> print('{0:.4f}'.format(gini_impurity([1, 1, 0, 1, 0, 0])))
0.5000
>>> print('{0:.4f}'.format(gini_impurity([1, 1, 1, 1])))
0.0000
```

In order to evaluate the quality of a split, we simply add up the Gini Impurity of all resulting subgroups, combining the proportions of each subgroup as corresponding weight factors. And again, the smaller the weighted sum of Gini Impurity, the better the split.

Take a look at the following self-driving car ad example, where we split the data based on user's gender and interest in technology respectively:

User gender	Interested in tech	Click	Group by gender
M	True	1	Group 1
F	False	0	Group 2
F	True	1	Group 2
M	False	0	Group 1
M	False	1	Group 1

User gender	Interested in tech	Click	Group by interest
M	True	1	Group 1
F	False	0	Group 2
F	True	1	Group 1
M	False	0	Group 2
M	False	1	Group 2

#1 split based on gender   #2 split based on interest in tech

The weighted Gini Impurity of the first split can be calculated as follows:

$$\#1 \ Gini \ Impurity = \frac{3}{5}\left[1 - \left(\frac{2^2}{3} + \frac{1^2}{3}\right)\right] + \frac{2}{5}\left[1 - \left(\frac{1^2}{2} + \frac{1^2}{2}\right)\right] = 0.467$$

The second split is as follows:

$$\#2 \ Gini \ Impurity = \frac{2}{5}[1 - (1^2 + 0^2)] + \frac{3}{5}\left[1 - \left(\frac{1^2}{3} + \frac{2^2}{3}\right)\right] = 0.267$$

Thus, splitting based on the user's interest in technology is a better strategy than gender.

Another metric, **Information Gain**, measures the improvement of purity after splitting, or in other words, the reduction of uncertainty due to a split. Higher Information Gain implies better splitting. We obtain the Information Gain of a split by comparing the **entropy** before and after the split.

Entropy is the probabilistic measure of uncertainty. Given a K-class dataset, and $f_k (0 \leq f_k \leq 1)$ denoted as the fraction of data from class $k (1 \leq k \leq K)$, the *entropy* of the dataset is defined as follows:

$$Entropy = -\sum_{k=1}^{K} f_k * log_2 f_k$$

Lower entropy implies a purer dataset with less ambiguity. In a perfect case where the dataset contains only one class, the entropy is $-(1 * log_2 1 + 0) = 0$. In the coin flip example, the entropy becomes $-(0.5 * log_2 0.5 + 0.5 * log_2 0.5) = 1$.

Similarly, we can visualize how entropy changes with different values of the positive class's fraction in binary cases using the following lines of codes:

```
>>> pos_fraction = np.linspace(0.00, 1.00, 1000)
>>> ent = - (pos_fraction * np.log2(pos_fraction) +
            (1 - pos_fraction) * np.log2(1 - pos_fraction))
>>> plt.plot(pos_fraction, ent)
>>> plt.xlabel('Positive fraction')
>>> plt.ylabel('Entropy')
>>> plt.ylim(0, 1)
>>> plt.show()
```

This will give us the following output:

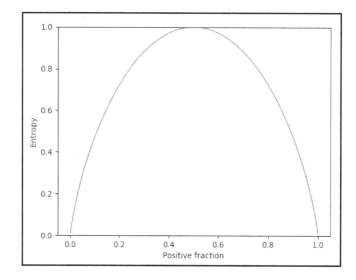

Given the labels of a dataset, the `entropy` calculation function can be implemented as follows:

```
>>> def entropy(labels):
...     if not labels:
...         return 0
...     counts = np.unique(labels, return_counts=True)[1]
...     fractions = counts / float(len(labels))
...     return - np.sum(fractions * np.log2(fractions))
```

Test it out with some examples:

```
>>> print('{0:.4f}'.format(entropy([1, 1, 0, 1, 0])))
0.9710
>>> print('{0:.4f}'.format(entropy([1, 1, 0, 1, 0, 0])))
1.0000
>>> print('{0:.4f}'.format(entropy([1, 1, 1, 1])))
-0.0000
```

Now that we have fully understood entropy, we can look into how Information Gain measures how much uncertainty was reduced after splitting, which is defined as the difference in entropy before a split (parent) and after the split (children):

$$InformationGain = Entropy(before) - Entropy(after)$$
$$= Entropy(parent) - Entropy(children)$$

Entropy after a split is calculated as the weighted sum of the entropy of each child, similarly to the weighted Gini Impurity.

During the process of constructing a node at a tree, our goal is to search for the splitting point where the maximum Information Gain is obtained. As the entropy of the parent node is unchanged, we just need to measure the entropy of the resulting children due to a split. The best split is the one with the lowest entropy of its resulting children.

To understand it better, let's look at the self-driving car ad example again.

For the first option, the *entropy* after the split can be calculated as follows:

$$\#1\ entropy = \frac{3}{5}\left[-\left(\frac{2}{3}*log_2\frac{2}{3}+\frac{1}{3}*log_2\frac{1}{3}\right)\right]+\frac{2}{5}\left[-\left(\frac{1}{2}*log_2\frac{1}{2}+\frac{1}{2}*log_2\frac{1}{2}\right)\right]=0.951$$

The second way of splitting is as follows:

$$\#2\ entropy = \frac{2}{5}[-1*log_21+0)]+\frac{3}{5}\left[-\left(\frac{1}{3}*log_2\frac{1}{3}+\frac{2}{3}*log_2\frac{2}{3}\right)\right]=0.551$$

For exploration, we can also calculate their *Information Gain* by:

$$Entropy\ before = -\left(\frac{3}{5}*log_2\frac{2}{3}+\frac{2}{5}*log_2\frac{2}{5}\right)=0.971$$
$$\#1\ Information\ Gain = 0.971 - 0.951 = 0.020$$
$$\#2\ Information\ Gain = 0.971 - 0.551 = 0.420$$

According to the Information Gain = entropy-based evaluation, the second split is preferable, which is the conclusion of the Gini Impurity criterion.

In general, the choice of two metrics, Gini Impurity and Information Gain, has little effect on the performance of the trained decision tree. They both measure the weighted impurity of the children after a split. We can combine them into one function to calculate the weighted impurity:

```
>>> criterion_function = {'gini': gini_impurity,
                          'entropy': entropy}
>>> def weighted_impurity(groups, criterion='gini'):
...     """
...     Calculate weighted impurity of children after a split
...     @param groups: list of children, and a child consists a
                       list of class labels
...     @param criterion: metric to measure the quality of a split,
...         'gini' for Gini Impurity or 'entropy' for Information Gain
...     @return: float, weighted impurity
...     """
...     total = sum(len(group) for group in groups)
...     weighted_sum = 0.0
...     for group in groups:
...         weighted_sum += len(group) / float(total) *
                            criterion_function[criterion](group)
...     return weighted_sum
```

Test it with the example we just hand-calculated, as follows:

```
>>> children_1 = [[1, 0, 1], [0, 1]]
>>> children_2 = [[1, 1], [0, 0, 1]]
>>> print('Entropy of #1 split:
        {0:.4f}'.format(weighted_impurity(children_1, 'entropy')))
Entropy of #1 split: 0.9510
>>> print('Entropy of #2 split:
        {0:.4f}'.format(weighted_impurity(children_2, 'entropy')))
Entropy of #2 split: 0.5510
```

Implementing a decision tree from scratch

With a solid understanding of partitioning evaluation metrics, let's practice the CART tree algorithm by hand on a toy dataset:

User interest	User occupation	Click
Tech	Professional	1
Fashion	Student	0
Fashion	Professional	0
Sports	Student	0
Tech	Student	1
Tech	Retired	0
Sports	Professional	1

To begin, we decide on the first splitting point, the root, by trying out all possible values for each of the two features. We utilize the `weighted_impurity` function we just defined to calculate the weighted Gini Impurity for each possible combination as follows:

Gini(interest, tech) = weighted_impurity([[1, 1, 0], [0, 0, 0, 1]]) = 0.405
Gini(interest, Fashion) = weighted_impurity([[0, 0], [1, 0, 1, 0, 1]]) = 0.343
Gini(interest, Sports) = weighted_impurity([[0, 1], [1, 0, 0, 1, 0]]) = 0.486
Gini(occupation, professional) = weighted_impurity([[0, 0, 1, 0], [1, 0, 1]]) = 0.405
Gini(occupation, student) = weighted_impurity([[0, 0, 1, 0], [1, 0, 1]]) = 0.405
Gini(occupation, retired) = weighted_impurity([[1, 0, 0, 0, 1, 1], [1]]) = 0.429

The root goes to the user interest feature with the fashion value, as this combination achieves the lowest weighted impurity, or the highest Information Gain. We can now build the first level of the tree as follows:

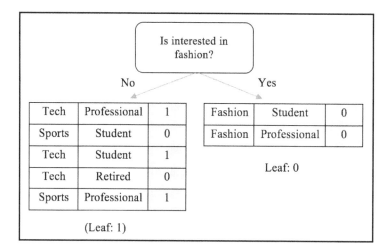

If we are satisfied with a one-level-deep tree, we can stop here by assigning the right branch label **0** and the left branch label **1** as the majority class. Alternatively, we can go further down the road, constructing the second level from the left branch (the right branch cannot be further split):

Gini(interest, tech) = weighted_impurity([[0, 1], [1, 1, 0]]) = 0.467
Gini(interest, Sports) = weighted_impurity([[1, 1, 0], [0, 1]]) = 0.467
Gini(occupation, professional) = weighted_impurity([[0, 1, 0], [1, 1]]) = 0.267
Gini(occupation, student) = weighted_impurity([[1, 0, 1], [0, 1]]) = 0.467
Gini(occupation, retired) = weighted_impurity([[1, 0, 1, 1], [0]]) = 0.300

With the second splitting point specified by (occupation, professional) with the lowest Gini Impurity, our tree becomes this:

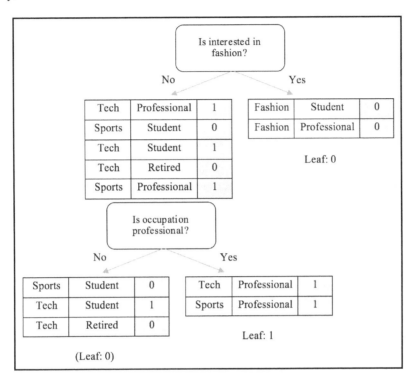

We can repeat the splitting process as long as the tree does not exceed the maximum depth and the node contains enough samples.

It is now time for coding after the process of tree construction has been made clear.

We start with the criterion of the best splitting point; the calculation of the weighted impurity of two potential children is what we defined previously, while that of two metrics are slightly different. The inputs now become NumPy arrays for computational efficiency:

```
>>> def gini_impurity_np(labels):
...     # When the set is empty, it is also pure
...     if labels.size == 0:
...         return 0
...     # Count the occurrences of each label
...     counts = np.unique(labels, return_counts=True)[1]
...     fractions = counts / float(len(labels))
...     return 1 - np.sum(fractions ** 2)
```

Also, take a look at the following code:

```
>>> def entropy_np(labels):
...         # When the set is empty, it is also pure
...         if labels.size == 0:
...             return 0
...         counts = np.unique(labels, return_counts=True)[1]
...         fractions = counts / float(len(labels))
...         return - np.sum(fractions * np.log2(fractions))
```

Also update the `weighted_impurity` function as follows:

```
>>> def weighted_impurity(groups, criterion='gini'):
...         """
...         Calculate weighted impurity of children after a split
...         @param groups: list of children, and a child consists a list
...                         of class labels
...         @param criterion: metric to measure the quality of a split,
...             'gini' for Gini Impurity or 'entropy' for Information Gain
...         @return: float, weighted impurity
...         """
...         total = sum(len(group) for group in groups)
...         weighted_sum = 0.0
...         for group in groups:
...             weighted_sum += len(group) / float(total) *
...                         criterion_function_np[criterion](group)
...         return weighted_sum
```

Next, we define a utility function to split a node into left and right children based on a feature and a value:

```
>>> def split_node(X, y, index, value):
...         """
...         Split dataset X, y based on a feature and a value
...         @param X: numpy.ndarray, dataset feature
...         @param y: numpy.ndarray, dataset target
...         @param index: int, index of the feature used for splitting
...         @param value: value of the feature used for splitting
...         @return: list, list, left and right child, a child is in the
...                         format of [X, y]
...         """
...         x_index = X[:, index]
...         # if this feature is numerical
...         if X[0, index].dtype.kind in ['i', 'f']:
...             mask = x_index >= value
...         # if this feature is categorical
...         else:
...             mask = x_index == value
```

```
...         # split into left and right child
...         left = [X[~mask, :], y[~mask]]
...         right = [X[mask, :], y[mask]]
...         return left, right
```

 We check whether the feature is numerical or categorical and split the data accordingly.

With the splitting measurement and generation functions available, we now define the greedy search function, which tries out all possible splits and returns the best one given a selection criterion, along with the resulting children:

```
>>> def get_best_split(X, y, criterion):
...         """
...         Obtain the best splitting point and resulting children for
...                                     the dataset X, y
...         @param X: numpy.ndarray, dataset feature
...         @param y: numpy.ndarray, dataset target
...         @param criterion: gini or entropy
...         @return: dict {index: index of the feature, value: feature
...                     value, children: left and right children}
...         """
...         best_index, best_value, best_score, children =
...                                     None, None, 1, None
...         for index in range(len(X[0])):
...             for value in np.sort(np.unique(X[:, index])):
...                 groups = split_node(X, y, index, value)
...                 impurity = weighted_impurity(
...                         [groups[0][1], groups[1][1]], criterion)
...                 if impurity < best_score:
...                     best_index, best_value, best_score, children =
...                                     index, value, impurity, groups
...         return {'index': best_index, 'value': best_value,
...                 'children': children}
```

The selection and splitting process occurs in a recursive manner on each of the subsequent children. When a stopping criterion is met, the process stops at a node and the major label will be assigned to this leaf node:

```
>>> def get_leaf(labels):
...         # Obtain the leaf as the majority of the labels
...         return np.bincount(labels).argmax()
```

And finally, the recursive function links all these together:

- It assigns a leaf node if one of two child nodes is empty
- It assigns a leaf node if the current branch depth exceeds the maximum depth allowed
- It assigns a leaf node if it does not contain sufficient samples required for a further split
- Otherwise, it proceeds with a further split with the optimal splitting point

This is done with the following function:

```
>>> def split(node, max_depth, min_size, depth, criterion):
...         """
...         Split children of a node to construct new nodes or assign
...         them terminals
...         @param node: dict, with children info
...         @param max_depth: int, maximal depth of the tree
...         @param min_size: int, minimal samples required to further
...                          split a child
...         @param depth: int, current depth of the node
...         @param criterion: gini or entropy
...         """
...         left, right = node['children']
...         del (node['children'])
...         if left[1].size == 0:
...             node['right'] = get_leaf(right[1])
...             return
...         if right[1].size == 0:
...             node['left'] = get_leaf(left[1])
...             return
...         # Check if the current depth exceeds the maximal depth
...         if depth >= max_depth:
...             node['left'], node['right'] =
...                             get_leaf(left[1]), get_leaf(right[1])
...             return
...         # Check if the left child has enough samples
...         if left[1].size <= min_size:
...             node['left'] = get_leaf(left[1])
...         else:
...             # It has enough samples, we further split it
...             result = get_best_split(left[0], left[1], criterion)
...             result_left, result_right = result['children']
...             if result_left[1].size == 0:
...                 node['left'] = get_leaf(result_right[1])
...             elif result_right[1].size == 0:
...                 node['left'] = get_leaf(result_left[1])
...             else:
```

```
...             node['left'] = result
...             split(node['left'], max_depth, min_size,
                                        depth + 1, criterion)
...         # Check if the right child has enough samples
...         if right[1].size <= min_size:
...             node['right'] = get_leaf(right[1])
...         else:
...             # It has enough samples, we further split it
...             result = get_best_split(right[0], right[1], criterion)
...             result_left, result_right = result['children']
...             if result_left[1].size == 0:
...                 node['right'] = get_leaf(result_right[1])
...             elif result_right[1].size == 0:
...                 node['right'] = get_leaf(result_left[1])
...             else:
...                 node['right'] = result
...                 split(node['right'], max_depth, min_size,
                                        depth + 1, criterion)
```

Finally, the entry point of the tree's construction is as follows:

```
>>> def train_tree(X_train, y_train, max_depth, min_size,
                   criterion='gini'):
...     """
...     Construction of a tree starts here
...     @param X_train: list of training samples (feature)
...     @param y_train: list of training samples (target)
...     @param max_depth: int, maximal depth of the tree
...     @param min_size: int, minimal samples required to further
                         split a child
...     @param criterion: gini or entropy
...     """
...     X = np.array(X_train)
...     y = np.array(y_train)
...     root = get_best_split(X, y, criterion)
...     split(root, max_depth, min_size, 1, criterion)
...     return root
```

Now, let's test it with the preceding hand-calculated example:

```
>>> X_train = [['tech', 'professional'],
...            ['fashion', 'student'],
...            ['fashion', 'professional'],
...            ['sports', 'student'],
...            ['tech', 'student'],
...            ['tech', 'retired'],
...            ['sports', 'professional']]
>>> y_train = [1, 0, 0, 0, 1, 0, 1]
>>> tree = train_tree(X_train, y_train, 2, 2)
```

To verify that the resulting tree from the model is identical to what we constructed by hand, we write a function displaying the tree:

```
>>> CONDITION = {'numerical': {'yes': '>=', 'no': '<'},
...              'categorical': {'yes': 'is', 'no': 'is not'}}
>>> def visualize_tree(node, depth=0):
...     if isinstance(node, dict):
...         if node['value'].dtype.kind in ['i', 'f']:
...             condition = CONDITION['numerical']
...         else:
...             condition = CONDITION['categorical']
...         print('{}|- X{} {} {}'.format(depth * '  ',
...             node['index'] + 1, condition['no'], node['value']))
...         if 'left' in node:
...             visualize_tree(node['left'], depth + 1)
...         print('{}|- X{} {} {}'.format(depth * '  ',
...             node['index'] + 1, condition['yes'], node['value']))
...         if 'right' in node:
...             visualize_tree(node['right'], depth + 1)
...     else:
...         print('{}[{}]'.format(depth * '  ', node))
>>> visualize_tree(tree)
|- X1 is not fashion
 |- X2 is not professional
   [0]
 |- X2 is professional
   [1]
|- X1 is fashion
 [0]
```

We can test it with a numerical example as follows:

```
>>> X_train_n = [[6, 7],
...              [2, 4],
...              [7, 2],
...              [3, 6],
```

```
...                   [4, 7],
...                   [5, 2],
...                   [1, 6],
...                   [2, 0],
...                   [6, 3],
...                   [4, 1]]
>>> y_train_n = [0, 0, 0, 0, 0, 1, 1, 1, 1, 1]
>>> tree = train_tree(X_train_n, y_train_n, 2, 2)
>>> visualize_tree(tree)
|- X2 < 4
  |- X1 < 7
    [1]
  |- X1 >= 7
    [0]
|- X2 >= 4
  |- X1 < 2
    [1]
  |- X1 >= 2
    [0]
```

The resulting trees from our decision tree model are the same as those we hand-crafted.

Now that we have a more solid understanding of decision trees by implementing one from scratch, we can try the decision tree package from scikit-learn, which is already well developed and optimized:

```
>>> from sklearn.tree import DecisionTreeClassifier
>>> tree_sk = DecisionTreeClassifier(criterion='gini',
                          max_depth=2, min_samples_split=2)
>>> tree_sk.fit(X_train_n, y_train_n)
```

To visualize the tree we just built, we utilize the built-in export_graphviz function, as follows:

```
>>> export_graphviz(tree_sk, out_file='tree.dot',
        feature_names=['X1', 'X2'], impurity=False, filled=True,
        class_names=['0', '1'])
```

Running this will generate a file called tree.dot, which can be converted to a PNG image file using **Graphviz** (introduction and installation instructions can be found at http://www.graphviz.org) by running the following command in the terminal:

```
dot -Tpng tree.dot -o tree.png
```

Refer to the following screenshot for the result:

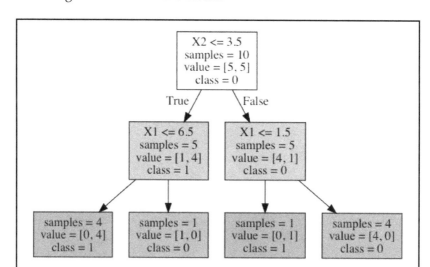

The generated tree is essentially the same as the one we had before.

Predicting ad click-through with decision tree

After several examples, it is now time to predict ad click-through with the decision tree algorithm we have just thoroughly learned about and practiced. We will use the dataset from a Kaggle machine learning competition, *Click-Through Rate Prediction* (`https://www.kaggle.com/c/avazu-ctr-prediction`). The dataset can be downloaded from `https://www.kaggle.com/c/avazu-ctr-prediction/data`.

Only the `train.gz` file contains labeled samples, so we only need to download this and unzip it (it will take a while). In this chapter, we focus on only the first 300,000 samples from the train file unzipped from `train.gz`.

The fields in the raw file are as follows:

Field	Description	Example values
id	ad identifier	such as '1000009418151094273', '10000169349117863715'
click	'0' for non-click, '1' for click	0, 1
hour	in the format of YYMMDDHH	'14102100'
C1	anonymized categorical variable	'1005', '1002'
banner_pos	where banner located	1, 0
site_id	site identifier	'1fbe01fe', 'fe8cc448', 'd6137915'
site_domain	hashed site domain	'bb1ef334', 'f3845767'
site_category	hashed site category	'28905ebd', '28905ebd'
app_id	mobile app identifier	'ecad2386'
app_domain	mobile app domain	'7801e8d9'
app_category	category of app	'07d7df22'
device_id	mobile device identifier	'a99f214a'
device_ip	IP address	'ddd2926e'
device_model	such as iphone 6, Samsung, hashed by the way	'44956a24'
device_type	such as tablet, smartphone, hashed	1
device_conn_type	Wi-Fi or 3G for example, again hashed in the data	0, 2
C14-C21	anonymized categorical variables	

We take a glance at the head of the file by running the following command:

```
head train | sed 's/,,/, ,/g;s/,,/, ,/g' | column -s, -t
```

Rather than simple `head train`, the output is cleaner as all the columns are aligned:

```
id                        click hour      C1    banner_pos site_id   site_domain site_category app_id
 app_domain  app_category  device_id  device_ip  device_model  device_type  device_conn_type  C14    C15
 C16  C17  C18  C19  C20     C21
1000009418151094273   0        14102100  1005  0                1fbe01fe  f3845767    28905ebd       ecad2386
7801e8d9     07d7df22      a99f214a  ddd2926e  44956a24      1            2                 15706  320
 50   1722  0    35   -1      79
10000169349117863715  0        14102100  1005  0                1fbe01fe  f3845767    28905ebd       ecad2386
7801e8d9     07d7df22      a99f214a  96809ac8  711ee120      1            0                 15704  320
 50   1722  0    35   100084  79
10000371904215119486  0        14102100  1005  0                1fbe01fe  f3845767    28905ebd       ecad2386
7801e8d9     07d7df22      a99f214a  b3cf8def  8a4875bd      1            0                 15704  320
 50   1722  0    35   100084  79
10000640724480838376  0        14102100  1005  0                1fbe01fe  f3845767    28905ebd       ecad2386
7801e8d9     07d7df22      a99f214a  e8275b8f  6332421a      1            0                 15706  320
 50   1722  0    35   100084  79
10000679056417042096  0        14102100  1005  1                fe8cc448  9166c161    0569f928       ecad2386
7801e8d9     07d7df22      a99f214a  9644d0bf  779d90c2      1            0                 18993  320
 50   2161  0    35   -1      157
10000720757801103869  0        14102100  1005  0                d6137915  bb1ef334    f028772b       ecad2386
7801e8d9     07d7df22      a99f214a  05241af0  8a4875bd      1            0                 16920  320
 50   1899  0    431  100077  117
10000724729988544911  0        14102100  1005  0                8fda644b  25d4cfcd    f028772b       ecad2386
7801e8d9     07d7df22      a99f214a  b264c159  be6db1d7      1            0                 20362  320
 50   2333  0    39   -1      157
10000918755742328737  0        14102100  1005  1                e151e245  7e091613    f028772b       ecad2386
7801e8d9     07d7df22      a99f214a  e6f67278  be74e6fe      1            0                 20632  320
 50   2374  3    39   -1      23
10000949271186029916  1        14102100  1005  0                1fbe01fe  f3845767    28905ebd       ecad2386
7801e8d9     07d7df22      a99f214a  37e8da74  5db079b5      1            2                 15707  320
 50   1722  0    35   -1      79
```

Don't be scared by the anonymized and hashed values. They are categorical features, and each possible value of them corresponds to a real and meaningful value, but is presented this way out of privacy policy. Maybe `C1` means user gender, and `1005` and `1002` represent male and female respectively.

Now, let's get started with reading the dataset using `pandas`. That's right, `pandas` is extremely good at handling data in a tabular format:

```
>>> import pandas as pd
>>> n_rows = 300000
>>> df = pd.read_csv("train.csv", nrows=n_rows)
```

The first 300,000 lines of the file are loaded and stored in a dataframe. Take a quick look at the first five rows of the dataframe:

```
>>> print(df.head(5))
   id   click       hour C1 banner_pos    site_id ... C16 C17 C18 C19      C20 C21
0  1.000009e+18       0 14102100 1005             0 1fbe01fe ... 50 1722 0   35
-1 79
1  1.000017e+19       0 14102100 1005             0 1fbe01fe ... 50 1722 0   35
100084 79
2  1.000037e+19       0 14102100 1005             0 1fbe01fe ... 50 1722 0   35
```

```
100084 79
3   1.000064e+19      0 14102100 1005      0 1fbe01fe ... 50 1722 0  35
100084 79
4   1.000068e+19      0 14102100 1005      1 fe8cc448 ... 50 2161 0  35
-1 157
```

The target variable is the `click` column:

```
>>> Y = df['click'].values
```

For the remaining columns, there are several columns that should be removed from the features (`id`, `hour`, `device_id`, and `device_ip`) as they do not contain much useful information:

```
>>> X = df.drop(['click', 'id', 'hour', 'device_id', 'device_ip'],
                axis=1).values
>>> print(X.shape)
(300000, 19)
```

Each sample has `19` predictive attributes.

Next, we need to split the data into training and testing sets. Normally, we do so by randomly picking samples. However, in our case, samples are in chronological order as indicated in the `hour` field. Obviously, we cannot use future samples to predict the past ones. Hence, we take the first 90% as training samples and the rest as testing samples:

```
>>> n_train = int(n_rows * 0.9)
>>> X_train = X[:n_train]
>>> Y_train = Y[:n_train]
>>> X_test = X[n_train:]
>>> Y_test = Y[n_train:]
```

As mentioned, decision tree models can take in categorical features. However, because the tree-based algorithms in `scikit-learn` (the current version is 0.20.0 as of the end of 2018) only allow numerical input, we need to transform categorical features into numerical ones. But note that in general we do not need to do so; for example, the decision tree classifier we developed from scratch earlier can directly take in categorical features.

We now transform string-based categorical features into one-hot encoded vectors using the `OneHotEncoder` module from `scikit-learn`. One-hot encoding was briefly mentioned in Chapter 1, *Getting Started with Machine Learning and Python*. To recap, it basically converts a categorical feature with k possible values into k binary features. For example, the site category feature with three possible values, `news`, `education`, and `sports`, will be encoded into three binary features, such as `is_news`, `is_education`, and `is_sports`, whose values are either 1 or 0.

Initialize a `OneHotEncoder` object as follows:

```
>>> from sklearn.preprocessing import OneHotEncoder
>>> enc = OneHotEncoder(handle_unknown='ignore')
```

Fit it on the training set as follows:

```
>>> X_train_enc = enc.fit_transform(X_train)
>>> X_train_enc[0]
<1x8385 sparse matrix of type '<class 'numpy.float64'>'
with 19 stored elements in Compressed Sparse Row format>
>>> print(X_train_enc[0])
  (0, 2) 1.0
  (0, 6) 1.0
  (0, 30) 1.0
  (0, 1471) 1.0
  (0, 2743) 1.0
  (0, 3878) 1.0
  (0, 4000) 1.0
  (0, 4048) 1.0
  (0, 6663) 1.0
  (0, 7491) 1.0
  (0, 7494) 1.0
  (0, 7861) 1.0
  (0, 8004) 1.
  (0, 8008) 1.0
  (0, 8085) 1.0
  (0, 8158) 1.0
  (0, 8163) 1.0
  (0, 8202) 1.0
  (0, 8383) 1.0
```

Each converted sample is a sparse vector.

Transform the testing set using the trained one-hot encoder as follows:

```
>>> X_test_enc = enc.transform(X_test)
```

Remember, we specify the `handle_unknown='ignore'` parameter in the one-hot encoder earlier. This is to prevent errors due to any unseen categorical values. Use the previous site category example, if there is a sample with the value `movie`, three converted binary features (`is_news`, `is_education`, and `is_sports`) all become 0s. If we do not specify `ignore`, an error will be raised.

Next, we train a decision tree model using grid search, which we learned about in Chapter 5, *Classifying Newsgroup Topics with a Support Vector Machine*. For demonstration purposes, we only tweak the `max_depth` hyperparameter. Other hyperparameters, such as `min_samples_split` and `class_weight`, are also highly recommended. The classification metric should be AUC of ROC, as it is an imbalanced binary case (only 51,211 out of 300,000 training samples are clicks, that, is a 17% positive click-through rate):

```
>>> from sklearn.tree import DecisionTreeClassifier
>>> parameters = {'max_depth': [3, 10, None]}
```

Pick three options for the maximal depth, `3`, `10`, and unbounded. Initialize a decision tree model with Gini Impurity as the metric and `30` as the minimum number of samples required to split further:

```
>>> decision_tree = DecisionTreeClassifier(criterion='gini',
                                     min_samples_split=30)
>>> from sklearn.model_selection import GridSearchCV
```

As for grid search, we use three-fold (as there are enough training samples) cross-validation and select the best performing hyperparameter measured by AUC:

```
>>> grid_search = GridSearchCV(decision_tree, parameters,
                       n_jobs=-1, cv=3, scoring='roc_auc')
```

Note `n_jobs=-1` means that we use all available CPU processors:

```
>>> grid_search.fit(X_train, y_train)
>>> print(grid_search.best_params_)
{'max_depth': 10}
```

Use the model with the optimal parameter to predict future test cases, as follows:

```
>>> decision_tree_best = grid_search.bestestimator
>>> pos_prob = decision_tree_best.predict_proba(X_test)[:, 1]
>>> from sklearn.metrics import roc_auc_score
>>> print('The ROC AUC on testing set is:
                {0:.3f}'.format(roc_auc_score(y_test, pos_prob)))
The ROC AUC on testing set is: 0.719
```

The AUC we can achieve with the optimal decision tree model is 0.72. It does not seem very high, but click-through involves many intricate human factors, which is why predicting it is not an easy problem. Although we can further optimize its hyperparameters, an AUC of 0.72 is pretty good, actually. Randomly selecting 17% of the samples to be click will generate an AUC of 0.496:

```
>>> pos_prob = np.zeros(len(Y_test))
>>> click_index = np.random.choice(len(Y_test),
 int(len(Y_test) * 51211.0/300000), replace=False)
>>> pos_prob[click_index] = 1
>>> roc_auc_score(Y_test, pos_prob)
0.496
```

Looking back, we can see that a decision tree is a sequence of greedy searches for the best splitting point at each step, based on the training dataset. However, this tends to cause overfitting as it is likely that the optimal points only work well for the training samples. Fortunately, ensembling is the technique to correct this, and random forest is an ensemble tree model that usually outperforms a simple decision tree.

Ensembling decision trees – random forest

The **ensemble** technique **bagging** (which stands for **bootstrap aggregating**), which we briefly mentioned in Chapter 1, *Getting Started with Machine Learning and Python*, can effectively overcome overfitting. To recap, different sets of training samples are randomly drawn with replacements from the original training data; each resulting set is used to fit an individual classification model. The results of these separately trained models are then combined together through a **majority vote** to make the final decision.

Tree bagging, described in the preceding section, reduces the high variance that a decision tree model suffers from and hence, in general, performs better than a single tree. However, in some cases, where one or more features are strong indicators, individual trees are constructed largely based on these features and as a result become highly correlated. Aggregating multiple correlated trees will not make much difference. To force each tree to be uncorrelated, random forest only consider a random subset of the features when searching for the best splitting point at each node. Individual trees are now trained based on different sequential sets of features, which guarantees more diversity and better performance. Random forest is a variant tree bagging model with additional **feature-based bagging**.

To employ random forest in our click-through prediction project, we use the package from `scikit-learn`. Similar to the way we implemented the decision tree in the preceding section, we only tweak the `max_depth` parameter:

```
>>> from sklearn.ensemble import RandomForestClassifier
>>> random_forest = RandomForestClassifier(n_estimators=100,
            criterion='gini', min_samples_split=30, n_jobs=-1)
```

Besides `max_depth`, `min_samples_split`, and `class_weight`, which are important hyperparameters related to a single decision tree, hyperparameters that are related to a random forest (a set of trees) such as `n_estimators` are also highly recommended:

```
>>> grid_search = GridSearchCV(random_forest, parameters,
                            n_jobs=-1, cv=3, scoring='roc_auc')
>>> grid_search.fit(X_train, y_train)
>>> print(grid_search.best_params_)
{'max_depth': None}
```

Use the model with the optimal parameter `None` for `max_depth` (nodes are expanded until another stopping criterion is met) to predict future unseen cases:

```
>>> random_forest_best = grid_search.bestestimator
>>> pos_prob = random_forest_best.predict_proba(X_test)[:, 1]
>>> print('The ROC AUC on testing set is:
    {0:.3f}'.format(roc_auc_score(y_test, pos_prob)))
The ROC AUC on testing set is: 0.759
```

It turns out that the random forest model gives a substantial lift to the performance.

Let's summarize several critical hyperparameters to tune in random forest:

- `max_depth`: This is the deepest individual tree. It tends to overfit if it is too deep, or to underfit if it is too shallow.
- `min_samples_split`: This hyperparameter represents the minimum number of samples required for further splitting at a node. Too small a value tends to cause overfitting, while too large a value is likely to introduce underfitting. `10`, `30`, and `50` might be good options to start with.

The preceding two hyperparameters are generally related to individual decision trees. The following two parameters are more related to a random forest, a collection of trees:

- `max_features`: This parameter represents the number of features to consider for each best splitting point search. Typically, for an *m*-dimensional dataset, $\sqrt{m}$ (rounded) is a recommended value for `max_features`. This can be specified as `max_features="sqrt"` in `scikit-learn`. Other options include `log2`, 20% of the original features to 50%.
- `n_estimators`: This parameter represents the number of trees considered for majority voting. Generally speaking, the more trees, the better the performance, but more computation time. It is usually set as 100, 200, 500, and so on.

Implementing random forest using TensorFlow

This is a bonus section where we implement a random forest with TensorFlow. Let's take a look at the following steps and see how it is done:

1. First, we import the modules we need, as follows:

```
>>> import tensorflow as tf
>>> from tensorflow.contrib.tensor_forest.python import
tensor_forest
>>> from tensorflow.python.ops import resources
```

2. Specify the parameters of the model, including `20` iterations during the training process, `10` trees in total, and `30000` maximal splitting nodes:

```
>>> n_iter = 20
>>> n_classes = 2
>>> n_features = int(X_train_enc.toarray().shape[1])
>>> n_trees = 10
>>> max_nodes = 30000
```

3. Next, we create placeholders and build the TensorFlow graph:

```
>>> x = tf.placeholder(tf.float32, shape=[None, n_features])
>>> y = tf.placeholder(tf.int64, shape=[None])
>>> hparams = tensor_forest.ForestHParams(num_classes=n_classes,
 num_features=n_features, num_trees=n_trees,
 max_nodes=max_nodes, split_after_samples=30).fill()
>>> forest_graph = tensor_forest.RandomForestGraphs(hparams)
```

4. After defining the graph for the random forest model, we get the training graph and loss, as well as the measurement of performance, the AUC:

```
>>> train_op = forest_graph.training_graph(x, y)
>>> loss_op = forest_graph.training_loss(x, y)
>>> infer_op, _, _ = forest_graph.inference_graph(x)
>>> auc = tf.metrics.auc(tf.cast(y, tf.int64), infer_op[:, 1])[1]
```

5. Then, initialize the variables and start a TensorFlow session:

```
>>> init_vars = tf.group(tf.global_variables_initializer(),
            tf.local_variables_initializer(),
resources.initialize_resources(resources.shared_resources()))
>>> sess = tf.Session()
>>> sess.run(init_vars)
```

5. In TensorFlow, models are usually trained in a batch. That is, the training set is split into many small chunks and the model fits them chunk by chunk. Here, we set the batch size to `1000` and define a function to get randomized chunks of samples in each training iteration:

```
>>> batch_size = 1000
>>> import numpy as np
>>> indices = list(range(n_train))
>>> def gen_batch(indices):
...         np.random.shuffle(indices)
...         for batch_i in range(int(n_train / batch_size)):
...             batch_index = indices[batch_i*batch_size:
                                    (batch_i+1)*batch_size]
...             yield X_train_enc[batch_index], Y_train[batch_index]
```

6. Finally, we start the training process and conduct a performance check-up for each iteration:

```
>>> for i in range(1, n_iter + 1):
...         for X_batch, Y_batch in gen_batch(indices):
...             _, l = sess.run([train_op, loss_op], feed_dict=
                                {x: X_batch.toarray(), y: Y_batch})
...         acc_train = sess.run(auc, feed_dict=
                                {x: X_train_enc.toarray(), y: Y_train})
...         print('Iteration %i, AUC of ROC on training set: %f' %
                                                    (i, acc_train))
...         acc_test = sess.run(auc, feed_dict=
                                {x: X_test_enc.toarray(), y: Y_test})
...         print("AUC of ROC on testing set:", acc_test)
Iteration 1, AUC of ROC on training set: 0.740271
AUC of ROC on testing set: 0.7418298
```

```
Iteration 2, AUC of ROC on training set: 0.745904
AUC of ROC on testing set: 0.74665743
Iteration 3, AUC of ROC on training set: 0.749690
AUC of ROC on testing set: 0.7501322
Iteration 4, AUC of ROC on training set: 0.752632
AUC of ROC on testing set: 0.7529533
Iteration 5, AUC of ROC on training set: 0.755357
AUC of ROC on testing set: 0.75560063
Iteration 6, AUC of ROC on training set: 0.757673
AUC of ROC on testing set: 0.75782216
Iteration 7, AUC of ROC on training set: 0.759688
AUC of ROC on testing set: 0.7597882
Iteration 8, AUC of ROC on training set: 0.761526
AUC of ROC on testing set: 0.76160187
Iteration 9, AUC of ROC on training set: 0.763228
AUC of ROC on testing set: 0.7632776
Iteration 10, AUC of ROC on training set: 0.764791
AUC of ROC on testing set: 0.76481616
Iteration 11, AUC of ROC on training set: 0.766269
AUC of ROC on testing set: 0.7662764
Iteration 12, AUC of ROC on training set: 0.767667
AUC of ROC on testing set: 0.76765794
Iteration 13, AUC of ROC on training set: 0.768994
AUC of ROC on testing set: 0.768983
Iteration 14, AUC of ROC on training set: 0.770247
AUC of ROC on testing set: 0.770225
Iteration 15, AUC of ROC on training set: 0.771437
AUC of ROC on testing set: 0.7714067
Iteration 16, AUC of ROC on training set: 0.772580
AUC of ROC on testing set: 0.772544
Iteration 17, AUC of ROC on training set: 0.773677
AUC of ROC on testing set: 0.7736392
Iteration 18, AUC of ROC on training set: 0.774740
AUC of ROC on testing set: 0.7746992
Iteration 19, AUC of ROC on training set: 0.775768
AUC of ROC on testing set: 0.77572197
Iteration 20, AUC of ROC on training set: 0.776747
AUC of ROC on testing set: 0.7766986
```

After 20 iterations, we are able to achieve 0.78 AUC using the TensorFlow random forest model.

Finally, you may wonder how to implement decision tree with TensorFlow. Well, that's easy. Simply use one tree (n_trees=1), and the whole random forest is basically a decision tree.

Summary

In this chapter, we started with an introduction to a typical machine learning problem, online advertising click-through prediction, and the inherent challenges, including categorical features. We then looked at tree-based algorithms that can take in both numerical and categorical features. We then had an in-depth discussion about the decision tree algorithm: the mechanics, different types, how to construct a tree, and two metrics (Gini Impurity and entropy) that measure the effectiveness of a split at a node. After constructing a tree in an example by hand, we implemented the algorithm from scratch. We also learned how to use the decision tree package from `scikit-learn` and applied it to predict click-through. We continued to improve the performance by adopting the feature-based random forest bagging algorithm and the chapter ended with some ways to tune a random forest model, as well as a bonus section in which we implemented a random forest with TensorFlow.

More practice is always good for honing skills. We recommend you complete the following exercise before going to the next chapter, where we will solve ad click-through prediction using another algorithm: **logistic regression**.

Exercise

- In the decision tree click-through prediction project, can you also tweak other hyperparameters, such as `min_samples_split` and `class_weight`? What is the highest AUC you are able to achieve?
- In the random forest-based click-through prediction project, can you also tweak other hyperparameters, such as `min_samples_split`, `max_features`, and `n_estimators`, in `scikit-learn`? What is the highest AUC you are able to achieve?

7
Predicting Online Ad Click-Through with Logistic Regression

In this chapter, we will be continuing our journey of tackling the billion-dollar worth problem of advertising click-through prediction. We will be focusing on learning a very (probably the most) scalable classification model—logistic regression. We will be exploring what logistic function is, how to train a logistic regression model, adding regularization to the model, and variants of logistic regression that are applicable to very large datasets. Besides the application in classification, we will also be discussing how logistic regression and random forest are used in picking significant features. Again, you won't get bored as there will be lots of implementations from scratch, and with scikit-learn and TensorFlow.

In this chapter, we will cover the following topics:

- Categorical feature encoding
- Logistic function
- What is logistic regression
- Training a logistic regression model via gradient descent
- Training a logistic regression model via stochastic gradient descent
- The implementations of logistic regression from scratch
- The implementations of logistic regression with scikit-learn
- The implementations of logistic regression with TensorFlow
- Click-through prediction with logistic regression
- Logistic regression with L1 and L2 regularization
- Logistic regression for feature selection
- Online learning
- Another way to select features—random forest

Converting categorical features to numerical – one-hot encoding and ordinal encoding

In the previous chapter, *Predicting Online Ads Click-through with Tree-Based Algorithms*, we mentioned how **one-hot encoding** transforms categorical features to numerical features in order to be used in the tree algorithms in scikit-learn and TensorFlow. This will not limit our choice to tree-based algorithms if we can adopt one-hot encoding to any other algorithms that only take in numerical features.

The simplest solution we can think of in terms of transforming a categorical feature with k possible values is to map it to a numerical feature with values from 1 to k. For example, [*Tech, Fashion, Fashion, Sports, Tech, Tech, Sports*] becomes [1, 2, 2, 3, 1, 1, 3]. However, this will impose an ordinal characteristic, such as *Sports* being greater than *Tech*, and a distance property, such as *Sports* being closer to *Fashion* than to *Tech*.

Instead, one-hot encoding converts the categorical feature to k binary features. Each binary feature indicates the presence or absence of a corresponding possible value. Hence, the preceding example becomes the following:

User interest	Interest: tech	Interest: fashion	Interest: sports
Tech	1	0	0
Fashion	0	1	0
Fashion	0	1	0
Sports	0	0	1
Tech	1	0	0
Tech	1	0	0
Sports	0	0	1

Previously, we have used `OneHotEncoder` from scikit-learn to convert a matrix of string into a binary matrix, but here, let's take a look at another module, `DictVectorizer`, which also provides an efficient conversion. It transforms dictionary objects (categorical feature: value) into one-hot encoded vectors.

For example, take a look at the following codes:

```
>>> from sklearn.feature_extraction import DictVectorizer
>>> X_dict = [{'interest': 'tech', 'occupation': 'professional'},
...           {'interest': 'fashion', 'occupation': 'student'},
...           {'interest': 'fashion','occupation':'professional'},
...           {'interest': 'sports', 'occupation': 'student'},
...           {'interest': 'tech', 'occupation': 'student'},
...           {'interest': 'tech', 'occupation': 'retired'},
...           {'interest': 'sports','occupation': 'professional'}]
>>> dict_one_hot_encoder = DictVectorizer(sparse=False)
>>> X_encoded = dict_one_hot_encoder.fit_transform(X_dict)
>>> print(X_encoded)
[[ 0.  0.  1.  1.  0.  0.]
 [ 1.  0.  0.  0.  0.  1.]
 [ 1.  0.  0.  1.  0.  0.]
 [ 0.  1.  0.  0.  0.  1.]
 [ 0.  0.  1.  0.  0.  1.]
 [ 0.  0.  1.  0.  1.  0.]
 [ 0.  1.  0.  1.  0.  0.]]
```

We can also see the mapping by executing the following:

```
>>> print(dict_one_hot_encoder.vocabulary_)
{'interest=fashion': 0, 'interest=sports': 1,
'occupation=professional': 3, 'interest=tech': 2,
'occupation=retired': 4, 'occupation=student': 5}
```

When it comes to new data, we can transform it by:

```
>>> new_dict = [{'interest': 'sports', 'occupation': 'retired'}]
>>> new_encoded = dict_one_hot_encoder.transform(new_dict)
>>> print(new_encoded)
[[ 0.  1.  0.  0.  1.  0.]]
```

We can inversely transform the encoded features back to the original features by:

```
>>> print(dict_one_hot_encoder.inverse_transform(new_encoded))
[{'interest=sports': 1.0, 'occupation=retired': 1.0}]
```

One important thing to note is that if a new (not seen in training data) category is encountered in new data, it should be ignored. `DictVectorizer` handles this implicitly (while `OneHotEncoder` needs to specify parameter `ignore`):

```
>>> new_dict = [{'interest': 'unknown_interest',
                 'occupation': 'retired'},
...             {'interest': 'tech', 'occupation':
                 'unseen_occupation'}]
```

```
>>> new_encoded = dict_one_hot_encoder.transform(new_dict)
>>> print(new_encoded)
[[ 0.  0. 0. 0.  1. 0.]
 [ 0.  0. 1. 0.  0. 0.]]
```

Sometimes, we do prefer transforming a categorical feature with *k* possible values into a numerical feature with values ranging from *1* to *k*. We conduct **ordinal encoding** in order to employ ordinal or ranking knowledge in our learning; for example, *large, medium,* and *small* become 3, 2, and 1 respectively, *good* and *bad* become 1 and 0, while one-hot encoding fails to preserve such useful information. We can realize ordinal encoding easily through the use of `pandas`, for example:

```
>>> import pandas as pd
>>> df = pd.DataFrame({'score': ['low',
...                               'high',
...                               'medium',
...                               'medium',
...                               'low']})
>>> print(df)
    score
0     low
1    high
2  medium
3  medium
4     low
>>> mapping = {'low':1, 'medium':2, 'high':3}
>>> df['score'] = df['score'].replace(mapping)
>>> print(df)
  score
0     1
1     3
2     2
3     2
4     1
```

We convert the string feature into ordinal values based on the mapping we define.

Classifying data with logistic regression

As seen in the last chapter, we trained the tree-based models only based on the first 300,000 samples out of 40 million. We did so simply because training a tree on a large dataset is extremely computationally expensive and time-consuming. Since we are now not limited to algorithms directly taking in categorical features thanks to one-hot encoding, we should turn to a new algorithm with high scalability to large datasets. Logistic regression is one of the most, or perhaps the most, scalable classification algorithms.

Getting started with the logistic function

Let's start with an introduction to the **logistic function** (which is more commonly referred to as the **sigmoid function**) as the algorithm core before we dive into the algorithm itself. It basically maps an input to an output of a value between *0* and *1*, and is defined as follows:

$$y(z) = \frac{1}{1 + exp(-z)}$$

We can visualize what it looks like by performing the following steps:

1. Define the logistic function:

    ```
    >>> import numpy as np
    >>> def sigmoid(input):
    ...       return 1.0 / (1 + np.exp(-input))
    ```

2. Input variables from −8 to 8, and the corresponding output, as follows:

    ```
    >>> z = np.linspace(-8, 8, 1000)
    >>> y = sigmoid(z)
    >>> import matplotlib.pyplot as plt
    >>> plt.plot(z, y)
    >>> plt.axhline(y=0, ls='dotted', color='k')
    >>> plt.axhline(y=0.5, ls='dotted', color='k')
    >>> plt.axhline(y=1, ls='dotted', color='k')
    >>> plt.yticks([0.0, 0.25, 0.5, 0.75, 1.0])
    >>> plt.xlabel('z')
    >>> plt.ylabel('y(z)')
    >>> plt.show()
    ```

Refer to the following screenshot for the end result:

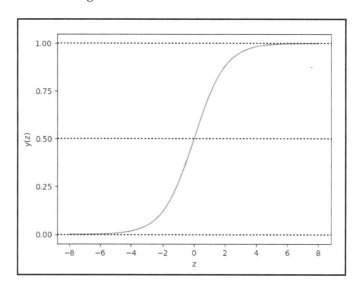

In the S-shaped curve, all inputs are transformed into the range from 0 to 1. For positive inputs, a greater value results in an output closer to 1; for negative inputs, a smaller value generates an output closer to 0; when the input is 0, the output is the midpoint, 0.5.

Jumping from the logistic function to logistic regression

Now that we have some knowledge of the logistic function, it is easy to map it to the algorithm that stems from it. In logistic regression, the function input z becomes the weighted sum of features. Given a data sample x with n features, $x_1, x_2, ..., x_n$ (x represents a feature vector and $x = (x_1, x_2, ..., x_n)$), and **weights** (also called **coefficients**) of the model w (w represents a vector $(w_1, w_2, ..., w_n)$), z is expressed as follows:

$$z = w_1 x_1 + w_2 x_2 + \cdots + w_n x_n = w^T x$$

Also, occasionally, the model comes with an **intercept** (also called **bias**), w_0. In this instance, the preceding linear relationship becomes:

$$z = w_0 + w_1 x_1 + w_2 x_2 + \cdots + w_n x_n = w^T x$$

As for the output y(z) in the range of 0 to 1, in the algorithm, it becomes the probability of the target being *1* or the positive class:

$$\hat{y} = P(y = 1 | x) = \frac{1}{1 + exp(-w^T x)}$$

Hence, logistic regression is a probabilistic classifier, similar to the Naïve Bayes classifier.

A logistic regression model or, more specifically, its weight vector *w* is learned from the training data, with the goal of predicting a positive sample as close to *1* as possible and predicting a negative sample as close to 0 as possible. In mathematical language, the weights are trained so as to minimize the cost defined as the **mean squared error (MSE)**, which measures the average of squares of difference between the truth and the prediction. Given *m* training samples, $(x^{(1)}, y^{(1)}), (x^{(2)}, y^{(2)}), \ldots (x^{(i)}, y^{(i)}) \ldots, (x^{(m)}, y^{(m)})$, where $y^{(i)}$ is either *1* (positive class) or 0 (negative class), the cost function *J(w)* regarding the weights to be optimized is expressed as follows:

$$J(w) = \frac{1}{m} \sum_{i=1}^{m} \frac{1}{2} \left(\hat{y}(x^{(i)}) - y^{(i)} \right)^2$$

However, the preceding cost function is **non-convex**, which means that, when searching for the optimal *w*, many local (suboptimal) optimums are found and the function does not converge to a global optimum.

Examples of the **convex** and **non-convex** functions are plotted respectively below:

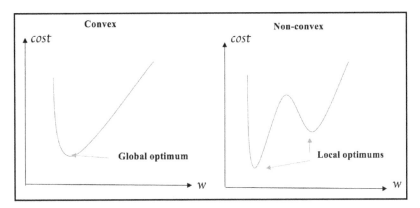

To overcome this, the cost function in practice is defined as follows:

$$J(w) = \frac{1}{m} \sum_{i=1}^{m} -\left[y^{(i)} log\big(\hat{y}(x^{(i)})\big) + (1 - y^{(i)})log\big(1 - \hat{y}(x^{(i)})\big) \right]$$

We can take a closer look at the cost of a single training sample:

$$j(w) = -y^{(i)} log\big(\hat{y}(x^{(i)})\big) - (1 - y^{(i)})log\big(1 - \hat{y}(x^{(i)})\big)$$

$$= \begin{cases} -log\big(\hat{y}(x^{(i)})\big), & if\ y^{(i)} = 1 \\ -log\big(1 - \hat{y}(x^{(i)})\big), if\ y^{(i)} = 0 \end{cases}$$

If $y^{(i)}$=1, when it predicts correctly (positive class in 100% probability), the sample cost j is 0; the cost keeps increasing when it is less likely to be the positive class; when it incorrectly predicts that there is no chance to be the positive class, the cost is infinitely high. We can visualize it as follows:

```
>>> y_hat = np.linspace(0, 1, 1000)
>>> cost = -np.log(y_hat)
>>> plt.plot(y_hat, cost)
>>> plt.xlabel('Prediction')
>>> plt.ylabel('Cost')
>>> plt.xlim(0, 1)
>>> plt.ylim(0, 7)
>>> plt.show()
```

Refer to the following screenshot for the end result:

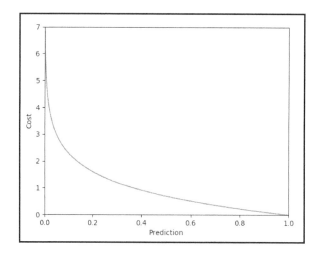

On the contrary, if $y^{(i)}=0$, when it predicts correctly (positive class in 0 probability, or negative class in 100% probability), the sample cost j is 0; the cost keeps increasing when it is more likely to be the positive class; when it incorrectly predicts that there is no chance to be the negative class, the cost goes infinitely high. We can visualize it using the following codes:

```
>>> y_hat = np.linspace(0, 1, 1000)
>>> cost = -np.log(1 - y_hat)
>>> plt.plot(y_hat, cost)
>>> plt.xlabel('Prediction')
>>> plt.ylabel('Cost')
>>> plt.xlim(0, 1)
>>> plt.ylim(0, 7)
>>> plt.show()
```

The following screenshot is the resultant output:

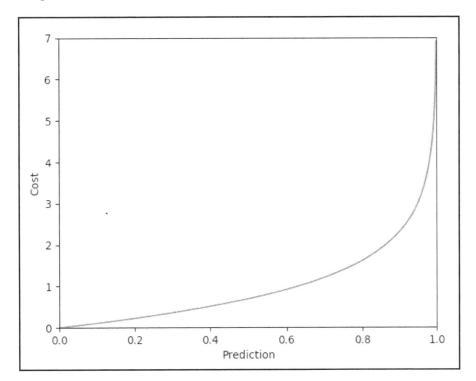

Minimizing this alternative cost function is actually equivalent to minimizing the MSE-based cost function. The advantages of choosing it over the other one include the following:

- Obviously, being convex, so that the optimal model weights can be found

- A summation of the logarithms of prediction $\hat{y}(x^{(i)})$ or $1 - \hat{y}(x^{(i)})$ simplifies the calculation of its derivative with respect to the weights, which we will talk about later

Due to the logarithmic function, the cost function
$J(w) = \frac{1}{m} \sum_{i=1}^{m} -\left[y^{(i)} log\left(\hat{y}(x^{(i)}) \right) + (1 - y^{(i)}) log\left(1 - \hat{y}(x^{(i)}) \right) \right]$ is also called **logarithmic loss**, or simply **log loss.**

Training a logistic regression model

Now, the question is how we can obtain the optimal w such that
$J(w) = \frac{1}{m} \sum_{i=1}^{m} -\left[y^{(i)} log\left(\hat{y}(x^{(i)}) \right) + (1 - y^{(i)}) log\left(1 - \hat{y}(x^{(i)}) \right) \right]$ is minimized. We can do so using gradient descent:

Training a logistic regression model using gradient descent

Gradient descent (also called **steepest descent**) is a procedure of minimizing an objective function by first-order iterative optimization. In each iteration, it moves a step that is proportional to the negative derivative of the objective function at the current point. This means the to-be-optimal point iteratively moves downhill towards the minimal value of the objective function. The proportion we just mentioned is called **learning rate**, or **step size**. It can be summarized in a mathematical equation as follows:

$$w := w - \eta \Delta w$$

Here, the left w is the weight vector after a learning step, and the right w is the one before moving, η is the learning rate, and Δw is the first-order derivative, the gradient.

In our case, let's start with the derivative of the cost function *J(w)* with respect to *w*. It might require some knowledge of calculus, but don't worry, we will walk through it step by step:

1. We first calculate the derivative of $\hat{y}(x)$ with respect to *w*. We herein take the *j-th* weight w_j, as an example (note $z = w^T x$, and we omit the $^{(i)}$ for simplicity):

$$
\begin{aligned}
\frac{\delta}{\delta w_j} \hat{y}(z) &= \frac{\delta}{\delta w_j} \frac{1}{1 + exp\,(-z)} \\
&= \frac{\delta}{\delta z} \frac{1}{1 + exp\,(-z)} \frac{\delta}{\delta w_j} z \\
&= \frac{1}{[1 + exp\,(-z)]^2} exp(-z) \frac{\delta}{\delta w_j} z \\
&= \frac{1}{1 + exp\,(-z)} \left[1 - \frac{1}{1 + exp\,(-z)} \right] \frac{\delta}{\delta w_j} z \\
&= \hat{y}(z)\big(1 - \hat{y}(z)\big) \frac{\delta}{\delta w_j} z
\end{aligned}
$$

2. Then, we calculate the derivative of the sample cost *J(w)* as follows:

$$
\begin{aligned}
\frac{\delta}{\delta w_j} J(w) &= -y \frac{\delta}{\delta w_j} log\big(\hat{y}(z)\big) + (1 - y) \frac{\delta}{\delta w_j} log\big(1 - \hat{y}(z)\big) \\
&= \left[-y \frac{1}{\hat{y}(z)} + (1 - y) \frac{1}{1 - \hat{y}(z)} \right] \frac{\delta}{\delta w_j} \hat{y}(z) \\
&= \left[-y \frac{1}{\hat{y}(z)} + (1 - y) \frac{1}{1 - \hat{y}(z)} \right] \hat{y}(z)\big(1 - \hat{y}(z)\big) \frac{\delta}{\delta w_j} z \\
&= \big(-y + \hat{y}(z)\big) x_j
\end{aligned}
$$

3. Finally, we calculate the entire cost over *m* samples as follows:

$$
\Delta w_j = \frac{\delta}{\delta w_j} J(w) = \frac{1}{m} \sum_{i=1}^{m} \big(-y^{(i)} + \hat{y}(z^{(i)})\big) x_j^{(i)}
$$

4. We then generalize it to *Δw*:

$$
\Delta w = \frac{1}{m} \sum_{i=1}^{m} \big(-y^{(i)} + \hat{y}(z^{(i)})\big) x^{(i)}
$$

5. Combined with the preceding derivations, the weights can be updated as follows:

$$w := w + \eta \frac{1}{m} \sum_{i=1}^{m} \left(y^{(i)} - \hat{y}(z^{(i)}) \right) x^{(i)}$$

Here, w gets updated in each iteration.

6. After a substantial number of iterations, the learned w and b are then used to classify a new sample x' by means of the following equation:

$$y' = \frac{1}{1 + exp\left(-w^T x' \right)}$$
$$\begin{cases} 1, if\ y' \geq 0.5 \\ 0, if\ y' < 0.5 \end{cases}$$

The decision threshold is *0.5* by default, but it definitely can be other values. In a case where a false negative is, by all means, supposed to be avoided, for example, when predicting fire occurrence (positive class) for alerts, the decision threshold can be lower than 0.5, such as 0.3, depending on how paranoid we are and how proactively we want to prevent the positive event from happening. On the other hand, when false positive class is the one should be evaded, for instance, when predicting the product success (positive class) rate for quality assurance, the decision threshold can be greater than 0.5, such as 0.7, based on how high the standard we set is.

With a thorough understanding of the gradient descent based training and predicting process, we now implement the logistic regression algorithm from scratch:

1. We begin by defining the function computing the prediction $\hat{y}(x)$ with current weights:

```
>>> def compute_prediction(X, weights):
...        """ Compute the prediction y_hat based on current weights
...        Args:
...            X (numpy.ndarray)
...            weights (numpy.ndarray)
...        Returns:
...            numpy.ndarray, y_hat of X under weights
...        """
...        z = np.dot(X, weights)
...        predictions = sigmoid(z)
...        return predictions
```

2. With this, we are able to continue with the function updating the weights
$w := w + \eta \dfrac{1}{m} \sum_{i=1}^{m} \left(y^{(i)} - \hat{y}(z^{(i)})\right) x^{(i)}$ by one step in a gradient descent
manner. Take a look at the following codes:

```
>>> def update_weights_gd(X_train, y_train, weights,
                                            learning_rate):
...         """ Update weights by one step
...         Args:
...             X_train, y_train (numpy.ndarray, training data set)
...             weights (numpy.ndarray)
...             learning_rate (float)
...         Returns:
...             numpy.ndarray, updated weights
...         """
...         predictions = compute_prediction(X_train, weights)
...         weights_delta = np.dot(X_train.T, y_train - predictions)
...         m = y_train.shape[0]
...         weights += learning_rate / float(m) * weights_delta
...         return weights
```

3. Then, the function calculating the cost *J(w)* is depicted as well:

```
>>> def compute_cost(X, y, weights):
...         """ Compute the cost J(w)
...         Args:
...             X, y (numpy.ndarray, data set)
...             weights (numpy.ndarray)
...         Returns:
...             float
...         """
...         predictions = compute_prediction(X, weights)
...         cost = np.mean(-y * np.log(predictions)
...                        - (1 - y) * np.log(1 - predictions))
...         return cost
```

4. Now, we connect all these functions to the model training function by executing the following:

- Updating the `weights` vector in each iteration
- Printing out the current cost for every `100` (can be other values) iterations to ensure `cost` is decreasing and that things are on the right track

Take a look at the following:

```
>>> def train_logistic_regression(X_train, y_train, max_iter,
                            learning_rate, fit_intercept=False):
```

```
...         """ Train a logistic regression model
...         Args:
...             X_train, y_train (numpy.ndarray, training data set)
...             max_iter (int, number of iterations)
...             learning_rate (float)
...             fit_intercept (bool, with an intercept w0 or not)
...         Returns:
...             numpy.ndarray, learned weights
...         """
...         if fit_intercept:
...             intercept = np.ones((X_train.shape[0], 1))
...             X_train = np.hstack((intercept, X_train))
...         weights = np.zeros(X_train.shape[1])
...         for iteration in range(max_iter):
...             weights = update_weights_gd(X_train, y_train,
                                             weights, learning_rate)
...             # Check the cost for every 100 (for example)
              iterations
...             if iteration % 100 == 0:
...                 print(compute_cost(X_train, y_train, weights))
...         return weights
```

5. Finally, predict the results of new inputs using the trained model as follows:

```
>>> def predict(X, weights):
...         if X.shape[1] == weights.shape[0] - 1:
...             intercept = np.ones((X.shape[0], 1))
...             X = np.hstack((intercept, X))
...         return compute_prediction(X, weights)
```

Implementing logistic regression is very simple, as we just saw. Let's now examine it using a brief example:

```
>>> X_train = np.array([[6, 7],
...                     [2, 4],
...                     [3, 6],
...                     [4, 7],
...                     [1, 6],
...                     [5, 2],
...                     [2, 0],
...                     [6, 3],
...                     [4, 1],
...                     [7, 2]])
>>> y_train = np.array([0,
...                     0,
...                     0,
...                     0,
...                     0,
```

```
...                    1,
...                    1,
...                    1,
...                    1,
...                    1])
```

Train a logistic regression model by 1000 iterations, at a learning rate of 0.1 based on intercept-included weights:

```
>>> weights = train_logistic_regression(X_train, y_train,
            max_iter=1000, learning_rate=0.1, fit_intercept=True)
0.574404237166
0.0344602233925
0.0182655727085
0.012493458388
0.00951532913855
0.00769338806065
0.00646209433351
0.00557351184683
0.00490163225453
0.00437556774067
```

The decreasing cost means that the model is being optimized over time. We can check the model's performance on new samples as follows:

```
>>> X_test = np.array([[6, 1],
...                    [1, 3],
...                    [3, 1],
...                    [4, 5]])
>>> predictions = predict(X_test, weights)
>>> predictions
array([ 0.9999478 , 0.00743991, 0.9808652 , 0.02080847])
```

To visualize this, execute the following codes:

```
>>> import matplotlib.pyplot as plt
>>> plt.scatter(X_train[:,0], X_train[:,1], c=['b']*5+['k']*5,
                                            marker='o')
```

Blue dots are training samples from class 0, while black dots are those from class 1. Use 0.5 as the classification decision threshold:

```
>>> colours = ['k' if prediction >= 0.5 else 'b'
                            for prediction in predictions]
>>> plt.scatter(X_test[:,0], X_test[:,1], marker='*', c=colours)
```

Blue stars are testing samples predicted from class 0, while black stars are those predicted from class 1:

```
>>> plt.xlabel('x1')
>>> plt.ylabel('x2')
>>> plt.show()
```

Refer to the following screenshot for the end result:

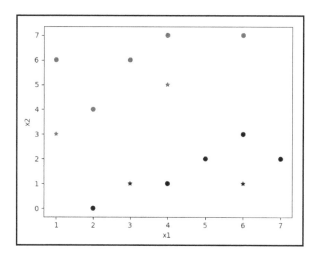

The model we trained correctly predicts classes of new samples (the stars).

Predicting ad click-through with logistic regression using gradient descent

After a brief example, we now deploy the algorithm we just developed in our click-through prediction project.

We herein start with only 10,000 training samples (you will soon see why we don't start with 270,000, as we did in the previous chapter):

```
>>> import pandas as pd
>>> n_rows = 300000
>>> df = pd.read_csv("train", nrows=n_rows)
>>> X = df.drop(['click', 'id', 'hour', 'device_id', 'device_ip'],
                                        axis=1).values
>>> Y = df['click'].values
>>> n_train = 10000
```

```
>>> X_train = X[:n_train]
>>> Y_train = Y[:n_train]
>>> X_test = X[n_train:]
>>> Y_test = Y[n_train:]
>>> from sklearn.preprocessing import OneHotEncoder
>>> enc = OneHotEncoder(handle_unknown='ignore')
>>> X_train_enc = enc.fit_transform(X_train)
>>> X_test_enc = enc.transform(X_test)
```

Train a logistic regression model over 10000 iterations, at a learning rate of 0.01 with bias:

```
>>> import timeit
>>> start_time = timeit.default_timer()
>>> weights = train_logistic_regression(X_train_enc.toarray(),
                Y_train, max_iter=10000, learning_rate=0.01,
                fit_intercept=True)
0.6820019456743648
0.4608619713011896
0.4503715555130051
...
...
...
0.41485094023829017
0.41477416506724385
0.41469802145452467
>>> print("--- %0.3fs seconds ---" % (timeit.default_timer() -
                                            start_time))

--- 232.756s seconds ---
```

It takes 232 seconds to optimize the model. The trained model performs on the testing set as follows:

```
>>> pred = predict(X_test_enc.toarray(), weights)
>>> from sklearn.metrics import roc_auc_score
>>> print('Training samples: {0}, AUC on testing set:
  {1:.3f}'.format(n_train, roc_auc_score(Y_test, pred)))
Training samples: 10000, AUC on testing set: 0.703
```

Now, let's use 100,000 training samples (n_train = 100000) and repeat the same process. It will take 5240.4 seconds, which is almost 1.5 hours. It takes 22 times longer to fit data of 10 times the size. As we mentioned at the beginning of the chapter, the logistic regression classifier can be good at training on large datasets. But our testing results seem to contradict this. How could we even handle larger training datasets efficiently, not just 100,000, but millions? Let's look at a more efficient way to train a logistic regression in the next section.

Training a logistic regression model using stochastic gradient descent

In gradient descent based logistic regression models, **all** training samples are used to update the weights in each single iteration. Hence, if the number of training samples is large, the whole training process will become very time-consuming and computationally expensive, as we just witnessed in our last example.

Fortunately, a small tweak will make logistic regression suitable for large-size data. For each weight update, **only one** training sample is consumed, instead of the **complete** training set. The model moves a step based on the error calculated by a single training sample. Once all samples are used, one iteration finishes. This advanced version of gradient descent is called **stochastic gradient descent (SGD)**. Expressed in a formula, for each iteration, we do the following:

$$for\ i\ in\ 1\ to\ m:$$
$$w := w + \eta\big(y^{(i)} - \hat{y}(z^{(i)})\big)x^{(i)}$$

SGD generally converges much faster than gradient descent where a large number of iterations is usually needed.

To implement SGD-based logistic regression, we just need to slightly modify the `update_weights_gd` function:

```
>>> def update_weights_sgd(X_train, y_train, weights,
                                         learning_rate):
...     """ One weight update iteration: moving weights by one
            step based on each individual sample
...     Args:
...     X_train, y_train (numpy.ndarray, training data set)
...     weights (numpy.ndarray)
...     learning_rate (float)
...     Returns:
...     numpy.ndarray, updated weights
...     """
...     for X_each, y_each in zip(X_train, y_train):
...         prediction = compute_prediction(X_each, weights)
...         weights_delta = X_each.T * (y_each - prediction)
...         weights += learning_rate * weights_delta
...     return weights
```

In the `train_logistic_regression` function, SGD is applied:

```
>>> def train_logistic_regression_sgd(X_train, y_train, max_iter,
                                learning_rate, fit_intercept=False):
...     """ Train a logistic regression model via SGD
...     Args:
...     X_train, y_train (numpy.ndarray, training data set)
...     max_iter (int, number of iterations)
...     learning_rate (float)
...     fit_intercept (bool, with an intercept w0 or not)
...     Returns:
...     numpy.ndarray, learned weights
...     """
...     if fit_intercept:
...         intercept = np.ones((X_train.shape[0], 1))
...         X_train = np.hstack((intercept, X_train))
...     weights = np.zeros(X_train.shape[1])
...     for iteration in range(max_iter):
...         weights = update_weights_sgd(X_train, y_train, weights,
                                            learning_rate)
...         # Check the cost for every 2 (for example) iterations
...         if iteration % 2 == 0:
...             print(compute_cost(X_train, y_train, weights))
...     return weights
```

Now, let's see how powerful SGD is. We work with 100,000 training samples and choose `10` as the number of iterations, `0.01` as the learning rate, and print out current costs every other iteration:

```
>>> start_time = timeit.default_timer()
>>> weights = train_logistic_regression_sgd(X_train_enc.toarray(),
            Y_train, max_iter=10, learning_rate=0.01, fit_intercept=True)
0.4127864859625796
0.4078504597223988
0.40545733114863264
0.403811787845451
0.4025431351250833
>>> print("--- %0.3fs seconds ---" %
                        (timeit.default_timer() - start_time))
--- 40.690s seconds ---
>>> pred = predict(X_test_enc.toarray(), weights)
>>> print('Training samples: {0}, AUC on testing set:
                {1:.3f}'.format(n_train, roc_auc_score(Y_test, pred)))
Training samples: 100000, AUC on testing set: 0.732
```

The training process finishes in just 40 seconds! And it also performs better than the previous one using gradient descent.

As usual, after successfully implementing the SGD-based logistic regression algorithm from scratch, we realize it using the `SGDClassifier` module of scikit-learn:

```
>>> from sklearn.linear_model import SGDClassifier
>>> sgd_lr = SGDClassifier(loss='log', penalty=None,
            fit_intercept=True, n_iter=10,
            learning_rate='constant', eta0=0.01)
```

Here, `'log'` for the `loss` parameter indicates that the cost function is log loss, `penalty` is the regularization term to reduce overfitting that we will discuss further in the next section, `n_iter` is the number of iterations, and the remaining two parameters mean the learning rate is `0.01` and unchanged during the course of training. It should be noted that the default `learning_rate` is `'optimal'`, where the learning rate slightly decreases as more and more updates are taken. This can be beneficial for finding the optimal solution on large datasets.

Now, train the model and test it:

```
>>> sgd_lr.fit(X_train_enc.toarray(), Y_train)
>>> pred = sgd_lr.predict_proba(X_test_enc.toarray())[:, 1]
>>> print('Training samples: {0}, AUC on testing set:
            {1:.3f}'.format(n_train, roc_auc_score(Y_test, pred)))
Training samples: 100000, AUC on testing set: 0.734
```

Quick and easy!

Training a logistic regression model with regularization

As we briefly mentioned in the previous section, the `penalty` parameter in the logistic regression `SGDClassifier` is related to model **regularization**. There are two basic forms of regularization, **L1** (also called **Lasso**) and **L2** (also called **ridge**). In either way, the regularization is an additional term on top on the original cost function:

$$J(w) = \frac{1}{m} \sum_{i=1}^{m} -\left[y^{(i)} log(\hat{y}(x^{(i)})) + (1 - y^{(i)}) log(1 - \hat{y}(x^{(i)})) \right] + \alpha \|w\|^q$$

Here, α is the constant that multiplies the regularization term, and q is either 1 or 2 representing L1 or L2 regularization where the following applies:

$$\|w\|^1 = \sum_{j=1}^{n} |w_j|$$
$$\|w\|^2 = \sum_{j=1}^{n} w_j^2$$

Training a logistic regression model is a process of reducing the cost as a function of weights w. If it gets to a point where some weights, such as w_i, w_j, and w_k are considerably large, the whole cost will be determined by these large weights. In this case, the learned model may just memorize the training set and fail to generalize to unseen data. The regularization term herein is introduced in order to penalize large weights, as the weights now become part of the cost to minimize. Regularization as a result eliminates overfitting. Finally, parameter α provides a trade-off between log loss and generalization. If α is too small, it is not able to compromise large weights and the model may suffer from high variance or overfitting; on the other hand, if α is too large, the model becomes over generalized and performs poorly in terms of fitting the dataset, which is the syndrome of underfitting. α is an important parameter to tune in order to obtain the best logistic regression model with regularization.

As for choosing between the L1 and L2 form, the rule of thumb is whether **feature selection** is expected. In machine learning classification, feature selection is the process of picking a subset of significant features for use in better model construction. In practice, not every feature in a dataset carries information useful for discriminating samples; some features are either redundant or irrelevant, and hence can be discarded with little loss. In a logistic regression classifier, feature selection can only be achieved with L1 regularization. To understand this, we consider two weight vectors, $w1=(1, 0)$ and $w2=(0.5, 0.5)$, and, supposing they produce the same amount of log loss, the L1 and L2 regularization terms of each weight vector are as follows:

$$|w_1|^1 = |1| + |0| = 1, |w_2|^1 = |0.5| + |0.5| = 1$$
$$|w_1|^2 = 1^2 + 0^2 = 1, |w_2|^2 = 0.5^2 + 0.5^2 = 0.5$$

The L1 term of both vectors is equivalent, while the L2 term of w_2 is less than that of w_1. This indicates that L2 regularization penalizes more on weights composed of significantly large and small weights than L1 regularization does. In other words, L2 regularization favors relative small values for all weights, and avoids significantly large and small values for any weight, while L1 regularization allows some weights with significantly small value, and some with significantly large value. Only with L1 regularization can some weights be compressed to close to or exactly 0, which enables feature selection.

In scikit-learn, the regularization type can be specified by the `penalty` parameter with options as `none` (without regularization), `"l1"`, `"l2"`, and `"elasticnet"` (a mixture of L1 and L2), and the multiplier α by the `alpha` parameter.

We herein examine L1 regularization for feature selection.

Initialize an SGD logistic regression model with L1 regularization, and train the model based on 10,000 samples:

```
>>> sgd_lr_l1 = SGDClassifier(loss='log', penalty='l1', alpha=0.0001,
                              fit_intercept=True, n_iter=10,
                              learning_rate='constant', eta0=0.01)
>>> sgd_lr_l1.fit(X_train_enc.toarray(), Y_train)
```

With the trained model, we obtain the absolute values of its coefficients:

```
>>> coef_abs = np.abs(sgd_lr_l1.coef_)
>>> print(coef_abs)
[[0. 0.09963329 0. ... 0. 0. 0.07431834]]
```

The bottom `10` coefficients and their values are printed as follows:

```
>>> print(np.sort(coef_abs)[0][:10])
[0. 0. 0. 0. 0. 0. 0. 0. 0. 0.]
>>> bottom_10 = np.argsort(coef_abs)[0][:10]
```

We can see what these 10 features are using the following codes:

```
>>> feature_names = enc.get_feature_names()
>>> print('10 least important features are:\n',
                              feature_names[bottom_10])
10 least important features are:
 ['x0_1001' 'x8_851897aa' 'x8_85119990' 'x8_84ebbcd4' 'x8_84eb6b0e'
  'x8_84dda655' 'x8_84c2f017' 'x8_84ace234' 'x8_84a9d4ba' 'x8_84915a27']
```

They are `1001` from the `0` column (that is the `C1` column) in `X_train`, `"851897aa"` from the `8` column (that is the `device_model` column), and so on and so forth.

Similarly, the top 10 coefficients and their values can be obtained as follows:

```
>>> print(np.sort(coef_abs)[0][-10:])
[0.67912376 0.70885933 0.79975917 0.8828797 0.98146351 0.98275124
 1.08313767 1.13261091 1.18445527 1.40983505]
>>> top_10 = np.argsort(coef_abs)[0][-10:]
>>> print('10 most important features are:\n', feature_names[top_10])
10 most important features are:
 ['x7_cef3e649' 'x3_7687a86e' 'x18_61' 'x18_15' 'x5_9c13b419'
'x5_5e3f096f' 'x2_763a42b5' 'x2_d9750ee7' 'x3_27e3c518'
'x5_1779deee']
```

They are "cef3e649" from the 7 column (that is `app_category`) in `X_train`, "7687a86e" from the third column (that is `site_domain`), and so on and so forth.

Training on large datasets with online learning

So far, we have trained our model on no more than 300,000 samples. If we go beyond this figure, memory might be overloaded since it holds too much data, and the program will crash. In this section, we will be presenting how to train on a large-scale dataset with **online learning**.

Stochastic gradient descent grows from gradient descent by sequentially updating the model with individual training samples one at a time, instead of the complete training set at once. We can scale up stochastic gradient descent further with online learning techniques. In online learning, new data for training is available in a sequential order or in real time, as opposed to all at once in an **offline learning** environment. A relatively small chunk of data is loaded and preprocessed for training at a time, which releases the memory used to hold the entire large dataset. Besides better computational feasibility, online learning is also used because of its adaptability to cases where new data is generated in real time and needed in modernizing the model. For instance, stock price prediction models are updated in an online learning manner with timely market data; click-through prediction models need to include the most recent data reflecting users' latest behaviors and tastes; spam email detectors have to be reactive to the ever-changing spammers by considering new features that are dynamically generated.

The existing model trained by previous datasets is now updated based on the most recently available dataset only, instead of rebuilt from scratch based on previous and recent datasets together, as in offline learning:

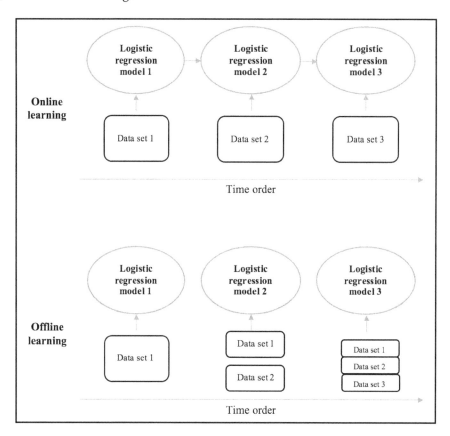

The SGDClassifier module in scikit-learn implements online learning with the partial_fit method (while the fit method is applied in offline learning, as we have seen). We train the model with 1,000,000 samples, where we feed in 100,000 samples at one time to simulate an online learning environment. And we will test the trained model on the next 100,000 samples as follows:

```
>>> n_rows = 100000 * 11
>>> df = pd.read_csv("train", nrows=n_rows)
>>> X = df.drop(['click', 'id', 'hour', 'device_id', 'device_ip'],
                                              axis=1).values
>>> Y = df['click'].values
>>> n_train = 100000 * 10
>>> X_train = X[:n_train]
```

```
>>> Y_train = Y[:n_train]
>>> X_test = X[n_train:]
>>> Y_test = Y[n_train:]
```

Fit the encoder on the whole training set as follows:

```
>>> enc = OneHotEncoder(handle_unknown='ignore')
>>> enc.fit(X_train)
```

Initialize an SGD logistic regression model where we set the number of iterations to 1 in order to partially fit the model and enable online learning:

```
>>> sgd_lr_online = SGDClassifier(loss='log', penalty=None,
                                  fit_intercept=True, n_iter=1,
                                  learning_rate='constant', eta0=0.01)
```

Loop over every `100000` samples and partially fit the model:

```
>>> start_time = timeit.default_timer()
>>> for i in range(10):
...     x_train = X_train[i*100000: (i+1)*100000]
...     y_train = Y_train[i*100000: (i+1)*100000]
...     x_train_enc = enc.transform(x_train)
...     sgd_lr_online.partial_fit(x_train_enc.toarray(), y_train,
                                  classes=[0, 1])
```

Again, we use the `partial_fit` method for online learning. Also, we specify the `classes` parameter, which is required in online learning:

```
>>> print("--- %0.3fs seconds ---" % (timeit.default_timer() -
                                       start_time))
--- 167.399s seconds ---
```

Apply the trained model on the testing set, the next 100,000 samples, as follows:

```
>>> x_test_enc = enc.transform(X_test)
>>> pred = sgd_lr_online.predict_proba(x_test_enc.toarray())[:, 1]
>>> print('Training samples: {0}, AUC on testing set:
          {1:.3f}'.format(n_train * 10, roc_auc_score(Y_test, pred)))
Training samples: 10000000, AUC on testing set: 0.761
```

With online learning, training based on a total of 1 million samples only takes 167 seconds and yields better accuracy.

Handling multiclass classification

One last thing worth noting is how logistic regression algorithms deal with multiclass classification. Although we interact with the scikit-learn classifiers in multiclass cases the same way as in binary cases, it is encouraging to understand how logistic regression works in multiclass classification.

Logistic regression for more than two classes is also called **multinomial logistic regression**, or better known latterly as **softmax regression**. As we have seen in the binary case, the model is represented by one weight vector w, the probability of the target being *1* or the positive class is written as follows:

$$\hat{y} = P(y = 1|x) = \frac{1}{1 + exp\left(-w^T x\right)}$$

In the *K* class case, the model is represented by *K* weight vectors, w_1, w_2, ..., w_K, and the probability of the target being class *k* is written as follows:

$$\widehat{y_k} = P(y = k|x) = \frac{exp\left(w_k^T x\right)}{\sum_{j=1}^{K} exp\left(w_j^T x\right)}$$

Note that the term $\sum_{j=1}^{K} exp(w_j^T x)$ normalizes probabilities $\widehat{y_k}$ (*k* from *1* to *K*) so that they total *1*. The cost function in the binary case is expressed as follows:

$$J(w) = \frac{1}{m} \sum_{i=1}^{m} -\left[y^{(i)} log\left(\hat{y}(x^{(i)})\right) + (1 - y^{(i)}) log\left(1 - \hat{y}(x^{(i)})\right)\right] + \alpha\|w\|^q$$

Similarly, the cost function in the multiclass case becomes the following:

$$J(w) = \frac{1}{m} \sum_{i=1}^{m} -\left[\sum_{j=1}^{K} 1\{y^{(i)} = j\} log\left(\widehat{y_k}(x^{(i)})\right)\right]$$

Here, function $1\{y^{(i)}=j\}$ is *1* only if $y^{(i)}=j$ is true, otherwise *0*.

With the cost function defined, we obtain the step Δw_j, for the *j* weight vector in the same way we derived the step Δw in the binary case:

$$\Delta w_j = \frac{1}{m} \sum_{i=1}^{m} \left(-1\{y^{(i)} = j\} + \widehat{y_k}(x^{(i)})\right)x^{(i)}$$

In a similar manner, all *K* weight vectors are updated in each iteration. After sufficient iterations, the learned weight vectors w_1, w_2, ..., w_K are then used to classify a new sample x' by means of the following equation:

$$y' = \underset{k}{argmax}\,\widehat{y_k} = \underset{k}{argmax}\,P(y = k|x')$$

To have a better sense, we experiment on it with a classic dataset, the handwritten digits for classification:

```
>>> from sklearn import datasets
>>> digits = datasets.load_digits()
>>> n_samples = len(digits.images)
```

As the image data is stored in 8*8 matrices, we need to flatten them, as follows:

```
>>> X = digits.images.reshape((n_samples, -1))
>>> Y = digits.target
```

We then split the data as follows:

```
>>> from sklearn.model_selection import train_test_split
>>> X_train, X_test, Y_train, Y_test = train_test_split(X, Y,
                              test_size=0.2, random_state=42)
```

We then combine grid search and cross-validation to find the optimal multiclass logistic regression model as follows:

```
>>> from sklearn.model_selection import GridSearchCV
>>> parameters = {'penalty': ['12', None],
...               'alpha': [1e-07, 1e-06, 1e-05, 1e-04],
...               'eta0': [0.01, 0.1, 1, 10]}
>>> sgd_lr = SGDClassifier(loss='log', learning_rate='constant',
                     eta0=0.01, fit_intercept=True, n_iter=10)
>>> grid_search = GridSearchCV(sgd_lr, parameters,
                         n_jobs=-1, cv=3)
>>> grid_search.fit(term_docs_train, label_train)
>>> print(grid_search.best_params_)
{'alpha': 1e-07, 'eta0': 0.1, 'penalty': None}
```

To predict using the optimal model, we apply the following:

```
>>> sgd_lr_best = grid_search.best_estimator_
>>> accuracy = sgd_lr_best.score(term_docs_test, label_test)
>>> print('The accuracy on testing set is:
                        {0:.1f}%'.format(accuracy*100))
The accuracy on testing set is: 94.2%
```

It doesn't look much different from the previous example, since `SGDClassifier` handles multiclass internally.

Implementing logistic regression using TensorFlow

This is a bonus section where we implement logistic regression with TensorFlow and use click prediction as example. We herein use 90% of the first 300,000 samples for training, the remaining 10% for testing, and assume that `X_train_enc`, `Y_train`, `X_test_enc`, and `Y_test` contain the correct data.

1. First, we import TensorFlow and specify parameters for the model, including 20 iterations during the training process and a learning rate of 0.001:

```
>>> import tensorflow as tf
>>> n_features = int(X_train_enc.toarray().shape[1])
>>> learning_rate = 0.001
>>> n_iter = 20
```

2. Then, we define placeholders and construct the model by computing the logits (output of logistic function based on the input and model coefficients):

```
>>> x = tf.placeholder(tf.float32, shape=[None, n_features])
>>> y = tf.placeholder(tf.float32, shape=[None])
>>> W = tf.Variable(tf.zeros([n_features, 1]))
>>> b = tf.Variable(tf.zeros([1]))
>>> logits = tf.add(tf.matmul(x, W), b)[:, 0]
>>> pred = tf.nn.sigmoid(logits)
```

3. After defining the graph for the model, we get the loss function, as well as the measurement of performance, the AUC:

```
>>> cost = tf.reduce_mean(
        tf.nn.sigmoid_cross_entropy_with_logits(labels=y,
    logits=logits))
>>> auc = tf.metrics.auc(tf.cast(y, tf.int64), pred)[1]
```

4. We then define a gradient descent optimizer that searches for the best coefficients by minimizing the loss. We herein use Adam as our optimizer, which is an advanced gradient descent with a learning rate adaptive to gradients:

```
>>> optimizer =
tf.train.AdamOptimizer(learning_rate).minimize(cost)
```

5. Now, we can initialize the variables and start a TensorFlow session:

```
>>> init_vars = tf.group(tf.global_variables_initializer(),
                          tf.local_variables_initializer())
>>> sess = tf.Session()
>>> sess.run(init_vars)
```

6. Again, the model is trained in a batch manner. We herein reuse the gen_batch function defined in the previous chapter and set the batch size to 1000:

```
>>> batch_size = 1000
>>> import numpy as np
>>> indices = list(range(n_train))
>>> def gen_batch(indices):
...     np.random.shuffle(indices)
...     for batch_i in range(int(n_train / batch_size)):
...         batch_index = indices[batch_i*batch_size:
                                    (batch_i+1)*batch_size]
...         yield X_train_enc[batch_index], Y_train[batch_index]
```

7. Finally, we start the training process and print out the loss after each iteration:

```
>>> for i in range(1, n_iter+1):
...     avg_cost = 0.
...     for X_batch, Y_batch in gen_batch(indices):
...         _, c = sess.run([optimizer, cost],
                            feed_dict={x: X_batch.toarray(), y:
Y_batch})
...         avg_cost += c / int(n_train / batch_size)
...     print('Iteration %i, training loss: %f' % (i, avg_cost))
Iteration 1, training loss: 0.464850
Iteration 2, training loss: 0.414757
Iteration 3, training loss: 0.409064
Iteration 4, training loss: 0.405977
Iteration 5, training loss: 0.403816
Iteration 6, training loss: 0.402151
Iteration 7, training loss: 0.400824
Iteration 8, training loss: 0.399730
Iteration 9, training loss: 0.398788
Iteration 10, training loss: 0.397975
Iteration 11, training loss: 0.397248
Iteration 12, training loss: 0.396632
Iteration 13, training loss: 0.396041
Iteration 14, training loss: 0.395555
Iteration 15, training loss: 0.395057
Iteration 16, training loss: 0.394610
Iteration 17, training loss: 0.394210
Iteration 18, training loss: 0.393873
```

```
Iteration 19, training loss: 0.393489
Iteration 20, training loss: 0.393181
```

8. We then conduct a performance check-up on the testing set afterward:

```
>>> auc_test = sess.run(auc,
                  feed_dict={x: X_test_enc.toarray(), y: Y_test})
>>> print("AUC of ROC on testing set:", auc_test)
AUC of ROC on testing set: 0.7713197
```

Feature selection using random forest

We have seen how feature selection works with L1-regularized logistic regression in one of the previous sections, where weights of unimportant features are compressed to close to, or exactly, 0. Besides L1-regularized logistic regression, random forest is another frequently used feature selection technique.

To recap, random forest is bagging over a set of individual decision trees. Each tree considers a random subset of the features when searching for the best splitting point at each node. And, as an essence of the decision tree algorithm, only those significant features (along with their splitting values) are used to constitute tree nodes. Consider the forest as a whole: the more frequently a feature is used in a tree node, the more important it is. In other words, we can rank the importance of features based on their occurrences in nodes among all trees, and select the top most important ones.

A trained `RandomForestClassifier` module in scikit-learn comes with an attribute, `feature_importances_`, indicating the feature importance, which are calculated as the proportions of occurrences in tree nodes. Again, we examine feature selection with random forest on the dataset with 100,000 ad click samples:

```
>>> from sklearn.ensemble import RandomForestClassifier
>>> random_forest = RandomForestClassifier(n_estimators=100,
                  criterion='gini', min_samples_split=30, n_jobs=-1)
>>> random_forest.fit(X_train_enc.toarray(), Y_train)
```

After fitting the random forest model, we obtain the feature importance scores by:

```
>>> feature_imp = random_forest.feature_importances_
>>> print(feature_imp)
[1.60540750e-05 1.71248082e-03 9.64485853e-04 ... 5.41025913e-04
 7.78878273e-04 8.24041944e-03]
```

Take a look at the bottom 10 feature scores and the corresponding 10 least important features:

```
>>> feature_names = enc.get_feature_names()
>>> print(np.sort(feature_imp)[:10])
[0. 0. 0. 0. 0. 0. 0. 0. 0. 0.]
>>> bottom_10 = np.argsort(feature_imp)[:10]
>>> print('10 least important features are:\n', feature_names[bottom_10])
10 least important features are:
 ['x8_ea4912eb' 'x8_c2d34e02' 'x6_2d332391' 'x2_ca9b09d0'
'x2_0273c5ad' 'x8_92bed2f3' 'x8_eb3f4b48' 'x3_535444a1' 'x8_8741c65a'
'x8_46cb77e5']
```

And now, take a look at the top 10 feature scores and the corresponding 10 most important features:

```
>>> print(np.sort(feature_imp)[-10:])
[0.00809279 0.00824042 0.00885188 0.00897925 0.01080301 0.01088246
 0.01270395 0.01392431 0.01532718 0.01810339]
>>> top_10 = np.argsort(feature_imp)[-10:]
>>> print('10 most important features are:\n', feature_names[top_10])
10 most important features are:
 ['x17_-1' 'x18_157' 'x12_300' 'x13_250' 'x3_98572c79' 'x8_8a4875bd'
'x14_1993' 'x15_2' 'x2_d9750ee7' 'x18_33']
```

Summary

In this chapter, we continued working on the online advertising click-through prediction project. This time, we overcame the categorical feature challenge by means of the one-hot encoding technique. We then resorted to a new classification algorithm logistic regression for its high scalability to large datasets. The in-depth discussion of the logistic regression algorithm stared with the introduction of the logistic function, which led to the mechanics of the algorithm itself. This was followed by how to train a logistic regression using gradient descent. After implementing a logistic regression classifier by hand and testing it on our click-through dataset, we learned how to train the logistic regression model in a more advanced manner, using stochastic gradient descent, and adjusted our algorithm accordingly. We also practiced how to use the SGD-based logistic regression classifier from scikit-learn and applied it to our project. We continued to tackle problems we might face in using logistic regression, including L1 and L2 regularization for eliminating overfitting, online learning techniques for training on large-scale datasets, and handling multiclass scenarios. We also learned how to implement logistic regression with TensorFlow. Finally, the chapter ended with applying the random forest model to feature selection, as an alternative to L1-regularized logistic regression.

You might be curious as to how we can efficiently train the model on the entire dataset of 40 million samples. In the next chapter, we will utilize tools such as **Spark** and the **PySpark** module to scale up our solution.

Exercises

- In the logistic regression-based click-through prediction project, can you also tweak hyperparameters such as `penalty`, `eta0`, and `alpha` in the `SGDClassifier` model? What is the highest testing AUC you are able to achieve?
- Can you try to use more training samples, for instance, 10 million samples, in the online learning solution?

8
Scaling Up Prediction to Terabyte Click Logs

In the previous chapter, we accomplished developing an ad click-through predictor using a logistic regression classifier. We proved that the algorithm is highly scalable by training efficiently on up to 1 million click log samples. Moving on to this chapter, we will be further boosting the scalability of the ad click-through predictor by utilizing a powerful parallel computing (or, more specifically, distributed computing) tool called Apache Spark. We will be demystifying how Apache Spark is used to scale up learning on massive data, as opposed to limiting model learning to one single machine. We will be using PySpark, which is the Python API, to explore the click log data, to develop classification solutions based on the entire click log dataset, and to evaluate performance, all in a distributed manner. Aside from this, we will be introducing two approaches to play around with the categorical features; one is related to hashing in computer science, while the other fuses multiple features. They will be implemented in Spark as well.

In this chapter, we will cover the following topics:

- The main components of Apache Spark
- Spark installation
- Deployment of Spark application
- Fundamental data structures in PySpark
- Core programming in PySpark
- The implementations of ad click-through predictions in PySpark
- Data exploratory analysis in PySpark
- Caching and persistence in Spark
- What feature hashing is
- The implementations of feature hashing in PySpark
- What is feature interaction?
- The implementations of feature interaction in PySpark

Learning the essentials of Apache Spark

Apache Spark is a distributed cluster-computing framework designed for fast and general-purpose computation. It is an open-source technology originally developed by Berkeley's AMPLab at the University of California. It provides an easy-to-use interface for programming interactive queries and stream processing of data. What makes it a popular big data analytics tool is its implicit data parallelism, where it automates operation on data in parallel across processors in the computing cluster. Users only need to focus on how they like to manipulate the data without worrying about how data is distributed among all computing nodes, or which part of the data a node is responsible for.

Bear in mind that this book is mainly about machine learning. Hence, we will only brief on the fundamentals of Spark, including its components, installation, deployment, data structure, and core programming.

Breaking down Spark

We start with the main components of Spark, which are depicted in the following diagram:

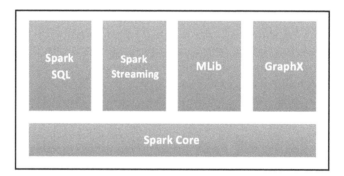

Now, let's explore all the main components of Spark:

- **Spark Core**: This is the foundation and the execution engine of the overall platform. It provides task distribution, scheduling, and in-memory computing. As its name implies, Spark Core is where all the other functionalities are built on top. It can also be exposed through an API of multiple languages, including Python, Java, Scala, and R.

- **Spark SQL**: This is a component built upon Spark Core that introduces a high-level data abstraction called **dataframes**. We will talk about data structures in Spark soon. Spark SQL supports SQL-like data manipulation in Python, Java, and Scala, which works great with structured and semi-structured data. We will be using modules from Spark SQL in this chapter.

- **Spark Streaming**: This performs real-time (or nearly real-time) data analytics by leveraging Spark Core's fast scheduling and in-memory computing capabilities.

- **MLlib**: Short for **machine learning library**, this is a distributed machine learning framework built on top of Spark Core. It allows learning on large-scale data efficiently thanks to the distributed architecture and in-memory computing capability. In in-memory computation, data are kept in the random-access memory (RAM) if it has sufficient capacity, instead of disk. This largely reduces the cost of memory and of reloading data back and forward during the iterative process. The training of a machine learning model is basically an iterative learning process. Hence, the in-memory computing capability of Spark makes it extremely applicable to machine learning modeling. According to major performance benchmarks, learning using MLlib is nearly ten times as fast as the disk-based solution. In this chapter, we will be using modules from Spark MLlib.

- **GraphX**: This is an another functionality built on top of Spark Core that focuses on distributed graph-based processing. PageRank and Pregel abstraction are two typical use cases.

> The main goal of this section is to understand Spark as distributed cluster computing designed for fast computation, and which facilitates both data analytics and iterative learning. If you are looking for more detailed information on Spark, there is a lot of useful documentation along with tutorials available online, such as `https://spark.apache.org/docs/latest/quick-start.html`.

Installing Spark

For learning purposes, let's now install Spark in the local computer (even though it is more frequently used in a cluster of servers). Full instructions can be found at: `https://spark.apache.org/downloads.html`.

There are many stable versions, and we take version **2.3.2 (Sep 24 2018)** as an example. As illustrated in the following screenshot, after selecting **2.3.2** in step 1, we choose **Pre-built for Apache Hadoop 2.7 and later** for step 2. Then, click the link in step 3 to download the `spark-2.3.2-bin-hadoop2.7.tgz` file. Unzip the file and the resulting folder contains a complete Spark package. The steps are in the following screenshot:

Download Apache Spark™

1. Choose a Spark release: 2.3.2 (Sep 24 2018) ⬍

2. Choose a package type: Pre-built for Apache Hadoop 2.7 and later ⬍

3. Download Spark: spark-2.3.2-bin-hadoop2.7.tgz

4. Verify this release using the 2.3.2 signatures and checksums and project release KEYS.

Before running any Spark program, we need to make sure the following dependencies are installed:

- Java 8+, and that it is included in the system environment variables
- Scala version 2.11

To check whether Spark is installed properly, we run the following tests:

1. First, we approximate the value of π using Spark by typing in the following command in Terminal (note `bin` is a folder in `spark-2.3.2-bin-hadoop2.7`):

   ```
   ./bin/run-example SparkPi 10
   ```

2. It should print out something similar to the following (the values may differ):

   ```
   Pi is roughly 3.141851141851142
   ```

   This test is actually similar to the following:

   ```
   ./bin/spark-submit examples/src/main/python/pi.py 10
   ```

3. Next, we test the interactive shell with the following command:

   ```
   ./bin/pyspark --master local[2]
   ```

This should open a Python interpreter, as shown in the following screenshot:

By now, the Spark program should be installed properly. We will talk about those commands (`pyspark`, and `spark-submit`) in the following sections.

Launching and deploying Spark programs

A Spark program can run by itself or over cluster managers. The first option is similar to running a program locally with multiple threads, and one thread is considered one Spark job worker. Of course, there is no parallelism at all, but it is a quick and easy way to launch a Spark application, and we will be deploying it in this model by way of demonstration, throughout the chapter. For example, we can run the following script to launch a Spark application:

```
./bin/spark-submit examples/src/main/python/pi.py
```

This is precisely as we did in the previous section. Or, we can specify the number of threads:

```
./bin/spark-submit --master local[4] examples/src/main/python/pi.py
```

In the previous code, we run Spark locally with four worker threads, or as many cores as there are on the machine by using the following command:

```
./bin/spark-submit --master local[*] examples/src/main/python/pi.py
```

Similarly, we can launch the interactive shell by replacing `spark-submit` with `pyspark`:

```
./bin/pyspark --master local[2] examples/src/main/python/pi.py
```

As for the cluster mode, it (version 2.3.2) currently supports the following approaches:

- **Standalone**: This is the simplest mode to launch a Spark application. It means that the master and workers are located on the same machine. Details of how to launch a Spark application in standalone cluster mode can be found at the following link: `https://spark.apache.org/docs/latest/spark-standalone.html`.
- **Apache Mesos**: As a centralized and fault-tolerant cluster manager, Mesos is designed for managing distributed computing environments. In Spark, when a driver submits tasks for scheduling, Mesos determines which machines handle which tasks. Refer to `https://spark.apache.org/docs/latest/running-on-mesos.html` for further details.
- **Apache Hadoop YARN**: The task scheduler in this approach becomes YARN, as opposed to Mesos in the previous one. **YARN**, which is short for **Yet Another Resource Negotiator**, is the resource manager in Hadoop. With YARN, Spark can be integrated into the Hadoop ecosystem (such as MapReduce, Hive, and File System) more easily. For more information, please go to the following link: `https://spark.apache.org/docs/latest/running-on-yarn.html`.
- **Kubernetes**: This is an open-source system providing container-centric infrastructure. It helps automate job deployment and management, and has gained in popularity over recent years. Kubernetes for Spark is still pretty new but, if you are interested, feel free to read more at the following link: `https://spark.apache.org/docs/latest/running-on-kubernetes.html`.

Programming in PySpark

This section provides a quick introduction to programming with Python in Spark. We will start with the basic data structures in Spark.

Resilient Distributed Datasets (**RDD**) is the primary data structure in Spark. It is a distributed collection of objects and has the following three main features:

- **Resilient**: When any node fails, affected partitions will be reassigned to healthy nodes, which makes Spark fault-tolerant
- **Distributed**: Data resides on one or more nodes in a cluster, which can be operated on in parallel
- **Dataset**: This contains a collection of partitioned data with their values or metadata

RDD was the main data structure in Spark before version 2.0. After that, it is replaced by the **DataFrame** , which is also a distributed collection of data but organized into named columns. DataFrame utilizes the optimized execution engine of Spark SQL. Therefore, it is conceptually similar to a table in a relational database or a `DataFrame` object in the Python `pandas` library.

 Although the current version of Spark still supports RDD, programming with DataFrames is highly recommended. Hence, we won't spent too much time here on programming with RDD. Refer to `https://spark.apache.org/docs/latest/rdd-programming-guide.html` if you are interested. We will go through the basics of programming with a dataframe.

The entry point to a Spark program is creating a Spark session, which can be done by using the following lines:

```
>>> from pyspark.sql import SparkSession
>>> spark = SparkSession \
...     .builder \
...     .appName("test") \
...     .getOrCreate()
```

Note that this is not needed if you run it in PySpark shell. Right after we spin up a PySpark shell, a Spark session is automatically created. We can check the running Spark application at the following link: `localhost:4040/jobs/`. Refer to the following screenshot for the resulting page:

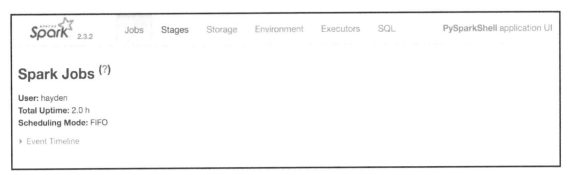

With a Spark session `spark`, a DataFrame object can be created by reading a file (which is usually the case) or manual input. In the following example, we create a DataFrame object from a CSV file:

```
>>> df = spark.read.csv("examples/src/main/resources/people.csv",
                                        header=True, sep=';')
```

Columns in the CSV file `people.csv` are separated by `;`.

Once this is done, we can see an accomplished job in `localhost:4040/jobs/`:

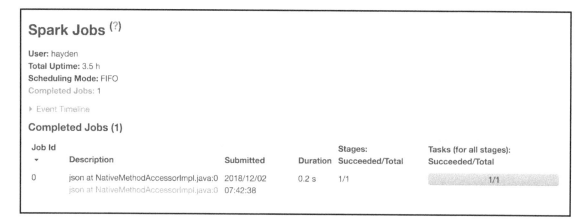

We can display the content of the `DataFrame` object by using the following command:

```
>>> df.show()
+-----+---+---------+
| name|age|      job|
+-----+---+---------+
|Jorge| 30|Developer|
|  Bob| 32|Developer|
+-----+---+---------+
```

We can count the number of rows by using the following command:

```
>>> df.count()
2
```

The schema of the DataFrame object can be displayed using the following command:

```
>>> df.printSchema()
root
 |-- name: string (nullable = true)
 |-- age: string (nullable = true)
 |-- job: string (nullable = true)
```

One or more columns can be selected as follows:

```
>>> df.select("name").show()
+-----+
| name|
+-----+
```

```
|Jorge|
|  Bob|
+-----+
>>> df.select(["name", "job"]).show()
+-----+---------+
| name|      job|
+-----+---------+
|Jorge|Developer|
|  Bob|Developer|
+-----+---------+
```

We can filter rows by condition, for instance, by the value of one column using the following command:

```
>>> df.filter(df['age'] > 31).show()
+----+---+---------+
|name|age|      job|
+----+---+---------+
| Bob| 32|Developer|
+----+---+---------+
```

We will continue programming in PySpark in the next section, where we use Spark to solve the ad click-through problem.

Learning on massive click logs with Spark

Normally, in order to take advantage of Spark, data is stored in a **Hadoop Distributed File System** (**HDFS**), which is a distributed filesystem designed to store large volumes of data, and computation occurs over multiple nodes on clusters. For demonstration purposes, we are keeping the data on a local machine and running Spark locally. It is no different from running it on a distributed computing cluster.

Loading click logs

To train a model on massive click logs, we first need to load the data in Spark. We do so by taking the following steps:

1. First, we spin up the PySpark shell by using the following command:

    ```
    ./bin/pyspark --master local[*]  --driver-memory 20G
    ```

    Here, we specify a large driver memory as we are dealing with a dataset of more than 6 GB.

2. Start a Spark session with an application named `CTR`:

```
>>> spark = SparkSession\
...        .builder\
...        .appName("CTR")\
...        .getOrCreate()
```

3. Then, we load the click log data from the `train` file into a DataFrame object. Note, the data load function `spark.read.csv` allows custom schema, which guarantees data is loaded as expected, as opposed to inferring by default. So first, we define the schema:

```
>>> from pyspark.sql.types import StructField, StringType,
          StructType, IntegerType
>>> schema = StructType([
...        StructField("id", StringType(), True),
...        StructField("click", IntegerType(), True),
...        StructField("hour", IntegerType(), True),
...        StructField("C1", StringType(), True),
...        StructField("banner_pos", StringType(), True),
...        StructField("site_id", StringType(), True),
...        StructField("site_domain", StringType(), True),
...        StructField("site_category", StringType(), True),
...        StructField("app_id", StringType(), True),
...        StructField("app_domain", StringType(), True),
...        StructField("app_category", StringType(), True),
...        StructField("device_id", StringType(), True),
...        StructField("device_ip", StringType(), True),
...        StructField("device_model", StringType(), True),
...        StructField("device_type", StringType(), True),
...        StructField("device_conn_type", StringType(), True),
...        StructField("C14", StringType(), True),
...        StructField("C15", StringType(), True),
...        StructField("C16", StringType(), True),
...        StructField("C17", StringType(), True),
...        StructField("C18", StringType(), True),
...        StructField("C19", StringType(), True),
...        StructField("C20", StringType(), True),
...        StructField("C21", StringType(), True),
... ])
```

Each field of the schema contains the name of the column (such as `id`, `click`, and `hour`), the data type (such as `integer`, and `string`), and whether missing values are allowed (allowed in this case).

With the defined schema, we create a DataFrame object:

```
>>> df = spark.read.csv("file://path_to_file/train", schema=schema,
                                                     header=True)
```

Remember to replace path_to_file with the absolute path of where the train data file is located. The file:// prefix indicates that data is read from a local file. Another prefix, dbfs://, is used for data stored in HDFS.

4. We will now double-check the schema as follows:

```
>>> df.printSchema()
root
 |-- id: string (nullable = true)
 |-- click: integer (nullable = true)
 |-- hour: integer (nullable = true)
 |-- C1: string (nullable = true)
 |-- banner_pos: string (nullable = true)
 |-- site_id: string (nullable = true)
 |-- site_domain: string (nullable = true)
 |-- site_category: string (nullable = true)
 |-- app_id: string (nullable = true)
 |-- app_domain: string (nullable = true)
 |-- app_category: string (nullable = true)
 |-- device_id: string (nullable = true)
 |-- device_ip: string (nullable = true)
 |-- device_model: string (nullable = true)
 |-- device_type: string (nullable = true)
 |-- device_conn_type: string (nullable = true)
 |-- C14: string (nullable = true)
 |-- C15: string (nullable = true)
 |-- C16: string (nullable = true)
 |-- C17: string (nullable = true)
 |-- C18: string (nullable = true)
 |-- C19: string (nullable = true)
 |-- C20: string (nullable = true)
 |-- C21: string (nullable = true)
```

5. And the data size is checked as follows:

```
>>> df.count()
40428967
```

6. Also, we need to drop several columns that provide little information. We will use the following code to do that:

```
>>> df =
    df.drop('id').drop('hour').drop('device_id').drop('device_ip')
```

7. We rename the column from `click` to `label`, as this will be consumed more often in the downstream operations:

```
>>> df = df.withColumnRenamed("click", "label")
```

8. Let's look at the current columns in the DataFrame object:

```
>>> df.columns
['label', 'C1', 'banner_pos', 'site_id', 'site_domain',
 'site_category', 'app_id', 'app_domain', 'app_category',
 'device_model', 'device_type', 'device_conn_type', 'C14', 'C15',
 'C16', 'C17', 'C18', 'C19', 'C20', 'C21']
```

Splitting and caching the data

Here, we split the data into a training and testing set, as follows:

```
>>> df_train, df_test = df.randomSplit([0.7, 0.3], 42)
```

Here, 70% of samples are used for training and the remaining for testing, with a random seed specified, as always, for reproduction.

Before we perform any heavy lifting (such as model learning) on the training set, `df_train`, it is good practice to cache the object. In Spark, **caching** and **persistence** is an optimization technique that reduces the computation overhead. It saves the intermediate results of RDD or DataFrame operations in memory and/or on disk. Without caching or persistence, whenever an intermediate DataFrame is needed, it will be recalculated again according to how it was created originally. Depending on the storage level, persistence behaves differently:

- `MEMORY_ONLY`: The object is only stored in memory. If it does not fit in memory, the remaining part will be recomputed each time it is needed.
- `DISK_ONLY`: The object is only kept on disk. A persisted object can be extracted directly from storage without being recalculated.

- MEMORY_AND_DISK: The object is stored in memory, and might be on disk as well. If the full object does not fit in memory, the remaining partition will be stored on disk, instead of being recalculated every time it is needed. This is the default mode for caching and persistence in Spark. It takes advantage of both fast retrieval of in-memory storage and the high accessibility and capacity of disk storage.

In PySpark, caching is simple. All that is required is a `cache` method.

Let's cache both the training and testing DataFrame:

```
>>> df_train.cache()
DataFrame[label: int, C1: string, banner_pos: string, site_id: string,
site_domain: string, site_category: string, app_id: string, app_domain:
string, app_category: string, device_model: string, device_type: string,
device_conn_type: string, C14: string, C15: string, C16: string, C17:
string, C18: string, C19: string, C20: string, C21: string]
>>> df_train.count()
28297027
>>> df_test.cache()
DataFrame[label: int, C1: string, banner_pos: string, site_id: string,
site_domain: string, site_category: string, app_id: string, app_domain:
string, app_category: string, device_model: string, device_type: string,
device_conn_type: string, C14: string, C15: string, C16: string, C17:
string, C18: string, C19: string, C20: string, C21: string]
>>> df_test.count()
12131940
```

Now, we have the training and testing data ready for downstream analysis.

One-hot encoding categorical features

Similar to the previous chapter, we need to encode categorical features into sets of multiple binary features by executing the following steps:

1. In our case, the categorical features include the following:

```
>>> categorical = df_train.columns
>>> categorical.remove('label')
>>> print(categorical)
['C1', 'banner_pos', 'site_id', 'site_domain', 'site_category',
'app_id', 'app_domain', 'app_category', 'device_model',
'device_type', 'device_conn_type', 'C14', 'C15', 'C16', 'C17',
'C18', 'C19', 'C20', 'C21']
```

In PySpark, one-hot encoding is not as direct as scikit-learn (specifically, with the `OneHotEncoder` module).

2. We first need to index each categorical column using the `StringIndexer` module:

```
>>> from pyspark.ml.feature import StringIndexer
>>> indexers = [
...         StringIndexer(inputCol=c, outputCol=
...             "{0}_indexed".format(c)).setHandleInvalid("keep")
...                                     for c in categorical
... ]
```

The `setHandleInvalid("keep")` handle makes sure it won't crash if any new categorical value occurs. Try to omit it and you will see error messages related to unknown values.

3. Then, we perform one-hot encoding on each individual indexed categorical column using the `OneHotEncoderEstimator` module:

```
>>> from pyspark.ml.feature import OneHotEncoderEstimator
>>> encoder = OneHotEncoderEstimator(
...     inputCols=[indexer.getOutputCol() for indexer in indexers],
...     outputCols=["{0}_encoded".format(indexer.getOutputCol())
...                                 for indexer in indexers]
... )
```

4. Next, we concatenate all sets of generated binary vectors into a single one using the `VectorAssembler` module:

```
>>> from pyspark.ml.feature import VectorAssembler
>>> assembler = VectorAssembler(
...                     inputCols=encoder.getOutputCols(),
...                     outputCol="features"
... )
```

This creates the final encoded vector column called `features`.

5. We chain all these three stages together into a pipeline with the `Pipeline` module in PySpark, which better organizes our one-hot encoding workflow:

```
>>> stages = indexers + [encoder, assembler]
>>> from pyspark.ml import Pipeline
>>> pipeline = Pipeline(stages=stages)
```

6. Finally, we can fit the `pipeline` one-hot encoding model over the training set:

```
>>> one_hot_encoder = pipeline.fit(df_train)
```

7. Once this is done, we use the trained encoder to transform both the training and testing sets. For the training set, we use the following code:

```
>>> df_train_encoded = one_hot_encoder.transform(df_train)
>>> df_train_encoded.show()
```

At this point, we skip displaying the results as there are dozens of columns with several additional ones added on top of df_train.

8. However, we can see the one we are looking for, the `features` column, which contains the one-hot encoded results. Hence, we only select this column along with the target variable:

```
>>> df_train_encoded = df_train_encoded.select(
                                ["label", "features"])
>>> df_train_encoded.show()
+-----+--------------------+
|label|            features|
+-----+--------------------+
|    0|(31458,[5,7,3527,...|
|    0|(31458,[5,7,788,4...|
|    0|(31458,[5,7,788,4...|
|    0|(31458,[5,7,788,4...|
|    0|(31458,[5,7,788,4...|
|    0|(31458,[5,7,788,4...|
|    0|(31458,[5,7,788,4...|
|    0|(31458,[5,7,788,4...|
|    0|(31458,[5,7,788,4...|
|    0|(31458,[5,7,788,4...|
|    0|(31458,[5,7,788,4...|
|    0|(31458,[5,7,788,4...|
|    0|(31458,[5,7,788,4...|
|    0|(31458,[5,7,1271,...|
|    0|(31458,[5,7,1271,...|
|    0|(31458,[5,7,1271,...|
|    0|(31458,[5,7,1271,...|
|    0|(31458,[5,7,1532,...|
|    0|(31458,[5,7,4366,...|
|    0|(31458,[5,7,14,45...|
+-----+--------------------+
only showing top 20 rows
```

The feature column contains sparse vectors of size 31,458.

9. Don't forget to cache `df_train_encoded`, as we will be using it to iteratively train our classification model:

```
>>> df_train_encoded.cache()
DataFrame[label: int, features: vector]
```

10. To release some space, we uncache `df_train`, since we will no longer need it:

```
>>> df_train.unpersist()
DataFrame[label: int, C1: string, banner_pos: string, site_id:
string, site_domain: string, site_category: string, app_id: string,
app_domain: string, app_category: string, device_model: string,
device_type: string, device_conn_type: string, C14: string, C15:
string, C16: string, C17: string, C18: string, C19: string, C20:
string, C21: string]
```

11. Now, we will repeat the preceding steps for the testing set:

```
>>> df_test_encoded = one_hot_encoder.transform(df_test)
>>> df_test_encoded = df_test_encoded.select(["label", "features"])
>>> df_test_encoded.show()
+-----+--------------------+
|label|            features|
+-----+--------------------+
|    0|(31458,[5,7,788,4...|
|    0|(31458,[5,7,788,4...|
|    0|(31458,[5,7,788,4...|
|    0|(31458,[5,7,788,4...|
|    0|(31458,[5,7,788,4...|
|    0|(31458,[5,7,14,45...|
|    0|(31458,[5,7,14,45...|
|    0|(31458,[5,7,14,45...|
|    0|(31458,[5,7,14,45...|
|    0|(31458,[5,7,14,45...|
|    0|(31458,[5,7,14,45...|
|    0|(31458,[5,7,14,45...|
|    0|(31458,[5,7,14,45...|
|    0|(31458,[5,7,14,45...|
|    0|(31458,[5,7,14,45...|
|    0|(31458,[5,7,14,45...|
|    0|(31458,[5,7,14,45...|
|    0|(31458,[5,7,14,45...|
|    0|(31458,[5,7,2859,...|
|    0|(31458,[1,7,651,4...|
+-----+--------------------+
only showing top 20 rows
>>> df_test_encoded.cache()
DataFrame[label: int, features: vector]
```

```
>>> df_test.unpersist()
DataFrame[label: int, C1: string, banner_pos: string, site_id:
string, site_domain: string, site_category: string, app_id: string,
app_domain: string, app_category: string, device_model: string,
device_type: string, device_conn_type: string, C14: string, C15:
string, C16: string, C17: string, C18: string, C19: string, C20:
string, C21: string]
```

12. If you check the Spark UI `localhost:4040/jobs/` in your browser, you will see several completed jobs, such as the following:

10	countByValue at StringIndexer.scala:140 countByValue at StringIndexer.scala:140	2018/12/03 18:59:12	4 s	2/2	96/96
9	countByValue at StringIndexer.scala:140 countByValue at StringIndexer.scala:140	2018/12/03 18:59:08	4 s	2/2	96/96
8	countByValue at StringIndexer.scala:140 countByValue at StringIndexer.scala:140	2018/12/03 18:59:04	4 s	2/2	96/96
7	countByValue at StringIndexer.scala:140 countByValue at StringIndexer.scala:140	2018/12/03 18:58:59	5 s	2/2	96/96
6	countByValue at StringIndexer.scala:140 countByValue at StringIndexer.scala:140	2018/12/03 18:58:55	4 s	2/2	96/96
5	countByValue at StringIndexer.scala:140 countByValue at StringIndexer.scala:140	2018/12/03 18:58:50	5 s	2/2	96/96
4	countByValue at StringIndexer.scala:140 countByValue at StringIndexer.scala:140	2018/12/03 18:58:46	4 s	2/2	96/96
3	countByValue at StringIndexer.scala:140 countByValue at StringIndexer.scala:140	2018/12/03 18:58:43	3 s	2/2	96/96
2	countByValue at StringIndexer.scala:140 countByValue at StringIndexer.scala:140	2018/12/03 18:58:28	15 s	2/2	96/96

Training and testing a logistic regression model

With the encoded training and testing set ready, we can now train our classification model. We use logistic regression as an example, but there are many other classification models supported in PySpark, such as decision tree classifiers, random forests, neural networks (which we will be studying in Chapter 9, *Stock Price Prediction with Regression Algorithms*), linear SVM, and Naïve Bayes. For further details, please refer to the following link: https:/ /spark.apache.org/docs/latest/ml-classification-regression.html#classification.

We train and test a logistic regression model by the following steps:

1. We first import the logistic regression module and initialize a model:

   ```
   >>> from pyspark.ml.classification import LogisticRegression
   >>> classifier = LogisticRegression(maxIter=20, regParam=0.001,
                                        elasticNetParam=0.001)
   ```

   Here, we set the maximum iterations as 20, and the regularization parameter as 0.001.

2. Now, fit the model on the encoded training set:

   ```
   >>> lr_model = classifier.fit(df_train_encoded)
   ```

   Be aware that this might take a while. You can check the running or completed jobs in the Spark UI in the meantime. Refer to the following screenshot for some completed jobs:

33	treeAggregate at RDDLossFunction.scala:61 treeAggregate at RDDLossFunction.scala:61	2018/12/03 19:49:50	20 s	2/2	54/54
32	treeAggregate at RDDLossFunction.scala:61 treeAggregate at RDDLossFunction.scala:61	2018/12/03 19:49:28	21 s	2/2	54/54
31	treeAggregate at RDDLossFunction.scala:61 treeAggregate at RDDLossFunction.scala:61	2018/12/03 19:49:07	20 s	2/2	54/54
30	treeAggregate at RDDLossFunction.scala:61 treeAggregate at RDDLossFunction.scala:61	2018/12/03 19:48:48	19 s	2/2	54/54
29	treeAggregate at RDDLossFunction.scala:61 treeAggregate at RDDLossFunction.scala:61	2018/12/03 19:48:24	23 s	2/2	54/54
28	treeAggregate at RDDLossFunction.scala:61 treeAggregate at RDDLossFunction.scala:61	2018/12/03 19:48:01	23 s	2/2	54/54
27	treeAggregate at RDDLossFunction.scala:61 treeAggregate at RDDLossFunction.scala:61	2018/12/03 19:47:38	23 s	2/2	54/54
26	treeAggregate at RDDLossFunction.scala:61 treeAggregate at RDDLossFunction.scala:61	2018/12/03 19:47:11	26 s	2/2	54/54
25	treeAggregate at LogisticRegression.scala:518 treeAggregate at LogisticRegression.scala:518	2018/12/03 19:28:25	19 min	2/2	54/54

Note that each **RDDLossFunction** represents an iteration of optimizing the logistic regression classifier.

3. After all iterations, we apply the trained model on the testing set:

   ```
   >>> predictions = lr_model.transform(df_test_encoded)
   ```

4. Cache the prediction results, as we will compute the prediction's performance:

```
>>> predictions.cache()
DataFrame[label: int, features: vector, rawPrediction: vector,
probability: vector, prediction: double]
Take a look at the prediction DataFrame:
>>> predictions.show()
+-----+--------------------+--------------------+------------------
--+----------+
|label|            features|       rawPrediction|
probability|prediction|
+-----+--------------------+--------------------+------------------
--+----------+
|
0|(31458,[5,7,788,4...|[2.80267740289335...|[0.94282033454271...|
0.0|
|
0|(31458,[5,7,788,4...|[2.72243908463177...|[0.93833781006061...|
0.0|
|
0|(31458,[5,7,788,4...|[2.72243908463177...|[0.93833781006061...|
0.0|
|
0|(31458,[5,7,788,4...|[2.82083664358057...|[0.94379146612755...|
0.0|
|
0|(31458,[5,7,788,4...|[2.82083664358057...|[0.94379146612755...|
0.0|
|
0|(31458,[5,7,14,45...|[4.44920221201642...|[0.98844714081261...|
0.0|
|
0|(31458,[5,7,14,45...|[4.44920221201642...|[0.98844714081261...|
0.0|
|
0|(31458,[5,7,14,45...|[4.44920221201642...|[0.98844714081261...|
0.0|
|
0|(31458,[5,7,14,45...|[4.54759977096521...|[0.98951842852058...|
0.0|
|
0|(31458,[5,7,14,45...|[4.54759977096521...|[0.98951842852058...|
0.0|
|
0|(31458,[5,7,14,45...|[4.38991492595212...|[0.98775013592573...|
0.0|
|
0|(31458,[5,7,14,45...|[4.38991492595212...|[0.98775013592573...|
```

```
0.0|
|
0| (31458, [5,7,14,45...| [4.38991492595212...| [0.98775013592573...|
0.0|
|
0| (31458, [5,7,14,45...| [4.38991492595212...| [0.98775013592573...|
0.0|
|
0| (31458, [5,7,14,45...| [5.58870435258071...| [0.99627406423617...|
0.0|
|
0| (31458, [5,7,14,45...| [5.66066729150822...| [0.99653187592454...|
0.0|
|
0| (31458, [5,7,14,45...| [5.66066729150822...| [0.99653187592454...|
0.0|
|
0| (31458, [5,7,14,45...| [5.61336061100621...| [0.99636447866332...|
0.0|
|
0| (31458, [5,7,2859, ...| [5.47553763410082...| [0.99582948965297...|
0.0|
|
0| (31458, [1,7,651,4...| [1.33424801682849...| [0.79154243844810...|
0.0|
+------+--------------------+--------------------+--------------------
--+----------+
only showing top 20 rows
```

This contains the predictive features, ground truth, probabilities of the two classes, and the final prediction (with a decision threshold of 0.5).

5. We evaluate the AUC of ROC on the testing set using the `BinaryClassificationEvaluator` function with the `areaUnderROC` evaluation metric:

```
>>> from pyspark.ml.evaluation import BinaryClassificationEvaluator
>>> ev = BinaryClassificationEvaluator(rawPredictionCol =
                "rawPrediction", metricName = "areaUnderROC")
>>> print(ev.evaluate(predictions))
0.7488839207716323
```

We are hereby able to obtain an AUC of 74.89%.

Feature engineering on categorical variables with Spark

We have demonstrated how to build an ad click predictor that learns from massive click logs using Spark. Thus far, we have been using one-hot encoding to employ the categorical inputs. In this section, we will be talking about two popular feature engineering techniques: feature hashing and feature interaction. One is an alternative to one-hot encoding, another is a variant of one-hot encoding. **Feature engineering** means generating new features based on domain knowledge or defined rules, in order to improve learning performance achieved with existing feature space.

Hashing categorical features

In machine learning, **feature hashing** (also called **hashing trick**) is an efficient way to encode categorical features. It is based on hashing functions in computer science that map data of variable sizes to data of a fixed (and usually smaller) size. It is easier to understand feature hashing through an example.

Let's say we have three features—**gender**, **site_domain**, and **device_model**, for example:

gender	site_domain	device_model
male	cnn	samsung
female	abc	iphone
male	nbc	huawei
male	facebook	xiaomi
female	abc	iphone

With one-hot encoding, this will become feature vectors of size 9, which come from 2 (from **gender**) + 4 (from **site_domain**) + 3 (from **device_model**). With feature hashing, we want to obtain a feature vector of size 4. We define a hash function as the sum of Unicode code points of each character, and then divide the result by 4 and take the remainder as the hashed output. Take the first row as an example, $ord(m) + ord(a) + ord(l) + ord(e) + ... + ord(s) + ord(u) + ord(n) + ord(g) = 109 + 97 + 108 + 101 + ... + 115 + 117 + 110 + 103 = 1500$, then 1500 % 4 = 0, which means **[1 0 0 0]**. If the remainder is 1, a sample is hashed into [0, 1, 0, 0]; [0, 0, 1, 0] for a sample with 2 as the remainder; [0, 0, 0, 1] for a sample with 3 as the remainder.

Similarly, for other rows, we have the following:

gender	site_domain	device_model	hash result
male	cnn	samsung	[1 0 0 0]
female	abc	iphone	[0 0 0 1]
male	nbc	huawei	[0 1 0 0]
male	facebook	xiaomi	[1 0 0 0]
female	abc	iphone	[0 0 0 1]

In the end, we use the four-dimension hashed vectors to represent the original data, instead of the nine-dimension one-hot encoded ones.

There are a few things to note about feature hashing:

- The same input will always be converted to the same output, for instance, the second and fifth rows.
- Two different inputs might be converted to the same output, such as the first and fourth rows. This phenomenon is called **hashing collision**.

- Hence, the choice of the resulting fixed size is important. It will result in serious collision and information loss if the size is too small. If it is too large, it is basically a redundant one-hot encoding. With the correct size, it will make it space-efficient and, at the same time, preserve important information, which further benefits downstream tasks.
- Hashing is one-way, which means we cannot revert the output to its input; while one-hot encoding is two-way mapping.

Let's now adopt feature hashing to our click prediction project. Recall that the one-hot encoded vectors are of size 31,458. If we choose 10,000 as the fixed hashing size, we will be able to cut the space to less than one third, and reduce the memory consumed by training the classification model. Also, we will see how quick it is to perform feature hashing compared to one-hot encoding, as there is no need to keep track of all unique values across all columns. It just maps each individual row of string values to a sparse vector through internal hash functions as follows:

1. We begin by importing the feature hashing module from PySpark and initialize a feature hasher with an output size of 10,000:

```
>>> from pyspark.ml.feature import FeatureHasher
>>> hasher = FeatureHasher(numFeatures=10000,
                inputCols=categorical, outputCol="features")
```

2. Use the defined hasher to convert the input DataFrame:

```
>>> hasher.transform(df_train).select("features").show()
+--------------------+
|            features|
+--------------------+
|(10000,[1228,1289...|
|(10000,[1228,1289...|
|(10000,[1228,1289...|
|(10000,[1228,1289...|
|(10000,[1228,1289...|
|(10000,[1228,1289...|
|(10000,[29,1228,1...|
|(10000,[1228,1289...|
|(10000,[1228,1289...|
|(10000,[1228,1289...|
|(10000,[1228,1289...|
|(10000,[1228,1289...|
|(10000,[1228,1289...|
|(10000,[1228,1289...|
|(10000,[1228,1289...|
|(10000,[1228,1289...|
|(10000,[1228,1289...|
|(10000,[746,1060,...|
|(10000,[675,1228,...|
|(10000,[1289,1695...|
+--------------------+
only showing top 20 rows
```

As we can see, the size of the resulting column, features, is 10,000. Again, there is no training or fitting in feature hashing. The hasher is a predefined mapping.

3. For better organization of the entire workflow, we chain the hasher and classification model together into a pipeline:

```
>>> classifier = LogisticRegression(maxIter=20, regParam=0.000,
                                     elasticNetParam=0.000)
>>> stages = [hasher, classifier]
>>> pipeline = Pipeline(stages=stages)
```

4. Fit the pipelined model on the training set as follows:

```
>>> model = pipeline.fit(df_train)
```

5. Apply the trained model on the testing set and record the prediction results:

```
>>> predictions = model.transform(df_test)
>>> predictions.cache()
```

6. Evaluate its performance in terms of AUC of ROC:

```
>>> ev = BinaryClassificationEvaluator(rawPredictionCol =
                  "rawPrediction", metricName = "areaUnderROC")
>>> print(ev.evaluate(predictions))
0.7448097180769776
```

We are able to achieve an AUC of 74.48%, which is close to the previous one of 74.89% with one-hot encoding. At the end of the day, we save a substantial amount of computational resources and attain a comparable prediction accuracy. That is a win.

 With feature hashing, we lose interpretability but gain computational advantage.

Combining multiple variables – feature interaction

Among all the features of the click log data, some are very weak signals in themselves. For example, gender itself doesn't tell you much regarding whether someone will click an ad, and the device model itself doesn't provide much information either. However, by combining multiple features, we will be able to create a stronger synthesized signal. **Feature interaction** is introduced for this purpose. For numerical features, it usually generates new features by multiplying multiples of them. We can also define whatever integration rules we want. For example, we generate an additional feature, **income/person**, from two original features, **household income** and **household size**:

household income	household size	income/person
300,000	2	150,000
100,000	1	100,000
400,000	4	100,000
300,000	5	60,000
200,000	2	100,000

For categorical features, feature interaction becomes an AND operation on two or more features. In the following example, we generate an additional feature, **gender:site_domain**, from two original features, **gender** and **site_domain**:

gender	site_domain	gender:site_domain
male	cnn	male:cnn
female	abc	female:abc
male	nbc	male:nbc
male	facebook	male:facebook
female	abc	female:abc

We then use one-hot encoding to transform string values. On top of six one-hot encoded features (two from **gender** and four from **site_domain**), feature interaction between **gender** and **site_domain** adds eight further features (two by four).

Let's now adopt feature interaction to our click prediction project. We take two features, C14 and C15, as an example of AND interaction:

1. First, we will import the feature interaction module, RFormula, from PySpark:

   ```
   >>> from pyspark.ml.feature import RFormula
   ```

   An RFormula model takes in a formula that describes how features interact. For instance, y ~ a + b means it takes in input features, *a* and *b*, and outputs *y*; y ~ a + b + a:b means it predicts y based on features *a*, *b*, and iteration term, *a* AND *b*; y ~ a + b + c + a:b means it predicts *y* based on features *a*, *b*, *c*, and iteration terms, *a* AND *b*.

2. We need to define an interaction formula accordingly:

   ```
   >>> cat_inter = ['C14', 'C15']
   >>> cat_no_inter = [c for c in categorical if c not in cat_inter]
   >>> concat = '+'.join(categorical)
   >>> interaction = ':'.join(cat_inter)
   >>> formula = "label ~ " + concat + '+' + interaction
   >>> print(formula)
   label ~
   C1+banner_pos+site_id+site_domain+site_category+app_id+app_domain+a
   pp_category+device_model+device_type+device_conn_type+C14+C15+C16+C
   17+C18+C19+C20+C21+C14:C15
   ```

3. Now, we can initialize a feature interactor with this formula:

```
>>> interactor = RFormula(
...         formula=formula,
...         featuresCol="features",
...         labelCol="label").setHandleInvalid("keep")
```

Again, the `setHandleInvalid("keep")` handle here makes sure it won't crash if any new categorical value occurs.

4. Use the defined feature interactor to fit and transform the input DataFrame:

```
>>>
interactor.fit(df_train).transform(df_train).select("features").
show()
+--------------------+
|            features|
+--------------------+
|(54930,[5,7,3527,...|
|(54930,[5,7,788,4...|
|(54930,[5,7,788,4...|
|(54930,[5,7,788,4...|
|(54930,[5,7,788,4...|
|(54930,[5,7,788,4...|
|(54930,[5,7,788,4...|
|(54930,[5,7,788,4...|
|(54930,[5,7,788,4...|
|(54930,[5,7,788,4...|
|(54930,[5,7,788,4...|
|(54930,[5,7,788,4...|
|(54930,[5,7,788,4...|
|(54930,[5,7,1271,...|
|(54930,[5,7,1271,...|
|(54930,[5,7,1271,...|
|(54930,[5,7,1271,...|
|(54930,[5,7,1532,...|
|(54930,[5,7,4366,...|
|(54930,[5,7,14,45...|
+--------------------+
only showing top 20 rows
```

More than 20,000 features are added to the feature space due to the interaction term of `C14` and `C15`.

5. Again, we chain the feature interactor and classification model together into a pipeline for better organizing the entire workflow:

```
>>> classifier = LogisticRegression(maxIter=20, regParam=0.000,
                                     elasticNetParam=0.000)
>>> stages = [interactor, classifier]
>>> pipeline = Pipeline(stages=stages)
>>> model = pipeline.fit(df_train)
>>> predictions = model.transform(df_test)
>>> predictions.cache()
>>> from pyspark.ml.evaluation import BinaryClassificationEvaluator
>>> ev = BinaryClassificationEvaluator(rawPredictionCol =
                        "rawPrediction", metricName = "areaUnderROC")
>>> print(ev.evaluate(predictions))
0.7490392990518315
```

An AUC of 74.90%, with additional interaction between features C14 and C15, is a boost from 74.89% without any interaction.

Summary

In this chapter, we continued working on the online advertising click-through prediction project. This time, we were able to train the classifier on the entire dataset with millions of records, with the help of the parallel computing tool, Apache Spark. We have discussed the basics of Spark, including its major components, deployment of Spark programs, programming essentials of PySpark, and the Python interface of Spark. And we programmed using PySpark to explore the click log data, perform one-hot encoding, cache intermediate results, develop classification solutions based on the entire click log dataset, and evaluate performance. In addition, we introduced two feature engineering techniques, feature hashing and feature interaction, in order to improve prediction performance. We had fun implementing them in PySpark as well.

Looking back on our learning journey, we have been working on classification problems since Chapter 4, *Detecting Spam Email with Naive Bayes*. Actually, we have covered all powerful and popular classification models in machine learning. And yes, we will move on to solving regression problems in the chapter, which is the sibling of classification in supervised learning. We will resort to regression models, including linear regression, decision trees for regression, and support vector regression, which all sound very familiar, as well as neural networks that have gained significantly in popularity recently.

Exercises

- In the one-hot encoding solution, can you use different classifiers supported in PySpark instead of logistic regression, such as decision tree, random forest, and linear SVM?
- In the feature hashing solution, can you try other hash sizes, such as 5,000, and 20,000? What do you observe?
- In the feature interaction solution, can you try other interactions, such as C1 and C20?
- Can you first use feature interaction and then feature hashing in order to lower the expanded dimension? Are you able to obtain higher AUC?

9
Stock Price Prediction with Regression Algorithms

In this chapter, we will be solving a problem that absolutely interests everyone—predicting stock prices. Getting wealthy by means of smart investment—who isn't interested?! In fact, stock market movements and stock price predictions have been actively researched by a large number of financial, trading, and even technology corporations. A variety of methods have been developed to predict stock prices using machine learning techniques. Herein, we will be focusing on learning several popular regression algorithms, including linear regression, regression tree and regression forest, and support vector regression, as well as neural networks, and utilizing them to tackle this billion (or trillion) dollar problem.

We will cover the following topics in this chapter:

- An introduction to the stock market and stock prices
- What is regression
- Feature engineering
- Acquiring stock data and generating predictive features
- What is linear regression
- Mechanics of linear regression
- Implementations of linear regression (from scratch, and using scikit-learn and TensorFlow)
- What is decision tree regression
- Mechanics of regression tree
- Implementations of regression tree (from scratch and using scikit-learn)
- From regression tree to regression forest

- Implementations of regression forest (using scikit-learn and TensorFlow)
- What is support vector regression
- Mechanics of support vector regression
- Implementations of support vector regression with scikit-learn
- What is a neural network
- Mechanics of neural networks
- Implementations of neural networks (from scratch, and using scikit-learn, TensorFlow, and Keras)
- Regression performance evaluation
- Predicting stock prices with regression algorithms

Brief overview of the stock market and stock prices

The stock of a corporation signifies ownership in the corporation. A single share of the stock represents a claim on fractional assets and earnings of the corporation in proportion to the total number of shares. For example, if an investor owns 50 shares of stock in a company that has, in total, 1,000 outstanding shares, that investor (or shareholder) would own and have claim on 5% of the company's assets and earnings.

Stocks of a company can be traded between shareholders and other parties via stock exchanges and organizations. Major stock exchanges include New York Stock Exchange, NASDAQ, London Stock Exchange Group, Shanghai Stock Exchange, and Hong Kong Stock Exchange. The prices that a stock is traded at fluctuate essentially due to the law of supply and demand. At any one moment, the supply is the number of shares that are in the hands of public investors, the demand is the number of shares investors want to buy, and the price of the stock moves up and down in order to attain and maintain equilibrium.

In general, investors want to buy low and sell high. This sounds simple enough but it's very challenging to implement as it's monumentally difficult to say whether a stock price will go up or down. There are two main streams of studies attempting to understand factors and conditions that lead to price changes or even to forecast future stock prices, **fundamental analysis** and **technical analysis**:

- **Fundamental analysis**: This stream focuses on underlying factors that influence a company's value and business, including overall economy and industry conditions from macro perspectives, the company's financial conditions, management, and competitors from micro perspectives.

- **Technical analysis**: On the other hand, this stream predicts future price movements through the statistical study of past trading activity, including price movement, volume, and market data. Predicting prices via machine learning techniques is an important topic in technical analysis nowadays. Many quant trading firms have been using machine learning to empower automated and algorithmic trading. In this chapter, we'll be working as a quantitative analyst/researcher, exploring how to predict stock prices with several typical **machine learning regression** algorithms.

What is regression?

Regression is another main instance of supervised learning in machine learning. Given a training set of data containing observations and their associated continuous output values, the goal of regression is to explore the relationships between the observations (also called features) and the targets, and to output a **continuous** value based on the input features of an unknown sample, which is depicted in the following diagram:

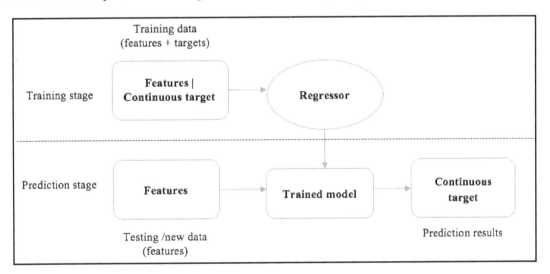

The major difference between regression and classification is that the output values in regression are continuous while they are discrete in classification. This leads to different application areas for these two supervised learning methods. Classification is basically used in determining the desired memberships or characteristics as we've seen in previous chapters, such as email being spam or not, newsgroup topics, ad click-through or not. On the other hand, regression mainly involves estimating an outcome or forecasting a response. An example of estimating continuous targets with linear regression is depicted as follows:

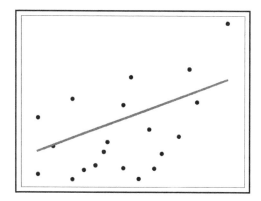

Typical machine learning regression problems include the following:

- Predicting house prices based on location, square footage, number of bedrooms, and bathrooms
- Estimating power consumption based on information of a system's processes and memory
- Forecasting retail inventory
- And of course, predicting stock prices

Mining stock price data

In theory, we can apply regression techniques in predicting prices of a particular stock. However, it's difficult to ensure the stock we pick is suitable enough for learning purposes—its price should follow some learnable patterns and it hasn't been affected by unprecedented instances or irregular events. Hence, we'll herein be focusing on one of the most popular **stock indexes** to better illustrate and generalize our price regression approach.

Let's first cover what an index is. A **stock index** is a statistical measure of the value of a portion of the overall stock market. An index includes several stocks that are diverse enough to represent a section of the whole market. And the price of an index is typically computed as the weighted average of the prices of selected stocks.

The **Dow Jones Industrial Average** (**DJIA**) is one of the longest established and most commonly watched indexes in the world. It consists of 30 of the most significant stocks in the U.S., such as Microsoft, Apple, General Electric, and the Walt Disney Company, and represents around a quarter of the value of the entire U.S. market. We can view its daily prices and performance in Yahoo Finance at `https://finance.yahoo.com/quote/%5EDJI/history?p=%5EDJI`:

Time Period: Dec 21, 2016 - Feb 21, 2017 ∨	Show: Historical Prices ∨		Frequency: Daily ∨		Apply
Currency in USD					⬇ Download Data
Date	Open	High	Low	Close	Adj Close*	Volume
Feb 21, 2017	20,663.43	20,757.64	20,663.37	20,743.00	20,743.00	336,880,000
Feb 17, 2017	20,564.13	20,624.05	20,532.61	20,624.05	20,624.05	340,620,000
Feb 16, 2017	20,627.31	20,639.87	20,556.83	20,619.77	20,619.77	354,120,000
Feb 15, 2017	20,504.27	20,620.45	20,496.03	20,611.86	20,611.86	384,380,000
Feb 14, 2017	20,374.22	20,504.41	20,374.02	20,504.41	20,504.41	356,580,000
Feb 13, 2017	20,338.54	20,441.48	20,322.95	20,412.16	20,412.16	314,620,000
Feb 10, 2017	20,211.23	20,298.21	20,204.76	20,269.37	20,269.37	312,230,000
Feb 09, 2017	20,061.73	20,206.36	20,061.73	20,172.40	20,172.40	325,310,000
Feb 08, 2017	20,049.29	20,068.28	20,015.33	20,054.34	20,054.34	280,410,000
Feb 07, 2017	20,107.62	20,155.35	20,068.68	20,090.29	20,090.29	279,670,000
Feb 06, 2017	20,025.61	20,094.95	20,002.81	20,052.42	20,052.42	281,720,000
Feb 03, 2017	19,964.21	20,081.48	19,964.21	20,071.46	20,071.46	344,220,000

In each trading day, price of a stock changes and is recorded in real time. Five values illustrating movements in the price over one unit of time (usually one day, but can also be one week or one month) are key trading indicators. They are as follows:

- **Open**: The starting price for a given trading day
- **Close**: The final price on that day
- **High**: The highest prices at which the stock traded on that day
- **Low**: The lowest prices at which the stock traded on that day
- **Volume**: The total number of shares traded before the market is closed on that day

Other major indexes besides DJIA include the following:

- **S&P 500** (short for **S**tandard & Poor's 500) Index is made up of 500 of the most commonly traded stocks in the U.S., representing 80% of the value of the entire U.S. market (`https://finance.yahoo.com/quote/%5EGSPC/history?p=%5EGSPC`).
- **NASDAQ Composite** is composed of all stocks traded on NASDAQ (`https://finance.yahoo.com/quote/%5EIXIC/history?p=%5EIXIC`).
- **Russell 2000 (RUT)** index is a collection of the last 2,000 out of 3,000 largest publicly-traded companies in the U.S. (`https://finance.yahoo.com/quote/%5ERUT/history?p=%5ERUT`).
- London FTSE-100 is composed of the top 100 companies in market capitalization listed on the London Stock Exchange (`https://finance.yahoo.com/quote/%5EFTSE/`).

We will be focusing on DJIA and using its historical prices and performance to predict future prices. In the following sections, we will be exploring how to develop price prediction models, specifically regression models, and what can be used as indicators or predictive features.

Getting started with feature engineering

When it comes to a machine learning algorithm, the first question to ask is usually what features are available or what the predictive variables are.

The driving factors that are used to predict future prices of DJIA, the **close** prices, include historical and current **open** prices as well as historical performance (**high, low,** and **volume**). Note that current or same-day performance (**high, low,** and **volume**) shouldn't be included because we simply can't foresee the highest and lowest prices at which the stock traded or the total number of shares traded before the market is closed on that day.

Predicting the close price with only those preceding four indicators doesn't seem promising and might lead to underfitting. So we need to think of ways to generate more features in order to increase predictive power. To recap, in machine learning, **feature engineering** is the process of creating domain-specific features based on existing features in order to improve the performance of a machine learning algorithm. Feature engineering usually requires sufficient domain knowledge and can be very difficult and time-consuming. In reality, features used to solve a machine learning problem are not usually directly available and need to be particularly designed and constructed, for example, term frequency or tf-idf features in spam email detection and newsgroup classification. Hence, feature engineering is essential in machine learning and is usually where we spend most efforts in solving a practical problem.

When making an investment decision, investors usually look at historical prices over a period of time, not just the price the day before. Therefore, in our stock price prediction case, we can compute the average close price over the past week (five trading days), over the past month and over the past year as three new features. We can also customize the time window to the size we want, such as the past quarter or the past six months. On top of these three averaged price features, we can generate new features associated with the price trend by computing the ratios between each pair of average prices in three different time frames. For instance, the ratio between the average price over the past week and that over the past year. Besides prices, volume is another important factor that investors analyze. Similarly, we can generate new volume-based features by computing the average volumes in several different time frames and ratios between each pair of averaged values.

Besides historical averaged values in a time window, investors also greatly consider stock volatility. Volatility describes the degree of variation of prices for a given stock or index over time. In statistical term, it's basically the standard deviation of the close prices. We can easily generate new sets of features by computing the standard deviation of close prices in a particular time frame, as well as the standard deviation of volumes traded. In a similar manner, ratios between each pair of standard deviation values can be included in our engineered feature pool.

Last but not least, return is a significant financial metric that investors closely watch for. Return is the percentage of gain or loss of close price for a stock/index in a particular period. For example, daily return and annual return are financial terms we frequently hear. They are calculated as follows:

$$return_{i:i-1} = \frac{price_i - price_{i-1}}{price_{i-1}}$$

$$return_{i:i-365} = \frac{price_i - price_{i-365}}{price_{i-365}}$$

Here, *price*$_i$ is the price on the ith day and *price*$_{i-1}$ is the price on the day before. Weekly and monthly returns can be computed in a similar way. Based on daily returns, we can produce a moving average over a particular number of days. For instance, given daily returns of the past week, *return*$_{i:i-1}$, *return*$_{i-1:i-2}$, *return*$_{i-2:i-3}$, *return*$_{i-3:i-4}$, *return*$_{i-4:i-5}$, we can calculate the moving average over that week as follows:

$$MovingAvg_{i\_5} = \frac{(return_{i:i-1} + return_{i-1:i-2} + return_{i-2:i-3} + return_{i-3:i-4} + return_{i-4:i-5})}{5}$$

In summary, we can generate the following predictive variables by applying feature engineering techniques:

$AvgPrice_5$	The average close price over the past five days
$AvgPrice_{30}$	The average close price over the past month
$AvgPrice_{365}$	The average close price over the past year
$\dfrac{AvgPrice_5}{AvgPrice_{30}}$	The ratio between the average price over the past week and that over the past month
$\dfrac{AvgPrice_5}{AvgPrice_{365}}$	The ratio between the average price over the past week and that over the past year
$\dfrac{AvgPrice_{30}}{AvgPrice_{365}}$	The ratio between the average price over the past month and that over the past year
$AvgVolume_5$	The average volume over the past five days
$AvgVolume_{30}$	The average volume over the past month
$AvgVolume_{365}$	The average volume over the past year
$\dfrac{AvgVolume_5}{AvgVolume_{30}}$	The ratio between the average volume over the past week and that over the past month
$\dfrac{AvgVolume_5}{AvgVolume_{365}}$	The ratio between the average volume over the past week and that over the past year
$\dfrac{AvgVolume_{30}}{AvgVolume_{365}}$	The ratio between the average volume over the past month and that over the past year
$StdPrice_5$	The standard deviation of the close prices over the past five days
$StdPrice_{30}$	The standard deviation of the close prices over the past month
$StdPrice_{365}$	The standard deviation of the close prices over the past year

$\dfrac{\text{StdPrice}_5}{\text{StdPrice}_{30}}$	The ratio between the standard deviation of the prices over the past week and that over the past month
$\dfrac{\text{StdPrice}_5}{\text{StdPrice}_{365}}$	The ratio between the standard deviation of the prices over the past week and that over the past year
$\dfrac{\text{StdPrice}_{30}}{\text{StdPrice}_{365}}$	The ratio between the standard deviation of the prices over the past month and that over the past year
StdVolume_5	The standard deviation of the volumes over the past five days
StdVolume_{30}	The standard deviation of the volumes over the past month
StdVolume_{365}	The standard deviation of the volumes over the past year
$\dfrac{\text{StdVolume}_5}{\text{StdVolume}_{30}}$	The ratio between the standard deviation of the volumes over the past week and that over the past month
$\dfrac{\text{StdVolume}_5}{\text{StdVolume}_{365}}$	The ratio between the standard deviation of the volumes over the past week and that over the past year
$\dfrac{\text{StdVolume}_{30}}{\text{StdVolume}_{365}}$	The ratio between the standard deviation of the volumes over the past month and that over the past year
$\text{return}_{i:i-1}$	Daily return of the past day
$\text{return}_{i:i-5}$	Weekly return of the past week
$\text{return}_{i:i-30}$	Monthly return of the past month
$\text{return}_{i:i-365}$	Yearly return of the past year
MovingAvg_{i_5}	Moving average of the daily returns over the past week
MovingAvg_{i_30}	Moving average of the daily returns over the past month
MovingAvg_{i_365}	Moving average of the daily returns over the past year

Eventually, we are able to generate in total 31 sets of features, along with the following six original features:

- *OpenPrice$_i$*: This feature represents the open price
- *OpenPrice$_{i-1}$*: This feature represents the open price on the past day
- *ClosePrice$_{i-1}$*: This feature represents the close price on the past day
- *HighPrice$_{i-1}$*: This feature represents the highest price on the past day
- *LowPrice$_{i-1}$*: This feature represents the lowest price on the past day
- *Volume$_{i-1}$*: This feature represents the volume on the past day

Acquiring data and generating features

For easier reference, we will implement the code for generating features here rather than in later sections. We will start with obtaining the dataset we need for our project.

Throughout the entire project, we acquire stock index price and performance data from Yahoo Finance. For example, in the **Historical Data** page, `https://finance.yahoo.com/quote/%5EDJI/history?p=%5EDJI`, we can change the **Time Period** to **Dec 01, 2005 - Dec10, 2005**, select **Historical Prices** in **Show**, and **Daily** in **Frequency** (or open this link directly: `https://finance.yahoo.com/quote/%5EDJI/history?period1=1133413200` `amp;period2=1134190800amp;interval=1damp;filter=historyamp;frequency=1d`), then click on the **Apply** button. Click the **Download data** button to download the data and name the file `20051201_20051210.csv`.

We can load the data we just downloaded as follows:

```
>>> mydata = pd.read_csv('20051201_20051210.csv', index_col='Date')
>>> mydata
                  Open          High          Low          Close
Date
2005-12-01  10806.030273  10934.900391  10806.030273  10912.570312
2005-12-02  10912.009766  10921.370117  10861.660156  10877.509766
2005-12-05  10876.950195  10876.950195  10810.669922  10835.009766
2005-12-06  10835.410156  10936.200195  10835.410156  10856.860352
2005-12-07  10856.860352  10868.059570  10764.009766  10810.910156
2005-12-08  10808.429688  10847.250000  10729.669922  10755.120117
2005-12-09  10751.759766  10805.950195  10729.910156  10778.580078

                  Volume      Adjusted Close
Date
2005-12-01  256980000.0       10912.570312
2005-12-02  214900000.0       10877.509766
2005-12-05  237340000.0       10835.009766
2005-12-06  264630000.0       10856.860352
2005-12-07  243490000.0       10810.910156
2005-12-08  253290000.0       10755.120117
2005-12-09  238930000.0       10778.580078
```

Note the output is a `pandas dataframe` object. The `Date` column is the index column, and the rest columns are the corresponding financial variables. If you have not installed `pandas`, the powerful package designed to simplify data analysis on **relational** (or table-like) data, you can do so via the following command line:

```
pip install pandas
```

Next, we implement feature generation by starting with a sub-function that directly creates features from the original six features, as follows:

```
>>> def add_original_feature(df, df_new):
...     df_new['open'] = df['Open']
...     df_new['open_1'] = df['Open'].shift(1)
...     df_new['close_1'] = df['Close'].shift(1)
...     df_new['high_1'] = df['High'].shift(1)
...     df_new['low_1'] = df['Low'].shift(1)
...     df_new['volume_1'] = df['Volume'].shift(1)
```

Then we develop a sub-function that generates six features related to average close prices:

```
>>> def add_avg_price(df, df_new):
...     df_new['avg_price_5'] = df['Close'].rolling(5).mean().shift(1)
...     df_new['avg_price_30'] = df['Close'].rolling(21).mean().shift(1)
...     df_new['avg_price_365'] = df['Close'].rolling(252).mean().shift(1)
...     df_new['ratio_avg_price_5_30'] =
                    df_new['avg_price_5'] / df_new['avg_price_30']
...     df_new['ratio_avg_price_5_365'] =
                    df_new['avg_price_5'] / df_new['avg_price_365']
...     df_new['ratio_avg_price_30_365'] =
                    df_new['avg_price_30'] / df_new['avg_price_365']
```

Similarly, a sub-function that generates six features related to average volumes is as follows:

```
>>> def add_avg_volume(df, df_new):
...     df_new['avg_volume_5'] = df['Volume'].rolling(5).mean().shift(1)
...     df_new['avg_volume_30'] = df['Volume'].rolling(21).mean().shift(1)
...     df_new['avg_volume_365'] =
                    df['Volume'].rolling(252).mean().shift(1)
...     df_new['ratio_avg_volume_5_30'] =
                    df_new['avg_volume_5'] / df_new['avg_volume_30']
...     df_new['ratio_avg_volume_5_365'] =
                    df_new['avg_volume_5'] / df_new['avg_volume_365']
...     df_new['ratio_avg_volume_30_365'] =
                    df_new['avg_volume_30'] / df_new['avg_volume_365']
```

As for the standard deviation, we develop the following sub-function for the price-related features:

```
>>> def add_std_price(df, df_new):
...     df_new['std_price_5'] = df['Close'].rolling(5).std().shift(1)
...     df_new['std_price_30'] = df['Close'].rolling(21).std().shift(1)
...     df_new['std_price_365'] = df['Close'].rolling(252).std().shift(1)
...     df_new['ratio_std_price_5_30'] =
                    df_new['std_price_5'] / df_new['std_price_30']
```

```
...          df_new['ratio_std_price_5_365'] =
                          df_new['std_price_5'] / df_new['std_price_365']
...          df_new['ratio_std_price_30_365'] =
                          df_new['std_price_30'] / df_new['std_price_365']
```

Similarly, a sub-function that generates six volume-based standard deviation features is as follows:

```
>>> def add_std_volume(df, df_new):
...          df_new['std_volume_5'] = df['Volume'].rolling(5).std().shift(1)
...          df_new['std_volume_30'] = df['Volume'].rolling(21).std().shift(1)
...          df_new['std_volume_365'] = df['Volume'].rolling(252).std().shift(1)
...          df_new['ratio_std_volume_5_30'] =
                          df_new['std_volume_5'] / df_new['std_volume_30']
...          df_new['ratio_std_volume_5_365'] =
                          df_new['std_volume_5'] / df_new['std_volume_365']
...          df_new['ratio_std_volume_30_365'] =
                          df_new['std_volume_30'] / df_new['std_volume_365']
```

And seven return-based features are generated using the following sub-function:

```
>>> def add_return_feature(df, df_new):
...          df_new['return_1'] = ((df['Close'] - df['Close'].shift(1)) /
                          df['Close'].shift(1)).shift(1)
...          df_new['return_5'] = ((df['Close'] - df['Close'].shift(5)) /
                          df['Close'].shift(5)).shift(1)
...          df_new['return_30'] = ((df['Close'] - df['Close'].shift(21)) /
                          df['Close'].shift(21)).shift(1)
...          df_new['return_365'] = ((df['Close'] - df['Close'].shift(252)) /
                          df['Close'].shift(252)).shift(1)
...          df_new['moving_avg_5'] =
                          df_new['return_1'].rolling(5).mean().shift(1)
...          df_new['moving_avg_30'] =
                          df_new['return_1'].rolling(21).mean().shift(1)
...          df_new['moving_avg_365'] =
                          df_new['return_1'].rolling(252).mean().shift(1)
```

Finally, we put together the main feature generation function that calls all preceding sub-functions:

```
>>> def generate_features(df):
...          """
...          Generate features for a stock/index based on historical price
                  and performance
...          @param df: dataframe with columns "Open", "Close", "High",
                      "Low", "Volume", "Adjusted Close"
...          @return: dataframe, data set with new features
...          """
```

```
...        df_new = pd.DataFrame()
...        # 6 original features
...        add_original_feature(df, df_new)
...        # 31 generated features
...        add_avg_price(df, df_new)
...        add_avg_volume(df, df_new)
...        add_std_price(df, df_new)
...        add_std_volume(df, df_new)
...        add_return_feature(df, df_new)
...        # the target
...        df_new['close'] = df['Close']
...        df_new = df_new.dropna(axis=0)
...        return df_new
```

It is noted that the window sizes here are 5, 21, and 252, instead of 7, 30, and 365 representing the weekly, monthly, and yearly window. This is because there are 252 (rounded) trading days in a year, 21 trading days in a month, and 5 in a week.

We can apply this feature engineering strategy on the DJIA data queried from 1988 to 2016 as follows:

```
>>> data_raw = pd.read_csv('19880101_20161231.csv', index_col='Date')
>>> data = generate_features(data_raw)
```

Take a look at what the data with the new features looks like:

```
>>> print(data.round(decimals=3).head(5))
```

The preceding command line generates the following output:

```
              open   open_1  close_1  high_1   low_1   volume_1  avg_price_5   ...    return_5
return_30  return_365  moving_avg_5  moving_avg_30  moving_avg_365   close
Date                                                                    ...

1989-01-04  2153.75  2163.21  2144.64  2168.39  2127.14  17310000.0    2165.000  ...     -0.011
   0.020       0.056        0.001          0.001            0.000   2177.68
1989-01-05  2184.29  2153.75  2177.68  2183.39  2146.61  15710000.0    2168.000  ...      0.007
   0.041       0.069       -0.002          0.001            0.000   2190.54
1989-01-06  2195.89  2184.29  2190.54  2205.18  2173.04  20310000.0    2172.822  ...      0.011
  ·0.031       0.068        0.001          0.002            0.000   2194.29
1989-01-09  2194.82  2195.89  2194.29  2213.75  2182.32  16500000.0    2175.144  ...      0.005
   0.021       0.148        0.002          0.001            0.000   2199.46
1989-01-10  2205.36  2194.82  2199.46  2209.11  2185.00  18420000.0    2181.322  ...      0.014
   0.021       0.131        0.001          0.001            0.001   2193.21

[5 rows x 38 columns]
```

Since all features and driving factors are ready, we should now focus on regression algorithms that estimate the continuous target variables based on these predictive features.

Estimating with linear regression

The first regression model that comes to our mind is **linear regression**. Does it mean fitting data points using a linear function, as its name implies? Let's explore it.

How does linear regression work?

In simple terms, linear regression tries to fit as many of the data points as possible with a line in two-dimensional space or a plane in three-dimensional space, and so on. It explores the linear relationship between observations and targets and the relationship is represented in a linear equation or weighted sum function. Given a data sample x with n features, $x_1, x_2, ..., x_n$ (x represents a feature vector and $x = (x_1, x_2, ..., x_n)$), and **weights** (also called **coefficients**) of the linear regression model w (w represents a vector $(w_1, w_2, ..., w_n)$), the target y is expressed as follows:

$$y = w_1 x_1 + w_2 x_2 + ... + w_n x_n = w^T x$$

Also, sometimes, the linear regression model comes with an **intercept** (also called **bias**) w_0, so the preceding linear relationship becomes as follows:

$$y = w_0 + w_1 x_1 + w_2 x_2 + ... + w_n x_n = w^T x$$

Doesn't it look familiar? The **logistic regression** algorithm we learned in `Chapter 7`, *Predicting Online Ads Click-through with Logistic Regression*, is just an addition of logistic transformation on top of the linear regression, which maps the continuous weighted sum to *0* (negative) or *1* (positive) class. Similarly, a linear regression model, or specifically, its weight vector w is learned from the training data, with the goal of minimizing the estimation error defined as **mean squared error** (MSE), which measures the average of squares of difference between the truth and prediction. Give m training samples, $(x^{(1)}, y^{(1)})$, $(x^{(2)}, y^{(2)}), ... (x^{(i)}, y^{(i)})..., (x^{(m)}, y^{(m)})$, the cost function $J(w)$ regarding the weights to be optimized is expressed as follows:

$$J(w) = \frac{1}{m} \sum_{i=1}^{m} \frac{1}{2} \left(\hat{y}(x^{(i)}) - y^{(i)} \right)^2$$

Here, $\hat{y}(x^{(i)}) = w^T x^{(i)}$ is the prediction.

Again, we can obtain the optimal w so that $J(w)$ is minimized using gradient descent. The first-order derivative, the gradient Δw, is derived as follows:

$$\Delta w = \frac{1}{m} \sum_{i=1}^{m} \left(-y^{(i)} + \hat{y}(x^{(i)}) \right) x^{(i)}$$

Combined with the gradient and learning rate η, the weight vector w can be updated in each step as follows:

$$w := w + \eta \frac{1}{m} \sum_{i=1}^{m} \left(y^{(i)} - \hat{y}(x^{(i)}) \right) x^{(i)}$$

After a substantial number of iterations, the learned w is then used to predict a new sample x' as follows:

$$y' = w^T x'$$

Implementing linear regression

With a thorough understanding of the gradient descent based linear regression, we'll now implement it from scratch.

We start with defining the function computing the prediction $\hat{y}(x)$ with the current weights:

```
>>> def compute_prediction(X, weights):
...     """ Compute the prediction y_hat based on current weights
...     Args:
...         X (numpy.ndarray)
...         weights (numpy.ndarray)
...     Returns:
...         numpy.ndarray, y_hat of X under weights
...     """
...     predictions = np.dot(X, weights)
...     return predictions
```

Then, we can continue with the function updating the weight w by one step in a gradient descent manner, as follows:

```
>>> def update_weights_gd(X_train, y_train, weights, learning_rate):
...         """ Update weights by one step
...         Args:
...             X_train, y_train (numpy.ndarray, training data set)
...             weights (numpy.ndarray)
...             learning_rate (float)
...         Returns:
...             numpy.ndarray, updated weights
...         """
...         predictions = compute_prediction(X_train, weights)
...         weights_delta = np.dot(X_train.T, y_train - predictions)
...         m = y_train.shape[0]
...         weights += learning_rate / float(m) * weights_delta
...         return weights
```

Then we add the function that calculates the cost $J(w)$ as well:

```
>>> def compute_cost(X, y, weights):
...         """ Compute the cost J(w)
...         Args:
...             X, y (numpy.ndarray, data set)
...             weights (numpy.ndarray)
...         Returns:
...             float
...         """
...         predictions = compute_prediction(X, weights)
...         cost = np.mean((predictions - y) ** 2 / 2.0)
...         return cost
```

Now, put all functions together with a model training function by performing the following tasks:

1. Update the weight vector in each iteration
2. Print out the current cost for every 100 (or can be any) iterations to ensure cost is decreasing and things are on the right track

Let's see how it's done by executing the following commands:

```
>>> def train_linear_regression(X_train, y_train, max_iter,
                                learning_rate, fit_intercept=False):
...     """ Train a linear regression model with gradient descent
...     Args:
...         X_train, y_train (numpy.ndarray, training data set)
...         max_iter (int, number of iterations)
...         learning_rate (float)
...         fit_intercept (bool, with an intercept w0 or not)
...     Returns:
...         numpy.ndarray, learned weights
...     """
...     if fit_intercept:
...         intercept = np.ones((X_train.shape[0], 1))
...         X_train = np.hstack((intercept, X_train))
...     weights = np.zeros(X_train.shape[1])
...     for iteration in range(max_iter):
...         weights = update_weights_gd(
                        X_train, y_train, weights, learning_rate)
...         # Check the cost for every 100 (for example) iterations
...         if iteration % 100 == 0:
...             print(compute_cost(X_train, y_train, weights))
...     return weights
```

Finally, predict the results of new input values using the trained model as follows:

```
>>> def predict(X, weights):
...     if X.shape[1] == weights.shape[0] - 1:
...         intercept = np.ones((X.shape[0], 1))
...         X = np.hstack((intercept, X))
...     return compute_prediction(X, weights)
```

Implementing linear regression is very similar to logistic regression as we just saw. Let's examine it with a small example:

```
>>> X_train = np.array([[6], [2], [3], [4], [1],
                        [5], [2], [6], [4], [7]])
>>> y_train = np.array([5.5, 1.6, 2.2, 3.7, 0.8,
                        5.2, 1.5, 5.3, 4.4, 6.8])
```

Train a linear regression model by 100 iterations, at a learning rate of 0.01 based on intercept-included weights:

```
>>> weights = train_linear_regression(X_train, y_train,
            max_iter=100, learning_rate=0.01, fit_intercept=True)
```

Check the model's performance on new samples as follows:

```
>>> X_test = np.array([[1.3], [3.5], [5.2], [2.8]])
>>> predictions = predict(X_test, weights)
>>> import matplotlib.pyplot as plt
>>> plt.scatter(X_train[:, 0], y_train, marker='o', c='b')
>>> plt.scatter(X_test[:, 0], predictions, marker='*', c='k')
>>> plt.xlabel('x')
>>> plt.ylabel('y')
>>> plt.show()
```

Refer to the following screenshot for the end result:

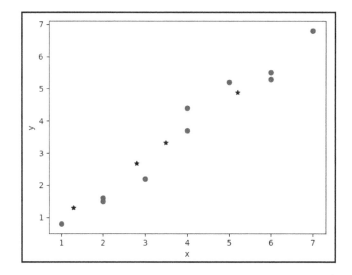

The model we trained correctly predicts new samples (depicted by the stars).

Let's try it on another dataset, the diabetes dataset from scikit-learn:

```
>>> from sklearn import datasets
>>> diabetes = datasets.load_diabetes()
>>> print(diabetes.data.shape)
(442, 10)
>>> num_test = 30
>>> X_train = diabetes.data[:-num_test, :]
>>> y_train = diabetes.target[:-num_test]
```

Train a linear regression model by `5000` iterations, at a learning rate of `1` based on intercept-included weights (the cost is displayed every 500 iterations):

```
>>> weights = train_linear_regression(X_train, y_train,
                  max_iter=5000, learning_rate=1, fit_intercept=True)
2960.1229915
1539.55080927
1487.02495658
1480.27644342
1479.01567047
1478.57496091
1478.29639883
1478.06282572
1477.84756968
1477.64304737
>>> X_test = diabetes.data[-num_test:, :]
>>> y_test = diabetes.target[-num_test:]
>>> predictions = predict(X_test, weights)
>>> print(predictions)
[ 232.22305668 123.87481969 166.12805033 170.23901231
  228.12868839 154.95746522 101.09058779 87.33631249
  143.68332296 190.29353122 198.00676871 149.63039042
  169.56066651 109.01983998 161.98477191 133.00870377
  260.1831988 101.52551082 115.76677836 120.7338523
  219.62602446 62.21227353 136.29989073 122.27908721
  55.14492975 191.50339388 105.685612 126.25915035
  208.99755875 47.66517424]
>>> print(y_test)
[ 261. 113. 131. 174. 257. 55. 84. 42. 146. 212. 233.
  91. 111. 152. 120. 67. 310. 94. 183. 66. 173. 72.
  49. 64. 48. 178. 104. 132. 220. 57.]
```

The estimate is pretty close to the ground truth.

So far, we have been using gradient descent in weight optimization but, the same as logistic regression, linear regression is also open to **stochastic gradient descent** (SGD). To realize it, we can simply replace the `update_weights_gd` function with `update_weights_sgd` we created in Chapter 7, *Predicting Online Ads Click-through with Logistic Regression*.

We can also directly use the SGD-based regression algorithm, `SGDRegressor`, from scikit-learn:

```
>>> from sklearn.linear_model import SGDRegressor
>>> regressor = SGDRegressor(loss='squared_loss', penalty='l2',
    alpha=0.0001, learning_rate='constant', eta0=0.01, n_iter=1000)
```

Here `'squared_loss'` for the `loss` parameter indicates the cost function is MSE; `penalty` is the regularization term and it can be `None`, `l1`, or `l2`, which is similar to `SGDClassifier` in `Chapter 7`, *Predicting Online Ads Click-through with Logistic Regression*, in order to reduce overfitting; `n_iter` is the number of iterations; and the remaining two parameters mean the learning rate is `0.01` and unchanged during the course of training. Train the model and output prediction on the testing set as follows:

```
>>> regressor.fit(X_train, y_train)
>>> predictions = regressor.predict(X_test)
>>> print(predictions)
[ 231.03333725 124.94418254 168.20510142 170.7056729
  226.52019503 154.85011364 103.82492496 89.376184
  145.69862538 190.89270871 197.0996725 151.46200981
  170.12673917 108.50103463 164.35815989 134.10002755
  259.29203744 103.09764563 117.6254098 122.24330421
  219.0996765 65.40121381 137.46448687 123.25363156
  57.34965405 191.0600674 109.21594994 128.29546226
  207.09606669 51.10475455]
```

Of course, we won't miss its implementation in TensorFlow. First, we import TensorFlow and specify the parameters of the model, including `1000` iterations during the training process and a `0.5` learning rate:

```
>>> import tensorflow as tf
>>> n_features = int(X_train.shape[1])
>>> learning_rate = 0.5
>>> n_iter = 1000
```

Then, we define `placeholder` and `Variable`, including the weights and bias of the model as follows:

```
>>> x = tf.placeholder(tf.float32, shape=[None, n_features])
>>> y = tf.placeholder(tf.float32, shape=[None])
>>> W = tf.Variable(tf.ones([n_features, 1]))
>>> b = tf.Variable(tf.zeros([1]))
```

Construct the model by computing the prediction as follows:

```
>>> pred = tf.add(tf.matmul(x, W), b)[:, 0]
```

After assembling the graph for the model, we define the loss function, the MSE, and a gradient descent optimizer that searches for the best coefficients by minimizing the loss:

```
>>> cost = tf.losses.mean_squared_error(labels=y, predictions=pred)
>>> optimizer =
    tf.train.GradientDescentOptimizer(learning_rate).minimize(cost)
```

Now we can initialize the variables and start a TensorFlow session:

```
>>> init_vars = tf.initialize_all_variables()
>>> sess = tf.Session()
>>> sess.run(init_vars)
```

Finally, we start the training process and print out loss after every 100 iterations as follows:

```
>>> for i in range(1, n_iter+1):
...     _, c = sess.run([optimizer, cost],
                        feed_dict={x: X_train, y: y_train})
...     if i % 100 == 0:
...         print('Iteration %i, training loss: %f' % (i, c))
Iteration 100, training loss: 3984.505859
Iteration 200, training loss: 3465.406494
Iteration 300, training loss: 3258.358398
Iteration 400, training loss: 3147.374023
Iteration 500, training loss: 3080.261475
Iteration 600, training loss: 3037.964111
Iteration 700, training loss: 3010.845947
Iteration 800, training loss: 2993.270752
Iteration 900, training loss: 2981.771240
Iteration 1000, training loss: 2974.175049
Apply the trained model on the testing set:
>>> predictions = sess.run(pred, feed_dict={x: X_test})
>>> print(predictions)
[230.2237 124.89581 170.9626 170.43433 224.11993 153.07018
 105.98048 90.66377 149.22597 191.74197 194.04721 153.0992
 170.85931 104.24113 169.2757 135.45589 260.55713 102.38674
 118.585556 123.41965 219.20732 67.479996 138.3001 122.41016
  57.012245 189.88608 114.48331 131.13383 202.2418 53.08335 ]
```

Estimating with decision tree regression

After linear regression, the next regression algorithm we'll be learning is **decision tree regression**, which is also called **regression tree**. It is easy to understand regression trees by comparing it with its sibling, the classification trees, which you are familiar with.

Transitioning from classification trees to regression trees

In classification, a decision tree is constructed by recursive binary splitting and growing each node into left and right children. In each partition, it greedily searches for the most significant combination of feature and its value as the optimal splitting point. The quality of separation is measured by the weighted purity of labels of two resulting children, specifically via metric **Gini Impurity** or **Information Gain**. In regression, the tree construction process is almost identical to the classification one, with only two differences due to the fact that the target becomes continuous:

- The quality of splitting point is now measured by the **weighted mean squared error** (**MSE**) of two children; the MSE of a child is equivalent to the variance of all target values, and the smaller the weighted MSE, the better the split.
- The **average** value of targets in a terminal node becomes the leaf value, instead of the majority of labels in the classification tree.

To make sure we understand regression tree, let's work on a small example of house price estimation:

Type	Number of bedrooms	Price (thousand)
Semi	3	600
Detached	2	700
Detached	3	800
Semi	2	400
Semi	4	700

We first define the MSE and weighted MSE computation functions as they'll be used in our calculation:

```
>>> def mse(targets):
...     # When the set is empty
...     if targets.size == 0:
...         return 0
...     return np.var(targets)
>>> def weighted_mse(groups):
...     """ Calculate weighted MSE of children after a split
...     Args:
...         groups (list of children, and a child consists a list
...             of targets)
```

```
...         Returns:
...             float, weighted impurity
...         """
...         total = sum(len(group) for group in groups)
...         weighted_sum = 0.0
...         for group in groups:
...             weighted_sum += len(group) / float(total) * mse(group)
...         return weighted_sum
```

Test things out by executing the following commands:

```
>>> print('{0:.4f}'.format(mse(np.array([1, 2, 3]))))
0.6667
>>> print('{0:.4f}'.format(weighted_mse([np.array([1, 2, 3]),
                                         np.array([1, 2])])))
0.5000
```

To build the house price regression tree, we first exhaust all possible pairs of feature and value and compute the corresponding MSE:

$$MSE(type, \textit{semi}) = \texttt{weighted\_mse}([[600, 400, 700], [700, 800]]) = 10333$$
$$MSE(bedroom, 2) = \texttt{weighted\_mse}([[700, 400], [600, 800, 700]]) = 13000$$
$$MSE(bedroom, 3) = \texttt{weighted\_mse}([[600, 800], [700, 400, 700]]) = 16000$$
$$MSE(bedroom, 4) = \texttt{weighted\_mse}([[700], [600, 700, 800, 400]]) = 17500$$

The lowest MSE is achieved with the `type, semi` pair, and the root node is then formed by such a splitting point:

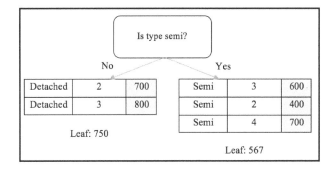

If we are satisfied with a one level deep regression tree, we can stop here by assigning both branches as leaf nodes with value as the average of targets of the samples included. Alternatively, we can go further down the road constructing the second level from the right branch (the left branch can't be further split):

$$MSE(bedroom, 2) = weighted\_mse([[], [600, 400, 700]]) = 15556$$
$$MSE(bedroom, 3) = weighted\_mse([[400], [600, 700]]) = 1667$$
$$MSE(bedroom, 4) = weighted\_mse([[400, 600], [700]]) = 6667$$

With the second splitting point specified by the `bedroom, 3` pair with the least MSE, our tree becomes as shown in the following diagram:

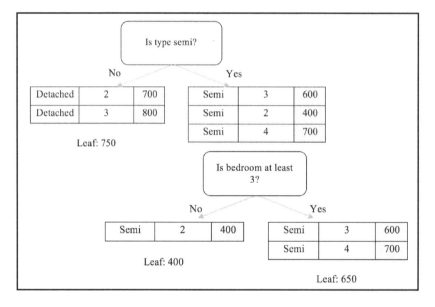

We can finish up the tree by assigning average values to both leaf nodes.

Implementing decision tree regression

It's now time for coding after we're clear about the regression tree construction process.

The node splitting utility function we define as follow is identical to what we had in `Chapter 6`, *Predicting Online Ads Click-through with Tree-Based Algorithms*, which separates samples in a node into left and right branches based on a pair of feature and value:

```
>>> def split_node(X, y, index, value):
...     """ Split data set X, y based on a feature and a value
```

```
...        Args:
...            X, y (numpy.ndarray, data set)
...            index (int, index of the feature used for splitting)
...            value (value of the feature used for splitting)
...        Returns:
...            list, list: left and right child, a child is in the
...                            format of [X, y]
...        """
...        x_index = X[:, index]
...        # if this feature is numerical
...        if type(X[0, index]) in [int, float]:
...            mask = x_index >= value
...        # if this feature is categorical
...        else:
...        mask = x_index == value
...        # split into left and right child
...        left = [X[~mask, :], y[~mask]]
...        right = [X[mask, :], y[mask]]
...        return left, right
```

Next, we define the greedy search function trying out all possible splits and returning the one with the least weighted MSE:

```
>>> def get_best_split(X, y):
...        """ Obtain the best splitting point and resulting children
...            for the data set X, y
...        Args:
...            X, y (numpy.ndarray, data set)
...            criterion (gini or entropy)
...        Returns:
...            dict {index: index of the feature, value: feature
...                value, children: left and right children}
...        """
...        best_index, best_value, best_score, children =
...                                    None, None, 1e10, None
...        for index in range(len(X[0])):
...            for value in np.sort(np.unique(X[:, index])):
...                groups = split_node(X, y, index, value)
...                impurity = weighted_mse([groups[0][1],
...                                        groups[1][1]])
...                if impurity < best_score:
...                    best_index, best_value, best_score, children =
...                                    index, value, impurity, groups
...        return {'index': best_index, 'value': best_value,
...                                    'children': children}
```

The preceding selection and splitting process occurs in a recursive manner on each of subsequent children. When a stopping criterion is met, the process at a node stops, and the mean value of the sample `targets` will be assigned to this terminal node:

```
>>> def get_leaf(targets):
...     # Obtain the leaf as the mean of the targets
...     return np.mean(targets)
```

And finally, the recursive function split that links all of these preceding together by checking whether any of stopping criteria is met and assigning the leaf node if so or proceeding with further separation otherwise:

```
>>> def split(node, max_depth, min_size, depth):
...     """ Split children of a node to construct new nodes or
...         assign them terminals
...     Args:
...         node (dict, with children info)
...         max_depth (int, maximal depth of the tree)
...         min_size (int, minimal samples required to further
...                   split a child)
...         depth (int, current depth of the node)
...     """
...     left, right = node['children']
...     del (node['children'])
...     if left[1].size == 0:
...         node['right'] = get_leaf(right[1])
...         return
...     if right[1].size == 0:
...         node['left'] = get_leaf(left[1])
...         return
...     # Check if the current depth exceeds the maximal depth
...     if depth >= max_depth:
...         node['left'], node['right'] =
...                     get_leaf(left[1]), get_leaf(right[1])
...         return
...     # Check if the left child has enough samples
...     if left[1].size <= min_size:
...         node['left'] = get_leaf(left[1])
...     else:
...         # It has enough samples, we further split it
...         result = get_best_split(left[0], left[1])
...         result_left, result_right = result['children']
...         if result_left[1].size == 0:
...             node['left'] = get_leaf(result_right[1])
...         elif result_right[1].size == 0:
...             node['left'] = get_leaf(result_left[1])
...         else:
```

```
...                 node['left'] = result
...                 split(node['left'], max_depth, min_size,
                                                    depth + 1)
...         # Check if the right child has enough samples
...         if right[1].size <= min_size:
...             node['right'] = get_leaf(right[1])
...         else:
...             # It has enough samples, we further split it
...             result = get_best_split(right[0], right[1])
...             result_left, result_right = result['children']
...             if result_left[1].size == 0:
...                 node['right'] = get_leaf(result_right[1])
...             elif result_right[1].size == 0:
...                 node['right'] = get_leaf(result_left[1])
...             else:
...                 node['right'] = result
...                 split(node['right'], max_depth, min_size,
                                                    depth + 1)
```

Finally, the entry point of the regression tree construction is as follows:

```
>>> def train_tree(X_train, y_train, max_depth, min_size):
...     """ Construction of a tree starts here
...     Args:
...         X_train, y_train (list, list, training data)
...         max_depth (int, maximal depth of the tree)
...         min_size (int, minimal samples required to further
...                     split a child)
...     """
...     root = get_best_split(X_train, y_train)
...     split(root, max_depth, min_size, 1)
...     return root
```

Now, let's test it with the preceding hand-calculated example:

```
>>> X_train = np.array([['semi', 3],
...                     ['detached', 2],
...                     ['detached', 3],
...                     ['semi', 2],
...                     ['semi', 4]], dtype=object)
>>> y_train = np.array([600, 700, 800, 400, 700])
>>> tree = train_tree(X_train, y_train, 2, 2)
```

To verify the trained tree is identical to what we constructed by hand, we write a function displaying the tree:

```
>>> CONDITION = {'numerical': {'yes': '>=', 'no': '<'},
...              'categorical': {'yes': 'is', 'no': 'is not'}}
```

```
>>> def visualize_tree(node, depth=0):
...     if isinstance(node, dict):
...         if type(node['value']) in [int, float]:
...             condition = CONDITION['numerical']
...         else:
...             condition = CONDITION['categorical']
...         print('{}|- X{} {} {}'.format(depth * '  ',
...             node['index'] + 1, condition['no'], node['value']))
...         if 'left' in node:
...             visualize_tree(node['left'], depth + 1)
...         print('{}|- X{} {} {}'.format(depth * '  ',
...             node['index'] + 1, condition['yes'], node['value']))
...         if 'right' in node:
...             visualize_tree(node['right'], depth + 1)
...     else:
...         print('{}[{}]'.format(depth * '  ', node))

>>> visualize_tree(tree)
|- X1 is not detached
  |- X2 < 3
    [400.0]
  |- X2 >= 3
    [650.0]
|- X1 is detached
  [750.0]
```

Now that we have a better understanding of regression tree by realizing it from scratch, we can directly use the DecisionTreeRegressor package from scikit-learn. Apply it on an example of predicting Boston house prices as follows:

```
>>> boston = datasets.load_boston()
>>> num_test = 10 # the last 10 samples as testing set
>>> X_train = boston.data[:-num_test, :]
>>> y_train = boston.target[:-num_test]
>>> X_test = boston.data[-num_test:, :]
>>> y_test = boston.target[-num_test:]
>>> from sklearn.tree import DecisionTreeRegressor
>>> regressor = DecisionTreeRegressor(max_depth=10,
                                    min_samples_split=3)
>>> regressor.fit(X_train, y_train)
>>> predictions = regressor.predict(X_test)
>>> print(predictions)
[12.7 20.9 20.9 20.2 20.9 30.8
 20.73076923 24.3 28.2 20.73076923]
```

Compare predictions with the ground truth as follows:

```
>>> print(y_test)
[ 19.7  18.3 21.2  17.5 16.8 22.4  20.6 23.9 22. 11.9]
```

Implementing regression forest

As seen in `Chapter 6`, *Predicting Online Ads Click-through with Tree-Based Algorithms*, we introduced **random forest** as an ensemble learning method by combining multiple decision trees that are separately trained and randomly subsampling training features in each node of a tree. In classification, a random forest makes a final decision by majority vote of all tree decisions. Applied to regression, a random forest regression model (also called **regression forest**) assigns the average of regression results from all decision trees to the final decision.

Here, we'll use the regression forest package, `RandomForestRegressor`, from scikit-learn and deploy it to our Boston house price prediction example:

```
>>> from sklearn.ensemble import RandomForestRegressor
>>> regressor = RandomForestRegressor(n_estimators=100,
                          max_depth=10, min_samples_split=3)
>>> regressor.fit(X_train, y_train)
>>> predictions = regressor.predict(X_test)
>>> print(predictions)
[ 19.34404351 20.93928947 21.66535354 19.99581433 20.873871
   25.52030056 21.33196685 28.34961905 27.54088571 21.32508585]
```

As a bonus section, we implement regression forest with TensorFlow. It is actually quite similar to the implementation of random forest in `Chapter 6`, *Predicting Online Ads Click-through with Tree-Based Algorithms*. First, we import the necessary modules as follows:

```
>>> import tensorflow as tf
>>> from tensorflow.contrib.tensor_forest.python import tensor_forest
>>> from tensorflow.python.ops import resources
```

And we specify the parameters of the model, including 20 iterations during training process, 10 trees in total, and 30000 maximal splitting nodes:

```
>>> n_iter = 20
>>> n_features = int(X_train.shape[1])
>>> n_trees = 10
>>> max_nodes = 30000
```

Next, we create placeholders and build the TensorFlow graph:

```
>>> x = tf.placeholder(tf.float32, shape=[None, n_features])
>>> y = tf.placeholder(tf.float32, shape=[None])
>>> hparams = tensor_forest.ForestHParams(num_classes=1,
                        regression=True, num_features=n_features,
                        num_trees=n_trees, max_nodes=max_nodes,
                        split_after_samples=30).fill()
>>> forest_graph = tensor_forest.RandomForestGraphs(hparams)
```

Note we need to set `num_classes` to `1` and `regression` to `True` as the forest is used for regression.

After defining the graph for the regression forest model, we specify the training graph and loss and the MSE:

```
>>> train_op = forest_graph.training_graph(x, y)
>>> loss_op = forest_graph.training_loss(x, y)
>>> infer_op, _, _ = forest_graph.inference_graph(x)
>>> cost = tf.losses.mean_squared_error(labels=y, predictions=infer_op[:,
0])
```

We then initialize the variables and start a TensorFlow session:

```
>>> init_vars = tf.group(tf.global_variables_initializer(),
            tf.local_variables_initializer(),
        resources.initialize_resources(resources.shared_resources()))
>>> sess = tf.Session()
>>> sess.run(init_vars)
```

Finally, we start the training process and conduct a performance check-up for each iteration:

```
>>> for i in range(1, n_iter + 1):
...         _, c = sess.run([train_op, cost], feed_dict={x: X_train, y:
y_train})
...         print('Iteration %i, training loss: %f' % (i, c))
Iteration 1, training loss: 596.255005
Iteration 2, training loss: 51.917843
Iteration 3, training loss: 35.395966
Iteration 4, training loss: 28.848433
Iteration 5, training loss: 22.499760
Iteration 6, training loss: 18.685938
Iteration 7, training loss: 16.956488
Iteration 8, training loss: 14.832330
Iteration 9, training loss: 13.048509
Iteration 10, training loss: 12.084823
Iteration 11, training loss: 11.044588
```

```
Iteration 12, training loss: 10.433226
Iteration 13, training loss: 9.818905
Iteration 14, training loss: 8.900123
Iteration 15, training loss: 7.952868
Iteration 16, training loss: 7.417612
Iteration 17, training loss: 6.849032
Iteration 18, training loss: 6.213216
Iteration 19, training loss: 5.869020
Iteration 20, training loss: 5.467315
```

After 20 iterations, we apply the trained model on the testing set as follows:

```
>>> pred = sess.run(infer_op, feed_dict={x: X_test})[:, 0]
>>> print(pred)
[15.446515 20.10433 21.38516 19.37373 19.593092 21.932205 22.259298
24.194878 24.095112 22.541391]
```

Estimating with support vector regression

The third regression algorithm that we want to explore is **support vector regression** (**SVR**). As the name implies, SVR is part of the support vector family and sibling of the **support vector machine** (**SVM**) for classification (or we can just call it **SVC**) we learned in Chapter 5, *Classifying Newsgroup Topic with Support Vector Machine*.

To recap, SVC seeks an optimal hyperplane that best segregates observations from different classes. Suppose a hyperplane is determined by a slope vector w and intercept b, the optimal hyperplane is picked so that the distance (which can be expressed as $\frac{1}{\|w\|}$) from its nearest points in each of segregated spaces to the hyperplane itself is maximized. Such optimal w and b can be learned and solved by the following optimization problem:

- Minimizing $\|w\|$
- Subject to $wx^{(i)}+b \geq 1$ *if* $y^{(i)}=1$ and $wx^{(i)}+b \leq 1$ *if* $y^{(i)}=-1$, given a training set of $(x^{(1)},y^{(1)})$, $(x^{(2)},y^{(2)}),\dots (x^{(i)},y^{(i)})\dots, (x^{(m)},y^{(m)})$.

In SVR, our goal is to find a hyperplane (defined by a slope vector w and intercept b) so that two hyperplanes, $wx+b=-\varepsilon$ and $wx+b=\varepsilon$, that are a distance away from itself covers most training data. In other words, most of data points are bounded in the ε bands of the optimal hyperplane. And at the same time, the optimal hyperplane is as flat as possible, which means $\|w\|$ is as small as possible, as shown in the following diagram:

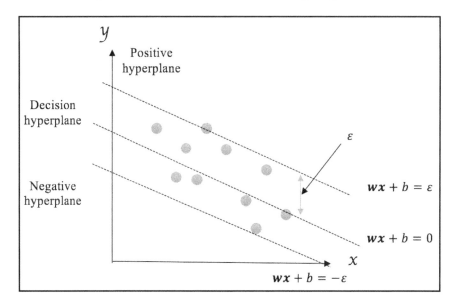

This translates into deriving the optimal w and b by solving the following optimization problem:

- Minimizing $\|w\|$
- Subject to $|y^{(i)}-(wx^{(i)}+b)| \leq \varepsilon$, given a training set of $(x^{(1)},y^{(1)})$, $(x^{(2)},y^{(2)})$,... $(x^{(i)},y^{(i)})$..., $(x^{(m)},y^{(m)})$

Implementing SVR

Again to solve the preceding optimization problem, we need to resort to quadratic programming techniques, which are beyond the scope of our learning journey. Therefore, we won't cover the computation methods in detail and will implement the regression algorithm using the SVR package from scikit-learn.

Important techniques of SVC, such as penalty as a trade off between bias and variance, kernel (RBF, for example) handling linear non-separation, are transferable to SVR. The SVR package from scikit-learn also supports these techniques.

Let's solve the previous house price prediction problem with SVR this time:

```
>>> from sklearn.svm import SVR
>>> regressor = SVR(C=0.1, epsilon=0.02, kernel='linear')
>>> regressor.fit(X_train, y_train)
>>> predictions = regressor.predict(X_test)
>>> print(predictions)
[ 14.59908201 19.32323741 21.16739294 18.53822876 20.1960847
  23.74076575 22.65713954 26.98366295 25.75795682 22.69805145]
```

Estimating with neural networks

Here comes our fourth model, **artificial neural networks** (**ANNs**) or more often we just call them **neural networks**. The neural network is probably the most frequently mentioned model in the media. It has been (falsely) considered equivalent to machine learning or artificial intelligence by the general public. Regardless, it is one of the most important machine learning models and has been rapidly evolving along with the revolution of **deep learning** (**DL**). Let's first understand how neural networks works.

Demystifying neural networks

A simple neural network is composed of three layers, the **Input layer**, **Hidden layer**, and **Output layer** as shown in the following diagram:

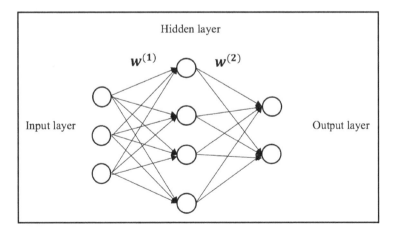

A layer is a conceptual collection of **nodes** (also called **units**), which simulate neurons in a biological brain. The input layer represents the input features x and each node is a predictive feature x. The output layer represents the target variable(s). In binary classification, the output layer contains only one node, whose value is the probability of the positive class. In multiclass classification, the output layer consists of n nodes where n is the number of possible classes and the value of each node is the probability of predicting that class. In regression, the output layer contains only one node the value of which is the prediction result. The hidden layer can be considered a composition of latent information extracted from the previous layer. There can be more than one hidden layer. Learning with a neural network with two or more hidden layers is called DL. We will focus on one hidden layer to begin with.

Two adjacent layers are connected by conceptual edges, sort of like the synapses in a biological brain, which transmit signal from one neuron in a layer to another neuron in the next layer. The **edges** are parameterized by the weights W of the model. For example, $W^{(1)}$ in the preceding diagram connects the input and hidden layers and $W^{(2)}$ connects the hidden and output layers.

In a standard neural network, data are conveyed only from the input layer to the output layer, through hidden layer(s). Hence, this kind of network is called **feed-forward** neural network. Basically, logistic regression is a feed-forward neural network with no hidden layer where the output layer connects directly with the input. Neural networks with one or more hidden layer between the input and output layer should be able to learn more about the the underneath relationship between the input data and target.

Suppose input x is of n dimension and the hidden layer is composed of H hidden units, the weight matrix $W^{(1)}$ connecting the input and hidden layer is of size n by H where each column $w_h^{(1)}$ represents the coefficients associating the input with the h-th hidden unit. The output (also called **activation**) of the hidden layer can be expressed mathematically as follows:

$$a^{(2)} = f(z^{(2)}) = f(W^{(1)}x)$$

Here *f(z)* is an **activation function**. As its name implies, the activation function checks how activated each neuron is simulating the way our brains work. Typical activation functions include the logistic function (more often called the **sigmoid** function in neural networks) and the **tanh** function, which is considered a re-scaled version of logistic function, as well as **ReLU** (short for **Rectified Linear Unit**), which is often used in DL:

$$sigmoid(z) = \frac{1}{1 + e^{-z}}$$

$$tanh(z) = \frac{e^z - e^{-z}}{e^z + e^{-z}} = \frac{2}{1 + e^{-2z}} - 1$$

$$relu(z) = z^+ = max(0, z)$$

We plot the following three activation functions as follows:

- The **logistic** (**sigmoid**) function plot is as follows:

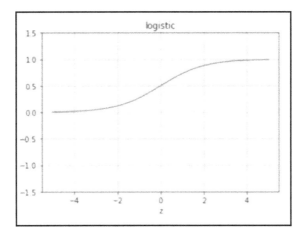

- The **tanh** function plot is as follows:

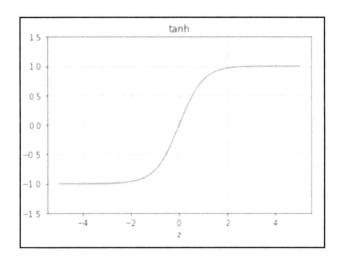

- The **relu** function plot is as follows:

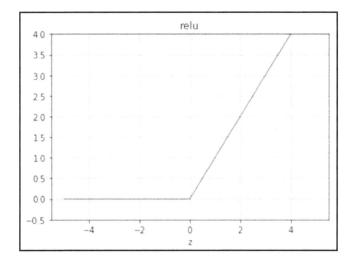

As for the output layer, let's assume there's one output unit (regression or binary classification) and the weight matrix $W^{(2)}$ connecting the hidden layer to the output layer is of the size H by 1. In regression, the output can be expressed mathematically as follows (for consistency, we here denote it as $a^{(3)}$ instead of y):

$$a^{(3)} = f(z^{(3)}) = W^{(2)} a^{(2)}$$

So, how can we obtain the optimal weights $W = \{W^{(1)}, W^{(2)}\}$ of the model? Similar to logistic regression, we learn all weights using gradient descent with the goal of minimizing the MSE cost $J(W)$. The difference is that the gradients ΔW are computed through **backpropagation**. In a single-layer network, the detailed steps of backpropagation are as follows:

1. We travel through the network from the input to output and compute the output values $a^{(2)}$ of the hidden layer as well as the output layer $a^{(3)}$. This is the feedforward step.

2. For the last layer, we calculate the derivative of the cost function with regards to the input to the output layer:

$$\delta^{(3)} = \frac{\delta}{\delta z^{(3)}} J(W) = -(y - a^{(3)}) \cdot f'(z^{(3)}) = a^{(3)} - y$$

3. For the hidden layer, we compute the derivative of the cost function with regards to the input to the hidden layer:

$$\delta^{(2)} = \frac{\delta}{\delta z^{(2)}} J(W) = \frac{\delta z^{(3)}}{\delta z^{(2)}} \frac{\delta}{\delta z^{(3)}} J(W) = ((W^{(2)})^T \delta^{(3)}) \cdot f'(z^{(2)})$$

4. We compute the gradients by applying the **chain rule**:

$$\Delta W^{(2)} = \frac{\partial J(W)}{\partial z_k^{(3)}} \frac{\partial z_k^{(3)}}{\partial W^{(2)}} = \delta^{(3)} (a^{(2)})^T$$

$$\Delta W^{(1)} = \frac{\partial J(W)}{\partial z_k^{(2)}} \frac{\partial z_k^{(2)}}{\partial W^{(1)}} = \delta^{(2)} (x)^T$$

5. We update the weights with the computed gradients and learning rate *a*:

$$W^{(1)} := W^{(1)} - \frac{1}{m}\alpha\Delta W^{(1)}$$

$$W^{(2)} := W^{(2)} - \frac{1}{m}\alpha\Delta W^{(2)}$$

6. We repeatedly update all weights by taking these steps with the latest weights until the cost function converges or it goes through enough iterations.

This might not be easy to digest at first glance, so let's implement it from scratch, which will help you to understand neural networks better.

Implementing neural networks

We herein use sigmoid as the activation function as an example. We first need to define the `sigmoid` function and its derivative function:

```
>>> def sigmoid(z):
...        return 1.0 / (1 + np.exp(-z))
>>> def sigmoid_derivative(z):
...        return sigmoid(z) * (1.0 - sigmoid(z))
```

You can derive the derivative yourselves if you want to verify it.

We then define the training function, which takes in the training dataset, the number of units in the hidden layer (we only use one hidden layer as an example), and the number of iterations:

```
>>> def train(X, y, n_hidden, learning_rate, n_iter):
...        m, n_input = X.shape
...        W1 = np.random.randn(n_input, n_hidden)
...        b1 = np.zeros((1, n_hidden))
...        W2 = np.random.randn(n_hidden, 1)
...        b2 = np.zeros((1, 1))
...        for i in range(1, n_iter+1):
...            Z2 = np.matmul(X, W1) + b1
...            A2 = sigmoid(Z2)
...            Z3 = np.matmul(A2, W2) + b2
...            A3 = Z3
...            dZ3 = A3 - y
...            dW2 = np.matmul(A2.T, dZ3)
...            db2 = np.sum(dZ3, axis=0, keepdims=True)
...            dZ2 = np.matmul(dZ3, W2.T) * sigmoid_derivative(Z2)
```

```
...            dW1 = np.matmul(X.T, dZ2)
...            db1 = np.sum(dZ2, axis=0)
...            W2 = W2 - learning_rate * dW2 / m
...            b2 = b2 - learning_rate * db2 / m
...            W1 = W1 - learning_rate * dW1 / m
...            b1 = b1 - learning_rate * db1 / m
...            if i % 100 == 0:
...                cost = np.mean((y - A3) ** 2)
...                print('Iteration %i, training loss: %f' % (i, cost))
...        model = {'W1': W1, 'b1': b1, 'W2': W2, 'b2': b2}
...        return model
```

Note besides weights W, we also employ bias b. Before training, we first randomly initialize weights and biases. In each iteration, we feed all layers of the network with the latest weights and biases, then calculate the gradients using the backpropagation algorithm, and finally update the weights and biases with the resulting gradients. For training performance inspection, we print out the loss and the MSE for every 100 iterations.

Again, we use Boston house prices as the toy dataset. As a reminder, data normalization is usually recommended whenever gradient descent is used. Hence, we standardize the input data by removing the mean and scaling to unit variance:

```
>>> boston = datasets.load_boston()
>>> num_test = 10 # the last 10 samples as testing set
>>> from sklearn import preprocessing
>>> scaler = preprocessing.StandardScaler()
>>> X_train = boston.data[:-num_test, :]
>>> X_train = scaler.fit_transform(X_train)
>>> y_train = boston.target[:-num_test].reshape(-1, 1)
>>> X_test = boston.data[-num_test:, :]
>>> X_test = scaler.transform(X_test)
>>> y_test = boston.target[-num_test:]
```

With the scaled dataset, we can now train a one-layer neural network with 20 hidden units, a 0.1 learning rate, and 2000 iterations:

```
>>> n_hidden = 20
>>> learning_rate = 0.1
>>> n_iter = 2000
>>> model = train(X_train, y_train, n_hidden, learning_rate, n_iter)
Iteration 100, training loss: 13.500649
Iteration 200, training loss: 9.721267
Iteration 300, training loss: 8.309366
Iteration 400, training loss: 7.417523
Iteration 500, training loss: 6.720618
Iteration 600, training loss: 6.172355
Iteration 700, training loss: 5.748484
```

```
Iteration 800, training loss: 5.397459
Iteration 900, training loss: 5.069072
Iteration 1000, training loss: 4.787303
Iteration 1100, training loss: 4.544623
Iteration 1200, training loss: 4.330923
Iteration 1300, training loss: 4.141120
Iteration 1400, training loss: 3.970357
Iteration 1500, training loss: 3.814482
Iteration 1600, training loss: 3.673037
Iteration 1700, training loss: 3.547397
Iteration 1800, training loss: 3.437391
Iteration 1900, training loss: 3.341110
Iteration 2000, training loss: 3.255750
```

Then, we define a `prediction` function, which takes in a model and produces regression results:

```
>>> def predict(x, model):
...     W1 = model['W1']
...     b1 = model['b1']
...     W2 = model['W2']
...     b2 = model['b2']
...     A2 = sigmoid(np.matmul(x, W1) + b1)
...     A3 = np.matmul(A2, W2) + b2
...     return A3
```

Finally, we apply the trained model on the testing set:

```
>>> predictions = predict(X_test, model)
>>> print(predictions)
[[16.28103034]
 [19.98591039]
 [22.17811179]
 [19.37515137]
 [20.5675095 ]
 [24.90457042]
 [22.92777643]
 [26.03651277]
 [25.35493394]
 [23.38112184]]
>>> print(y_test)
[19.7 18.3 21.2 17.5 16.8 22.4 20.6 23.9 22. 11.9]
```

After successfully building a neural network model from scratch, we move on with the implementation with `scikit-learn`. We utilize the `MLPRegressor` class (**MLP** stands for **multi-layer perceptron**, a nickname of neural networks):

```
>>> from sklearn.neural_network import MLPRegressor
>>> nn_scikit = MLPRegressor(hidden_layer_sizes=(20, 8),
...                          activation='logistic', solver='lbfgs',
...                          learning_rate_init=0.1, random_state=42,
...                          max_iter=2000)
```

The `hidden_layer_sizes` hyperparameter represents the number(s) of hidden neurons. In our previous example, the network contains two hidden layers with 20 and 8 nodes respectively.

We fit the neural network model on the training set and predict on the testing data:

```
>>> nn_scikit.fit(X_train, y_train)
>>> predictions = nn_scikit.predict(X_test)
>>> print(predictions)
[14.73064216 19.77077071 19.77422245 18.95256283 19.73320899 24.15010593
 19.78909311 28.36477319 24.17612634 19.80954273]
```

Neural networks are often implemented with TensorFlow, which is one of the most popular deep learning (multilayer neural network) frameworks.

First, we specify parameters of the model, including two hidden layers with 20 and 8 nodes respectively, 2000 iterations, and a 0.1 learning rate:

```
>>> n_features = int(X_train.shape[1])
>>> n_hidden_1 = 20
>>> n_hidden_2 = 8
>>> learning_rate = 0.1
>>> n_iter = 2000
```

Then, we define placeholders and construct the network from input to hidden layers to output:

```
>>> x = tf.placeholder(tf.float32, shape=[None, n_features])
>>> y = tf.placeholder(tf.float32, shape=[None, 1])
>>> layer_1 = tf.nn.sigmoid(tf.layers.dense(x, n_hidden_1))
>>> layer_2 = tf.nn.sigmoid(tf.layers.dense(layer_1, n_hidden_2))
>>> pred = tf.layers.dense(layer_2, 1)
```

After assembling the components for the model, we define the loss function, the MSE, and a gradient descent optimizer that searches for the best coefficients by minimizing the loss:

```
>>> cost = tf.losses.mean_squared_error(labels=y, predictions=pred)
>>> optimizer =
 tf.train.GradientDescentOptimizer(learning_rate).minimize(cost)
```

Now we can initialize the variables and start a TensorFlow session:

```
>>> init_vars = tf.initialize_all_variables()
>>> sess = tf.Session()
>>> sess.run(init_vars)
```

Finally, we start the training process and print out the loss after every 100 iterations:

```
>>> for i in range(1, n_iter+1):
...        _, c = sess.run([optimizer, cost],
                         feed_dict={x: X_train, y: y_train})
...        if i % 100 == 0:
...            print('Iteration %i, training loss: %f' % (i, c))
Iteration 100, training loss: 12.995015
Iteration 200, training loss: 8.587905
Iteration 300, training loss: 6.319847
Iteration 400, training loss: 5.524787
Iteration 500, training loss: 5.200356
Iteration 600, training loss: 4.217351
Iteration 700, training loss: 4.070641
Iteration 800, training loss: 3.825407
Iteration 900, training loss: 3.301410
Iteration 1000, training loss: 3.124229
Iteration 1100, training loss: 3.220546
Iteration 1200, training loss: 2.895406
Iteration 1300, training loss: 2.680367
Iteration 1400, training loss: 2.504926
Iteration 1500, training loss: 2.362953
Iteration 1600, training loss: 2.257992
Iteration 1700, training loss: 2.154428
Iteration 1800, training loss: 2.170816
Iteration 1900, training loss: 2.052284
Iteration 2000, training loss: 1.971042
```

We apply the trained model on the testing set:

```
>>> predictions = sess.run(pred, feed_dict={x: X_test})
>>> print(predictions)
[[16.431433]
 [17.861343]
 [20.286907]
```

```
[17.6935 ]
[18.380125]
[22.405527]
[19.216259]
[24.333553]
[23.02146 ]
[18.86538 ]]
```

A bonus section is its implementation in Keras (`https://keras.io/`), another popular package for neural networks. Keras is a high-level API written on top of TensorFlow and two other deep learning frameworks. It was developed for fast prototyping and experimenting neural network models. We can install Keras using PyPI:

```
pip install keras
```

We import the necessary modules after installation as follows:

```
>>> from keras import models
>>> from keras import layers
```

Then, we initialize a `Sequential` model of Keras:

```
>>> model = models.Sequential()
```

We add layer by layer, from the first hidden layer (20 units), to the second hidden layer (8 units), then the output layer:

```
>>> model.add(layers.Dense(n_hidden_1, activation="sigmoid",
                            input_shape=(n_features, )))
>>> model.add(layers.Dense(n_hidden_2, activation="sigmoid"))
>>> model.add(layers.Dense(1))
```

It's quite similar to building **LEGO**. We also need an optimizer, which we define as follows with a `0.01` learning rate:

```
>>> from keras import optimizers
>>> sgd = optimizers.SGD(lr=0.01)
```

Now we can compile the model by specifying the loss function and optimizer:

```
>>> model.compile(loss='mean_squared_error', optimizer=sgd)
```

Finally, we fit the model on the training set, with `100` iterations, and validate the performance on the testing set:

```
>>> model.fit(
...       X_train, y_train,
...       epochs=100,
```

```
...        validation_data=(X_test, y_test)
... )
Train on 496 samples, validate on 10 samples
Epoch 1/100
496/496 [==============================] - 0s 356us/step - loss: 255.7313 -
val_loss: 10.7765
Epoch 2/100
496/496 [==============================] - 0s 24us/step - loss: 83.0557 -
val_loss: 21.5385
Epoch 3/100
496/496 [==============================] - 0s 25us/step - loss: 70.7806 -
val_loss: 22.5854
Epoch 4/100
496/496 [==============================] - 0s 24us/step - loss: 58.7843 -
val_loss: 25.0963
Epoch 5/100
496/496 [==============================] - 0s 27us/step - loss: 51.1305 -
val_loss: 20.6070
......
......
Epoch 96/100
496/496 [==============================] - 0s 21us/step - loss: 6.4766 -
val_loss: 18.2094
Epoch 97/100
496/496 [==============================] - 0s 21us/step - loss: 6.2356 -
val_loss: 13.1832
Epoch 98/100
496/496 [==============================] - 0s 21us/step - loss: 6.0728 -
val_loss: 13.2538
Epoch 99/100
496/496 [==============================] - 0s 21us/step - loss: 6.0512 -
val_loss: 14.1940
Epoch 100/100
496/496 [==============================] - 0s 23us/step - loss: 6.2514 -
val_loss: 13.1176
```

In each iteration, the training loss and validation loss are displayed.

As usually, we obtain the prediction of the testing set using the trained model:

```
>>> predictions = model.predict(X_test)
>>> print(predictions)
[[16.521835]
 [18.425688]
 [19.65961 ]
 [19.23118 ]
 [18.676624]
 [21.917233]
```

```
[21.794016]
[25.537102]
[24.175468]
[22.05365 ]]
```

Evaluating regression performance

So far, we've covered in depth four popular regression algorithms and implemented them from scratch and by using several prominent libraries. Instead of judging how well a model works on testing sets by printing out the prediction, we need to evaluate its performance by the following metrics which give us better insight:

- The MSE, as we mentioned, measures the squared loss corresponding to the expected value. Sometimes the square root is taken on top of the MSE in order to convert the value back into the original scale of the target variable being estimated. This yields the **root mean squared error** (**RMSE**).
- The **mean absolute error** (**MAE**) on the other hand measures the absolute loss. It uses the same scale as the target variable and gives an idea of how close predictions are to the actual values.

 For both the MSE and MAE, the smaller value, the better regression model.

- R^2 (pronounced as r squared) indicates the goodness of the fit of a regression model. It ranges from 0 to 1, meaning from no fit to perfect prediction.

Let's compute these three measurements on a linear regression model using corresponding functions from scikit-learn:

1. We re-work on the diabetes dataset and fine-tune the parameters of linear regression model using the grid search technique:

```
>>> diabetes = datasets.load_diabetes()
>>> num_test = 30 # the last 30 samples as testing set
>>> X_train = diabetes.data[:-num_test, :]
>>> y_train = diabetes.target[:-num_test]
>>> X_test = diabetes.data[-num_test:, :]
>>> y_test = diabetes.target[-num_test:]
>>> param_grid = {
...      "alpha": [1e-07, 1e-06, 1e-05],
...      "penalty": [None, "12"],
```

```
...        "eta0": [0.001, 0.005, 0.01],
...        "n_iter": [300, 1000, 3000]
... }
>>> from sklearn.model_selection import GridSearchCV
>>> regressor = SGDRegressor(loss='squared_loss',
                             learning_rate='constant')
>>> grid_search = GridSearchCV(regressor, param_grid, cv=3)
```

2. We obtain the optimal set of parameters:

```
>>> grid_search.fit(X_train, y_train)
>>> print(grid_search.best_params_)
{'penalty': None, 'alpha': 1e-05, 'eta0': 0.01, 'n_iter': 300}
>>> regressor_best = grid_search.best_estimator_
```

3. We predict the testing set with the optimal model:

```
>>> predictions = regressor_best.predict(X_test)
```

4. We evaluate the performance on testing sets based on the MSE, MAE, and R^2 metrics:

```
>>> from sklearn.metrics import mean_squared_error,
    mean_absolute_error, r2_score
>>> mean_squared_error(y_test, predictions)
1862.0518552093429
>>> mean_absolute_error(y_test, predictions)
34.605923224169558
>>> r2_score(y_test, predictions)
0.63859162277753756
```

Predicting stock price with four regression algorithms

Now that we've learned four (or five, you could say) commonly used and powerful regression algorithms and performance evaluation metrics, let's utilize each of them to solve our stock price prediction problem.

We generated features based on data from 1988 to 2016 earlier, and we'll now continue with constructing the training set with data from 1988 to 2015 and the testing set with data from 2016:

```
>>> data_raw = pd.read_csv('19880101_20161231.csv', index_col='Date')
>>> data = generate_features(data_raw)
```

```
>>> start_train = '1988-01-01'
>>> end_train = '2015-12-31'
>>> start_test = '2016-01-01'
>>> end_test = '2016-12-31'
>>> data_train = data.ix[start_train:end_train]
>>> X_train = data_train.drop('close', axis=1).values
>>> y_train = data_train['close'].values
>>> print(X_train.shape)
(6804, 37)
>>> print(y_train.shape)
(6804,)
```

All fields in the `dataframe` data except `'close'` are feature columns, and `'close'` is the target column. We have 6,553 training samples and each sample is 37-dimensional. And we have 252 testing samples:

```
>>> print(X_test.shape)
(252, 37)
```

We first experiment with SGD-based linear regression. Before we train the model, we should realize that SGD-based algorithms are sensitive to data with features at largely different scales, for example, in our case, the average value of the `open` feature is around 8,856, while that of the `moving_avg_365` feature is 0.00037 or so. Hence, we need to normalize features into the same or a comparable scale. We do so by removing the mean and rescaling to unit variance:

```
>>> from sklearn.preprocessing import StandardScaler
>>> scaler = StandardScaler()
```

We rescale both sets with `scaler` taught by the training set:

```
>>> X_scaled_train = scaler.fit_transform(X_train)
>>> X_scaled_test = scaler.transform(X_test)
```

Now we can search for the SGD-based linear regression with the optimal set of parameters. We specify `l2` regularization and 1,000 iterations and tune the regularization term multiplier, `alpha`, and initial learning rate, `eta0`:

```
>>> param_grid = {
...     "alpha": [1e-5, 3e-5, 1e-4],
...     "eta0": [0.01, 0.03, 0.1],
... }
>>> lr = SGDRegressor(penalty='l2', n_iter=1000)
>>> grid_search = GridSearchCV(lr, param_grid, cv=5, scoring='r2')
>>> grid_search.fit(X_scaled_train, y_train)
```

Select the best linear regression model and make predictions of the testing samples:

```
>>> print(grid_search.best_params_)
{'alpha': 3e-05, 'eta0': 0.03}
>>> lr_best = grid_search.best_estimator_
>>> predictions_lr = lr_best.predict(X_scaled_test)
```

Measure the prediction performance via the MSE, MAE, and R^2:

```
>>> print('MSE: {0:.3f}'.format(
...             mean_squared_error(y_test, predictions_lr)))
MSE: 18934.971
>>> print('MAE: {0:.3f}'.format(
...             mean_absolute_error(y_test, predictions_lr))
MAE: 100.244
>>> print('R^2: {0:.3f}'.format(r2_score(y_test, predictions_lr)))
R^2: 0.979
```

We achieve 0.979 R^2 with a fine-tuned linear regression model.

Similarly, we experiment with random forest, where we specify 500 trees to ensemble and tune the the maximum depth of the tree, `max_depth`; the minimum number of samples required to further split a node, `min_samples_split`; and the number of features used for each tree, as well as the following:

```
>>> param_grid = {
...       'max_depth': [50, 70, 80],
...       'min_samples_split': [5, 10],
...       'max_features': ['auto', 'sqrt'],
...       'min_samples_leaf': [3, 5]
... }
>>> rf = RandomForestRegressor(n_estimators=500, n_jobs=-1)
>>> grid_search = GridSearchCV(rf, param_grid, cv=5, scoring='r2',
                                                n_jobs=-1)
>>> grid_search.fit(X_train, y_train)
```

Note this may take a while, hence we use all available CPU cores for training.

Select the best regression forest model and make predictions of the testing samples:

```
>>> print(grid_search.best_params_)
{'max_depth': 70, 'max_features': 'auto', 'min_samples_leaf': 3,
'min_samples_split': 5}
>>> rf_best = grid_search.best_estimator_
>>> predictions_rf = rf_best.predict(X_test)
```

Measure the prediction performance as follows:

```
>>> print('MSE: {0:.3f}'.format(mean_squared_error(y_test,
...        predictions_rf)))
MSE: 260349.365
>>> print('MAE: {0:.3f}'.format(mean_absolute_error(y_test,
...        predictions_rf)))
MAE: 299.344
>>> print('R^2: {0:.3f}'.format(r2_score(y_test, predictions_rf)))
R^2: 0.706
```

An R^2 of 0.706 is obtained with a tweaked forest regressor.

Next, we work with SVR with linear and RBF kernel and leave the penalty parameter C and ε as well as the kernel coefficient of RBF for fine tuning. Similar to SGD-based algorithms, SVR doesn't work well on data with feature scale disparity:

```
>>> param_grid = [
...     {'kernel': ['linear'], 'C': [100, 300, 500],
...         'epsilon': [0.00003, 0.0001]},
...     {'kernel': ['rbf'], 'gamma': [1e-3, 1e-4],
...         'C': [10, 100, 1000], 'epsilon': [0.00003, 0.0001]}
... ]
```

Again, to work around this, we use the rescaled data to train the SVR model:

```
>>> svr = SVR()
>>> grid_search = GridSearchCV(svr, param_grid, cv=5, scoring='r2')
>>> grid_search.fit(X_scaled_train, y_train)
```

Select the best SVR model and make predictions of the testing samples:

```
>>> print(grid_search.best_params_)
{'C': 500, 'epsilon': 3e-05, 'kernel': 'linear'}
>>> svr_best = grid_search.best_estimator_
>>> predictions_svr = svr_best.predict(X_scaled_test)
>>> print('MSE: {0:.3f}'.format(mean_squared_error(y_test,
predictions_svr)))
MSE: 17466.596
>>> print('MAE: {0:.3f}'.format(mean_absolute_error(y_test,
predictions_svr)))
MAE: 95.070
>>> print('R^2: {0:.3f}'.format(r2_score(y_test, predictions_svr)))
R^2: 0.980
```

With SVR, we're able to achieve R^2 0.980 on the testing set.

Finally, we experiment with the neural network where we fine-tune from the following options for hyperparameters including a list of hidden layer sizes, activation function, optimizer, learning rate, penalty factor, and mini-batch size:

```
>>> param_grid = {
...       'hidden_layer_sizes': [(50, 10), (30, 30)],
...       'activation': ['logistic', 'tanh', 'relu'],
...       'solver': ['sgd', 'adam'],
...       'learning_rate_init': [0.0001, 0.0003, 0.001, 0.01],
...       'alpha': [0.00003, 0.0001, 0.0003],
...       'batch_size': [30, 50]
... }
>>> nn = MLPRegressor(random_state=42, max_iter=2000)
>>> grid_search = GridSearchCV(nn, param_grid, cv=5, scoring='r2',
                               n_jobs=-1)
>>> grid_search.fit(X_scaled_train, y_train)
```

Select the best neural network model and make predictions of the testing samples:

```
>>> print(grid_search.best_params_)
{'activation': 'relu', 'alpha': 0.0003, 'hidden_layer_sizes': (50, 10),
 'learning_rate_init': 0.001, 'solver': 'adam'}
>>> nn_best = grid_search.best_estimator_
>>> predictions_nn = nn_best.predict(X_scaled_test)
>>> print('MSE: {0:.3f}'.format(mean_squared_error(y_test,
            predictions_nn)))
MSE: 19619.618
>>> print('MAE: {0:.3f}'.format(mean_absolute_error(y_test,
            predictions_nn)))
MAE: 100.956
>>> print('R^2: {0:.3f}'.format(r2_score(y_test, predictions_nn)))
R^2: 0.978
```

We're able to achieve a 0.978 R^2 with a fine-tuned neural network model.

We'll also plot the prediction generated by each of the three algorithms, along with the ground truth:

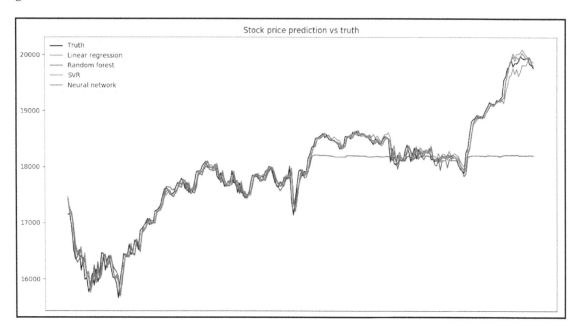

Summary

In this chapter, we worked on the last project of this entire book, predicting stock (specifically stock index) prices using machine learning regression techniques. We started with a short introduction to the stock market and factors that influence trading prices. To tackle this billion dollar problem, we investigated machine learning regression, which estimates a continuous target variable, as opposed to discrete output in classification. We followed with an in-depth discussion of three popular regression algorithms, linear regression, regression tree and regression forest, and SVR as well as neural networks. We covered the definition, mechanics, and implementation from scratch and with several popular frameworks including `scikit-learn`, `tensorflow`, and `keras`, along with their applications on toy datasets. We also learned the metrics used to evaluate a regression model. Finally, we applied what we learned in this whole chapter to solve our stock price prediction problem.

At last, recall that we briefly mentioned several major stock indexes besides DJIA. Is it possible to better the DJIA price prediction model we just developed by considering historical prices and performance of these major indexes? It's highly likely! The idea behind this is that no stock or index is isolated and that there are weak or strong influences between stocks and different financial markets. This should be intriguing to explore.

In the next and final chapter, we'll wrap up this book with best practices of real-world machine learning. It aims to foolproof your learning and get you ready for the entire machine learning workflow and productionization.

Exercise

As mentioned, can you add more signals to our stock prediction system, such as performance of other major indexes? Does this improve prediction?

Section 3: Python Machine Learning Best Practices

After working on several projects in the previous chapters, you will have got a broad overview of the machine learning ecosystem. However, there will be issues once you start working on projects in the real world. In this section, you will have a chance to fullproof your learning and get ready for production by following 21 best practices throughout the entire machine learning workflow.

This section contains the following chapter:

10
Machine Learning Best Practices

After working on multiple projects covering important machine learning concepts, techniques, and widely used algorithms, we have gathered a broad picture of the machine learning ecosystem, as well as solid experience in tackling practical problems using machine learning algorithms and Python. However, there will be issues once we start working on projects from scratch in the real world. This chapter aims to get us ready for it with 21 best practices to follow throughout the entire machine learning solution workflow.

We will cover the following topics in this chapter:

- Machine learning solution workflow
- Tasks in the data preparation stage
- Tasks in the training sets generation stage
- Tasks in the algorithm training, evaluation, and selection stage
- Tasks in the system deployment and monitoring stage
- Best practices in the data preparation stage
- Best practices in the training sets generation stage
- Word embedding
- Best practices in the model training, evaluation, and selection stage
- Best practices in the system deployment and monitoring stage

Machine learning solution workflow

In general, the main tasks involved in solving a machine learning problem can be summarized into four areas, as follows:

- Data preparation
- Training sets generation
- Model training, evaluation, and selection
- Deployment and monitoring

Starting from data sources to the final machine learning system, a machine learning solution basically follows the following paradigm:

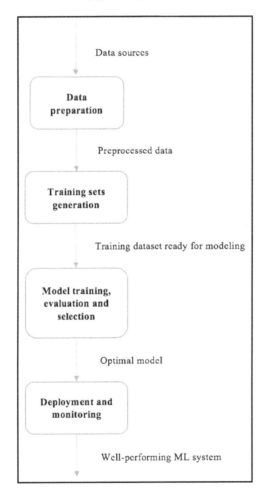

In the following sections, we will be learning about the typical tasks, common challenges, and best practices for each of these four stages.

Best practices in the data preparation stage

No machine learning system can be built without data. Therefore, **data collection** should be our first focus.

Best practice 1 – completely understanding the project goal

Before starting to collect data, we should make sure that the goal of the project and the business problem, is completely understood, as this will guide us on what data sources to look into, and where sufficient domain knowledge and expertise is also required. For example, in the previous chapter, Chapter 9, *Stock Price Prediction with Regression Algorithms*, our goal was to predict the future prices of the DJIA index, so we first collected data of its past performance, instead of past performance of an irrelevant European stock. In Chapter 6, *Predicting Online Ads Click-through with Tree-Based Algorithms*, and Chapter 7, *Predicting Online Ads Click-through with Logistic Regression*, the business problem was to optimize advertising targeting efficiency measured in click-through rate, so we collected the clickstream data of who clicked or did not click on what ad on what page, instead of merely how many ads were displayed in a web domain.

Best practice 2 – collecting all fields that are relevant

With a set goal in mind, we can narrow down potential data sources to investigate. Now the question becomes: is it necessary to collect the data of all fields available in a data source, or is a subset of attributes enough? It would be perfect if we knew in advance which attributes were key indicators or key predictive factors. However, it is in fact very difficult to ensure that the attributes hand-picked by a domain expert will yield the best prediction results. Hence, for each data source, it is recommended to collect **all** of the fields that are related to the project, especially in cases where recollecting the data is time consuming, or even impossible.

For example, in the stock price prediction example, we collected the data of all fields including **open**, **high**, **low**, and **volume**, even though we were initially not certain of how useful **high** and **low** predictions would be. Retrieving the stock data is quick and easy, however. In another example, if we ever want to collect data ourselves by scraping online articles for topic classification, we should store as much information as possible. Otherwise, if any piece of information is not collected but is later found valuable, such as hyperlinks in an article, the article might be already removed from the web page; if it still exists, rescraping those pages can be costly.

After collecting the datasets that we think are useful, we need to assure the data quality by inspecting its **consistency** and **completeness**. Consistency refers to how the distribution of data is changing over time. Completeness means how much data is present across fields and samples. They are explained in detail in the following two practices.

Best practice 3 – maintaining the consistency of field values

In a dataset that already exists, or in one we collect from scratch, oftentimes we see different values representing the same meaning. For example, there are American, US, and U.S.A in the country field, and male and M in the gender field. It is necessary to unify or standardize values in a field. For example, we can only keep M and F in the gender field and replace other alternatives. Otherwise it will mess up the algorithms in later stages as different feature values will be treated differently even if they have the same meaning. It is also a great practice to keep track of what values are mapped to the default value of a field.

In addition, the format of values in the same field should also be consistent. For instance, in the *age* field, there are true age values, such as 21 and 35, and incorrect age values, such as 1990 and 1978; in the *rating* field, both cardinal numbers and English numerals are found, such as 1, 2, and 3, and *one, two,* and *three*. Transformation and reformatting should be conducted in order to ensure data consistency.

Best practice 4 – dealing with missing data

Due to various reasons, datasets in the real world are rarely completely clean and often contain missing or corrupted values. They are usually presented as blanks, *Null, -1, 999999, unknown,* or any other placeholder. Samples with missing data not only provide incomplete predictive information, but also confuse the machine learning model as it can not tell whether *-1* or *unknown* holds a meaning. It is important to pinpoint and deal with missing data in order to avoid jeopardizing the performance of models in later stages.

Here are three basic strategies that we can use to tackle the missing data issue:

- Discarding samples containing any missing value
- Discarding fields containing missing values in any sample

- Inferring the missing values based on the known part from the attribute. This process is called **missing data imputation**. Typical imputation methods include replacing missing values with mean or median value of the field across all samples, or the most frequent value for categorical data.

The first two strategies are simple to implement; however, they come at the expense of the data lost, especially when the original dataset is not large enough. The third strategy doesn't abandon any data, but does try to fill in the blanks.

Let's look at how each strategy is applied in an example where we have a dataset (age, income) consisting of six samples (30, 100), (20, 50), (35, *unknown*), (25, 80), (30, 70), and (40, 60):

- If we process this dataset using the first strategy, it becomes (30, 100), (20, 50), (25, 80), (30, 70), and (40, 60)
- If we employ the second strategy, the dataset becomes (30), (20), (35), (25), (30), and (40), where only the first field remains
- If we decide to complete the unknown value instead of skipping it, the sample (35, *unknown*) can be transformed into (35, 72) with the mean of the rest values in the second field, or (35, 70), with the median value in the second field

In scikit-learn, the Imputer class provides a nicely written imputation transformer. We herein use it for the following small example:

```
>>> import numpy as np
>>> from sklearn.preprocessing import Imputer
```

Represent the unknown value by np.nan in numpy, as detailed in the following:

```
>>> data_origin = [[30, 100],
...                [20, 50],
...                [35, np.nan],
...                [25, 80],
...                [30, 70],
...                [40, 60]]
```

Initialize the imputation transformer with the mean value and obtain such information from the original data:

```
>>> imp_mean = Imputer(missing_values='NaN', strategy='mean')
>>> imp_mean.fit(data_origin)
```

Complete the missing value as follows:

```
>>> data_mean_imp = imp_mean.transform(data_origin)
>>> print(data_mean_imp)
[[ 30.  100.]
 [ 20.   50.]
 [ 35.   72.]
 [ 25.   80.]
 [ 30.   70.]
 [ 40.   60.]]
```

Similarly, initialize the imputation transformer with the median value, as detailed in the following:

```
>>> imp_median = Imputer(missing_values='NaN', strategy='median')
>>> imp_median.fit(data_origin)
>>> data_median_imp = imp_median.transform(data_origin)
>>> print(data_median_imp)
[[ 30.  100.]
 [ 20.   50.]
 [ 35.   70.]
 [ 25.   80.]
 [ 30.   70.]
 [ 40.   60.]]
```

When new samples come in, the missing values (in any attribute) can be imputed using the trained transformer, for example, with the mean value, as shown here:

```
>>> new = [[20, np.nan],
...        [30, np.nan],
...        [np.nan, 70],
...        [np.nan, np.nan]]
>>> new_mean_imp = imp_mean.transform(new)
>>> print(new_mean_imp)
[[ 20.  72.]
 [ 30.  72.]
 [ 30.  70.]
 [ 30.  72.]]
```

Note that 30 in the age field is the mean of those six age values in the original dataset.

Now that we have seen how imputation works as well as its implementation, let's explore how the strategy of imputing missing values and discarding missing data affects the prediction results through the following example:

1. First we load the diabetes dataset and simulate a corrupted dataset with missing values, as shown here:

```
>>> from sklearn import datasets
>>> dataset = datasets.load_diabetes()
>>> X_full, y = dataset.data, dataset.target
```

2. Simulate a corrupted dataset by adding 25% missing values:

```
>>> m, n = X_full.shape
>>> m_missing = int(m * 0.25)
>>> print(m, m_missing)
442 110
```

3. Randomly select the m_missing samples, as follows:

```
>>> np.random.seed(42)
>>> missing_samples = np.array([True] * m_missing +
                              [False] * (m - m_missing))
>>> np.random.shuffle(missing_samples)
```

4. For each missing sample, randomly select 1 out of n features:

```
>>> missing_features = np.random.randint(low=0, high=n,
                                  size=m_missing)
```

5. Represent missing values by nan, as shown here:

```
>>> X_missing = X_full.copy()
>>> X_missing[np.where(missing_samples)[0], missing_features] =
                                                np.nan
```

6. Then we deal with this corrupted dataset by discarding the samples containing a missing value:

```
>>> X_rm_missing = X_missing[~missing_samples, :]
>>> y_rm_missing = y[~missing_samples]
```

7. Measure the effects of using this strategy by estimating the averaged regression score, R^2, with a regression forest model in a cross-validation manner. Estimate R^2 on the dataset with the missing samples removed, as follows:

```
>>> from sklearn.ensemble import RandomForestRegressor
>>> from sklearn.model_selection import cross_val_score
>>> regressor = RandomForestRegressor(random_state=42,
                                      max_depth=10, n_estimators=100)
>>> score_rm_missing = cross_val_score(regressor, X_rm_missing,
                                       y_rm_missing).mean()
>>> print('Score with the data set with missing samples removed:
                                 {0:.2f}'.format(score_rm_missing))
Score with the data set with missing samples removed: 0.39
```

8. Now we approach the corrupted dataset differently by imputing missing values with the mean, shown here:

```
>>> imp_mean = Imputer(missing_values='NaN', strategy='mean')
>>> X_mean_imp = imp_mean.fit_transform(X_missing)
```

9. Similarly, measure the effects of using this strategy by estimating the averaged R^2, as follows:

```
>>> regressor = RandomForestRegressor(random_state=42,
                                      max_depth=10, n_estimators=100)
>>> score_mean_imp = cross_val_score(regressor, X_mean_imp,
                                     y).mean()
>>> print('Score with the data set with missing values replaced by
                            mean: {0:.2f}'.format(score_mean_imp))
Score with the data set with missing values replaced by mean: 0.42
```

10. An imputation strategy works better than discarding in this case. So, how far is the imputed dataset from the original full one? We can check it again by estimating the averaged regression score on the original dataset, as follows:

```
>>> regressor = RandomForestRegressor(random_state=42,
                                      max_depth=10, n_estimators=500)
>>> score_full = cross_val_score(regressor, X_full, y).mean()
>>> print 'Score with the full data set:
                            {0:.2f}'.format(score_full)
Score with the full data set: 0.44
```

It turns out that little information is comprised in the completed dataset.

However, there is no guarantee that an imputation strategy always works better, and sometimes dropping samples with missing values can be more effective. Hence, it is a great practice to compare the performances of different strategies via cross-validation as we have done previously.

Best practice 5 – storing large-scale data

With the ever-growing size of data, oftentimes we can't simply fit the data in our single local machine and need to store it on the cloud or distributed filesystems. As this is mainly a book on machine learning with Python, we will just touch on some basic areas that you can look into. The two main strategies of storing big data are **scale-up** and **scale-out**:

- A scale-up approach increases storage capacity if data exceeds the current system capacity, such as by adding more disks. This is useful in fast-access platforms.
- In a scale-out approach, storage capacity grows incrementally with additional nodes in a storage cluster. Apache Hadoop (`https://hadoop.apache.org/`) is used to store and process big data on scale-out clusters, where data is spread across hundreds or even thousands of nodes. Also, there are cloud-based distributed file services, such as S3 in Amazon Web Services (`https://aws.amazon.com/s3/`), and Google Cloud Storage in Google Cloud (`https://cloud.google.com/storage/`). They are massively scalable and are designed for secure and durable storage.

Best practices in the training sets generation stage

With well-prepared data, it is safe to move on with the training sets generation stage. Typical tasks in this stage can be summarized into two major categories: **data preprocessing** and **feature engineering**.

To begin, data preprocessing usually involves categorical feature encoding, feature scaling, feature selection, and dimensionality reduction.

Best practice 6 – identifying categorical features with numerical values

In general, categorical features are easy to spot, as they convey qualitative information, such as risk level, occupation, and interests. However, it gets tricky if the feature takes on a discreet and countable (limited) number of numerical values, for instance, 1 to 12 representing months of the year, and 1 and 0 indicating true and false. The key to identifying whether such a feature is categorical or numerical is whether it provides a mathematical or ranking implication: if so, it is a numerical feature, such as a product rating from 1 to 5; otherwise, it is categorical, such as the month, or day of the week.

Best practice 7 – deciding on whether or not to encode categorical features

If a feature is considered categorical, we need to decide whether we should encode it. This depends on what prediction algorithm(s) we will use in later stages. Naïve Bayes and tree-based algorithms can directly work with categorical features, while other algorithms in general cannot, in which case, encoding is essential.

As the output of the feature generation stage is the input of the model training stage, steps taken in the feature generation stage should be compatible with the prediction algorithm. Therefore, we should look at two stages of feature generation and predictive model training as a whole, instead of two isolated components. The following practical tips also emphasize this point.

Best practice 8 – deciding on whether or not to select features, and if so, how to do so

We have seen in `Chapter 7`, *Predicting Online Ads Click-through with Logistic Regression*, where feature selection was performed using L1-based regularized logistic regression and random forest. The benefits of feature selection include the following:

- Reducing the training time of prediction models, as redundant, or irrelevant features are eliminated
- Reducing overfitting for the preceding same reason
- Likely improving performance as prediction models will learn from data with more significant features

Note we used the word *likely* because there is no absolute certainty that feature selection will increase prediction accuracy. It is therefore good practice to compare the performances of conducting feature selection and not doing so via cross-validation. For example, by executing the following steps, we can measure the effects of feature selection by estimating the averaged classification accuracy with an `SVC` model in a cross-validation manner:

1. First, we load the handwritten digits dataset from `scikit-learn`, as follows:

```
>>> from sklearn.datasets import load_digits
>>> dataset = load_digits()
>>> X, y = dataset.data, dataset.target
>>> print(X.shape)
(1797, 64)
```

2. Next, estimate the accuracy of the original dataset, which is 64 dimensional, as detailed here:

```
>>> from sklearn.svm import SVC
>>> from sklearn.model_selection import cross_val_score
>>> classifier = SVC(gamma=0.005)
>>> score = cross_val_score(classifier, X, y).mean()
>>> print('Score with the original data set:
                                {0:.2f}'.format(score))
Score with the original data set: 0.88
```

3. Then conduct feature selection based on random forest and sort the features based on their importance scores:

```
>>> from sklearn.ensemble import RandomForestClassifier
>>> random_forest = RandomForestClassifier(n_estimators=100,
                                criterion='gini', n_jobs=-1)
>>> random_forest.fit(X, y)
>>> feature_sorted =
                np.argsort(random_forest.feature_importances_)
```

4. Now select a different number of top features to construct a new dataset, and estimate the accuracy on each dataset, as follows:

```
>>> K = [10, 15, 25, 35, 45]
>>> for k in K:
...        top_K_features = feature_sorted[-k:]
...        X_k_selected = X[:, top_K_features]
...        # Estimate accuracy on the data set with k
            selected features
...        classifier = SVC(gamma=0.005)
...        score_k_features =
                cross_val_score(classifier, X_k_selected, y).mean()
```

```
    ...         print('Score with the data set of top {0} features:
                            {1:.2f}'.format(k, score_k_features))
    ...
Score with the data set of top 10 features: 0.88
Score with the data set of top 15 features: 0.93
Score with the data set of top 25 features: 0.94
Score with the data set of top 35 features: 0.92
Score with the data set of top 45 features: 0.88
```

Best practice 9 – deciding on whether or not to reduce dimensionality, and if so, how to do so

Feature selection and dimensionality are different in the sense that the former chooses features from the original data space, while the latter does so from a projected space from the original space. Dimensionality reduction has the following advantages that are similar to feature selection, as follows:

- Reducing the training time of prediction models, as redundant, or correlated features are merged into new ones
- Reducing overfitting for the same reason as previously
- Likely improving performance as prediction models will learn from data with less redundant or correlated features

Again, it is not guaranteed that dimensionality reduction will yield better prediction results. In order to examine its effects, integrating dimensionality reduction in the model training stage is recommended. Reusing the preceding handwritten digits example, we can measure the effects of **principal component analysis** (**PCA**)-based dimensionality reduction, where we keep a different number of top components to construct a new dataset, and estimate the accuracy on each dataset:

```
>>> from sklearn.decomposition import PCA
>>> # Keep different number of top components
>>> N = [10, 15, 25, 35, 45]
>>> for n in N:
...     pca = PCA(n_components=n)
...     X_n_kept = pca.fit_transform(X)
...     # Estimate accuracy on the data set with top n components
...     classifier = SVC(gamma=0.005)
...     score_n_components =
                    cross_val_score(classifier, X_n_kept, y).mean()
...     print('Score with the data set of top {0} components:
                        {1:.2f}'.format(n, score_n_components))
Score with the data set of top 10 components: 0.95
```

```
Score with the data set of top 15 components: 0.95
Score with the data set of top 25 components: 0.91
Score with the data set of top 35 components: 0.89
Score with the data set of top 45 components: 0.88
```

Best practice 10 – deciding on whether or not to rescale features

As seen in `Chapter 9`, *Stock Price Prediction with Regression Algorithms*, SGD-based linear regression, SVR, and the neural network model require features to be standardized by removing the mean and scaling to unit variance. So, when is feature scaling needed and when is it not?

In general, Naïve Bayes and tree-based algorithms are not sensitive to features at different scales, as they look at each feature independently.

In most cases, an algorithm that involves any form of distance (or separation in spaces) of samples in learning requires scaled/standardized inputs, such as SVC, SVR, k-means clustering, and k-nearest neighbors (KNN) algorithms. Feature scaling is also a must for any algorithm using SGD for optimization, such as linear or logistic regression with gradient descent, and neural networks.

We have so far covered tips regarding data preprocessing and will next discuss best practices of feature engineering as another major aspect of training sets generation. We will do so from two perspectives.

Best practice 11 – performing feature engineering with domain expertise

If we are lucky enough to possess sufficient domain knowledge, we can apply it in creating domain-specific features; we utilize our business experience and insights to identify what is in the data and to formulate what from the data correlates to the prediction target. For example, in `Chapter 9`, *Stock Price Prediction with Regression Algorithms*, we designed and constructed feature sets for the prediction of stock prices based on factors that investors usually look at when making investment decisions.

While particular domain knowledge is required, sometimes we can still apply some general tips in this category. For example, in fields related to customer analytics, such as market and advertising, the time of the day, day of the week, and month are usually important signals. Given a data point with the value 2017/02/05 in the date column and 14:34:21 in the time column, we can create new features including afternoon, Sunday, and February. In retail, information over a period of time is usually aggregated to provide better insights. The number of times a customer visits a store for the past three months, or the average number of products purchased weekly for the previous year, for instance, can be good predictive indicators for customer behavior prediction.

Best practice 12 – performing feature engineering without domain expertise

If we unfortunately have very little domain knowledge, how can we generate features? Don't panic. There are several generic approaches that you can follow:

- **Binarization**: This is the process of converting a numerical feature to a binary one with a preset threshold. For example, in spam email detection, for the feature (or term) *prize*, we can generate a new feature *whether prize occurs*: any term frequency value greater than 1 becomes 1, otherwise it is 0. The feature *number of visits per week* can be used to produce a new feature *is frequent visitor* by judging whether the value is greater than or equal to 3. We implement such binarization using scikit-learn, as follows:

```
>>> from sklearn.preprocessing import Binarizer
>>> X = [[4], [1], [3], [0]]
>>> binarizer = Binarizer(threshold=2.9)
>>> X_new = binarizer.fit_transform(X)
>>> print(X_new)
[[1]
 [0]
 [1]
 [0]]
```

- **Discretization**: This is the process of converting a numerical feature to a categorical feature with limited possible values. Binarization can be viewed as a special case of discretization. For example, we can generate an *age group* feature: *"18-24"* for age from 18 to 24, *"25-34"* for age from 25 to 34, *"34-54"*, and *"55+"*.

- **Interaction**: This includes the sum, multiplication, or any operations of two numerical features, joint condition check of two categorical features. For example, *the number of visits per week* and *the number of products purchased per week* can be used to generate *the number of products purchased per visit* feature; *interest* and *occupation*, such as *sports* and *engineer*, can form *occupation AND interest*, such as *engineer interested in sports*.
- **Polynomial transformation**: This is a process of generating polynomial and interaction features. For two features, a and b, the two degree of polynomial features generated are a^2, ab, and b^2. In `scikit-learn`, we can use the `PolynomialFeatures` class to perform polynomial transformation, as follows:

```
>>> from sklearn.preprocessing import PolynomialFeatures
>>> X = [[2, 4],
...      [1, 3],
...      [3, 2],
...      [0, 3]]
>>> poly = PolynomialFeatures(degree=2)
>>> X_new = poly.fit_transform(X)
>>> print(X_new)
[[ 1.  2.  4.  4.  8. 16.]
 [ 1.  1.  3.  1.  3.  9.]
 [ 1.  3.  2.  9.  6.  4.]
 [ 1.  0.  3.  0.  0.  9.]]
```

Note the resulting new features consist of 1 (bias, intercept), a, b, a^2, ab, and b^2.

Best practice 13 – documenting how each feature is generated

We have covered the rules of feature engineering with domain knowledge and in general, there is one more thing worth noting: documenting how each feature is generated. It sounds trivial, but oftentimes we just forget about how a feature is obtained or created. We usually need to go back to this stage after some failed trials in the model training stage and attempt to create more features with the hope of improving performance. We have to be clear on what and how features are generated, in order to remove those that do not quite work out, and to add new ones that have more potential.

Best practice 14 – extracting features from text data

We have worked intensively with text data in Chapter 2, *Exploring the 20 Newsgroups Dataset with Text Analysis Techniques*, Chapter 3, *Mining the 20 Newsgroups Dataset with Clustering, and Topic Modeling Algorithms*, Chapter 4, *Detecting Spam Email with Naive Bayes*, and Chapter 5, *Classifying News Topics with a Support Vector Machine*, where we extracted features from text based on **term frequency** (**tf**) and **term frequency-inverse document frequency** (**tf-idf**). Both methods consider each document of words (terms) a collection of words, or a **bag of words** (**BoW**), disregarding the order of words, but keeping multiplicity. A tf approach simply uses the counts of tokens, while tf-idf extends tf by assigning each tf a weighting factor that is inversely proportional to the document frequency. With the idf factor incorporated, tf-idf diminishes the weight of common terms (such as *get*, *make*) that occur frequently, and emphasizes terms that rarely occur, but convey important meaning. Hence, oftentimes features extracted from tf-idf are more representative than those from tf.

As you may remember, a document is represented by a very sparse vector where only present terms have non-zero values. And its dimensionality is usually high, which is determined by the size of vocabulary and the number of unique terms. Also, such one-hot encoding approaching treats each term as an independent item and does not consider the relationship across words (referred to as "context" in linguistics).

On the contrary, another approach, called **word embedding,** is able to capture the meanings of words and their context. In this approach, a word is represented by a vector of float numbers. Its dimensionality is a lot lower than the size of vocabulary and is usually several hundreds only. For example, the word **machine** can be represented as [1.4, 2.1, 10.3, 0.2, 6.81]. So, how can we embed a word into a vector? One solution is word2vec, which trains a shallow neural network to predict a word given other words around it (called **CBOW**) or to predict words around a word (called **skip-gram**). The coefficients of the trained neural network are the embedding vectors for corresponding words.

CBOW is short for **Continuous Bag of Words**. Given a sentence *I love reading Python machine learning by example* in a corpus, and 5 as the size of word window, we can have the following training sets for the CBOW neural network:

Input of neural network	Output of neural network
(I, love, python, machine)	(reading)
(love, reading, machine, learning)	(python)
(reading, python, learning, by)	(machine)
(python, machine, by, example)	(learning)

Of course, the inputs and outputs of the neural network are one-hot encoding vectors, where values are either 1 for present words, or 0 for absent words. And we can have millions of training samples constructed from a corpus sentence by sentence. After the network is trained, the weights that connect the input layer and hidden layer embed individual input words. A skip-gram-based neural network embeds words in a similar way. But its input and output is an inverse version of CBOW. Given the same sentence *I love reading Python machine learning by example* and 5 as the size of word window, we can have the following training sets for the skip-gram neural network:

Input of neural network	Output of neural network
(reading)	(i)
(reading)	(love)
(reading)	(python)
(reading)	(machine)
(python)	(love)
(python)	(reading)
(python)	(machine)
(python)	(learning)
(machine)	(reading)
(machine)	(python)
(machine)	(learning)
(machine)	(by)
(learning)	(python)
(learning)	(machine)
(learning)	(by)
(learning)	(example)

The embedding vectors are of real values where each dimension encodes an aspect of meaning for words in the vocabulary. This helps reserve the semantics information of words, as opposed to discarding it as in the dummy one-hot encoding approach using tf or td-idf. An interesting phenomenon is that vectors from semantically similar words are proximate to each other in geometric space. For example, both the word *clustering* and *grouping* refer to unsupervised clustering in the context of machine learning, hence their embedding vectors are close together.

Training a word embedding neural network can be time-consuming and computationally expensive. Fortunately, there are several big tech companies that have trained word embedding models on different kinds of corpora and open sourced them. We can simply use these **pre-trained** models to map words to vectors. Some popular pretrained word embedding models are as follows:

Name	fasttext-wiki-news-subwords-300	
Corpus	Wikipedia 2017	
Vector size	300	
Vocabulary size	1 million	
File size	958 MB	
More information	https://fasttext.cc/docs/en/english-vectors.html	

Name	glove-twitter-100	glove-twitter-25
Corpus	Twitter (2 billion tweets)	
Vector size	100	25
Vocabulary size	1.2 million	
File size	387 MB	104 MB
More information	https://nlp.stanford.edu/projects/glove/	

Name	word2vec-google-news-300	
Corpus	Google News (about 100 billion words)	
Vector size	300	
Vocabulary size	3 million	
File size	1662 MB	
More information	https://code.google.com/archive/p/word2vec/	

Once we have embedding vectors for individual words, we can represent a document sample by averaging all of the vectors of present words in this document. The resulting vectors of document samples are then consumed by downstream predictive tasks, such as classification, similarity ranking in search engine, and clustering.

Now let's play around with `gensim`, a popular NLP package with powerful word embedding modules. If you have not installed the package in `Chapter 2`, *Exploring the 20 Newsgroups Dataset with Text Analysis Techniques*, you can do so using `pip`.

First, we import the package and load a pretrained model, `glove-twitter-25`, as follows:

```
>>> import gensim.downloader as api
>>> model = api.load("glove-twitter-25")
[==================================================] 100.0%
104.8/104.8MB downloaded
```

You will see the process bar if you first run this line of code. The `glove-twitter-25` model is one of the smallest ones so the download will not take very long.

We can obtain the embedding vector for a word (`computer`, for example), as follows:

```
>>> vector = model.wv['computer']
>>> print('Word computer is embedded into:\n', vector)
Word computer is embedded into:
 [ 0.64005 -0.019514 0.70148 -0.66123 1.1723 -0.58859 0.25917
-0.81541 1.1708 1.1413 -0.15405 -0.11369 -3.8414 -0.87233
   0.47489 1.1541 0.97678 1.1107 -0.14572 -0.52013 -0.52234
 -0.92349 0.34651 0.061939 -0.57375 ]
```

The result is a 25-dimension float vector as expected.

We can also get the top 10 words that are most contextually relevant to `computer` using the *most_similar* method, as follows:

```
>>> similar_words = model.most_similar("computer")
>>> print('Top ten words most contextually relevant to computer:\n',
            similar_words)
Top ten words most contextually relevant to computer:
 [('camera', 0.907833456993103), ('cell', 0.891890287399292), ('server',
0.8744666576385498), ('device', 0.869352400302887), ('wifi',
0.8631256818771362), ('screen', 0.8621907234191895), ('app',
0.8615544438362122), ('case', 0.8587921857833862), ('remote',
0.8583616018295288), ('file', 0.8575270771980286)]
```

The result looks promising.

Finally, we demonstrate how to generate representing vectors for a document with a simple example, as follows:

```
>>> doc_sample = ['i', 'love', 'reading', 'python', 'machine',
                  'learning', 'by', 'example']
>>> import numpy as np
>>> doc_vector = np.mean([model.wv[word] for word in doc_sample],
                                              axis=0)
>>> print('The document sample is embedded into:\n', doc_vector)
The document sample is embedded into:
 [-0.17100249 0.1388764 0.10616798 0.200275 0.1159925 -0.1515975
   1.1621187 -0.4241785 0.2912 -0.28199488 -0.31453252 0.43692702
  -3.95395 -0.35544625 0.073975 0.1408525 0.20736426 0.17444688
   0.10602863 -0.04121475 -0.34942 -0.2736689 -0.47526264 -0.11842456
  -0.16284864]
```

The resulting vector is the average of embedding vectors of eight input words.

In traditional NLP applications, such as text classification and topic modeling, tf or td-idf is still an outstanding solution for feature extraction. In more complicated areas, such as text summarization, machine translation, named entity resolution, question answering, and information retrieval, word embedding is used extensively and extracts far better features than the two traditional approaches.

Best practices in the model training, evaluation, and selection stage

Given a supervised machine learning problem, the first question many people ask is usually *what is the best classification or regression algorithm to solve it*. However, there is no one-size-fits-all solution, or no free lunch. No one could know which algorithm will work the best before trying multiple ones and fine-tuning the optimal one. We will be looking into best practices around this in the following sections.

Best practice 15 – choosing the right algorithm(s) to start with

Due to the fact that there are several parameters to tune for an algorithm, exhausting all algorithms and fine-tuning each one can be extremely time-consuming and computationally expensive. We should instead shortlist one to three algorithms to start with using the general guidelines that follow (note we herein focus on classification, but the theory transcends in regression and there is usually a counterpart algorithm in regression).

There are several things we need to be clear about before shortlisting potential algorithms, as described in the following:

- Size of the training dataset
- Dimensionality of the dataset
- Whether the data is linearly separable
- Whether features are independent
- Tolerance and trade-off of bias and variance
- Whether online learning is required

Naïve Bayes

This is a very simple algorithm. For a relatively small training dataset, if features are independent, Naïve Bayes will usually perform well. For a large dataset, Naïve Bayes will still work well as feature independence can be assumed in this case, regardless of the truth. The training of Naïve Bayes is usually faster than any other algorithms due to its computational simplicity. However, this may lead to a high bias (but a low variance).

Logistic regression

This is probably the most widely used classification algorithm, and the first algorithm that a machine learning practitioner usually tries when given a classification problem. It performs well when data is linearly separable or approximately **linearly separable**. Even if it is not linearly separable, it might be possible to convert the linearly non-separable features into separable ones and apply logistic regression afterward.

In the following instance, data in the original space is not linearly separable, but they become separable in a transformed space created from the interaction of two features:

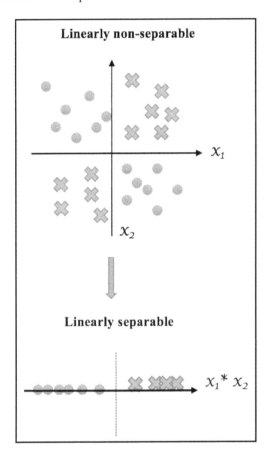

Also, logistic regression is extremely scalable to large datasets with SGD optimization, which makes it efficient in solving big data problems. Plus, it makes online learning feasible. Although logistic regression is a low-bias, high-variance algorithm, we overcome the potential overfitting by adding L1, L2, or a mix of two regularizations.

SVM

This is versatile enough to adapt to the linear separability of data. For a separable dataset, SVM, with linear kernel, performs comparably to logistic regression. Beyond this, SVM also works well for a non-separable one, if equipped with a non-linear kernel, such as RBF. For a high-dimensional dataset, the performance of logistic regression is usually compromised, while SVM still performs well. A good example of this can be in news classification, where the feature dimensionality is in the tens of thousands. In general, very high accuracy can be achieved by SVM with the right kernel and parameters. However, this might be at the expense of intense computation and high memory consumption.

Random forest (or decision tree)

Linear separability of data does not matter to the algorithm. And it works directly with categorical features without encoding, which provides great ease of use. Also, the trained model is very easy to interpret and explain to non-machine learning practitioners, which cannot be achieved with most other algorithms. Additionally, random forest boosts decision tree, which might lead to overfitting by ensembling a collection of separate trees. Its performance is comparable to SVM, while fine-tuning a random forest model is less difficult compared to SVM and neural networks.

Neural networks

These are extremely powerful, especially with the development of deep learning. However, finding the right topology (layers, nodes, activation functions, and so on) is not easy, not to mention the time-consuming model of training and tuning. Hence, they are not recommended as an algorithm to start with.

Best practice 16 – reducing overfitting

We've touched on ways to avoid overfitting when discussing the pros and cons of algorithms in the last practice. We herein formally summarize them, as follows:

- Cross-validation, a good habit that we have built over all of the chapters in this book.
- Regularization. It adds penalty terms to reduce the error caused by fitting the model perfectly on the given training set.

- Simplification, if possible. The more complex the mode is, the higher chance of overfitting. Complex models include a tree or forest with excessive depth, a linear regression with high degree polynomial transformation, and an SVM with a complicated kernel.
- Ensemble learning, combining a collection of weak models to form a stronger one.

Best practice 17 – diagnosing overfitting and underfitting

So, how can we tell whether a model suffers from overfitting, or the other extreme, underfitting? A **learning curve** is usually used to evaluate the bias and variance of a model. A learning curve is a graph that compares the cross-validated training and testing scores over a various number of training samples.

For a model that fits well on the training samples, the performance of training samples should be above desire. Ideally, as the number of training samples increases, the model performance on testing samples improves; eventually the performance on testing samples becomes close to that on training samples.

When the performance on testing samples converges at a value far from the performance on training samples, overfitting can be concluded. In this case, the model fails to generalize to instances that are not seen.

For a model that does not even fit well on the training samples, underfitting is easily spotted: both performances on training and testing samples are below desire in the learning curve.

Here is an example of the learning curve in an ideal case:

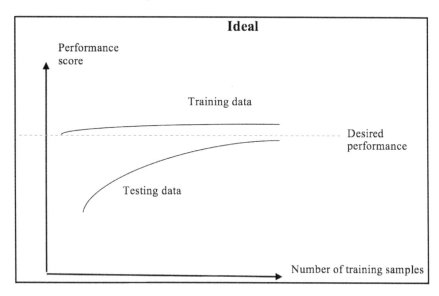

An example of the learning curve for an overfitted model is shown in the following diagram:

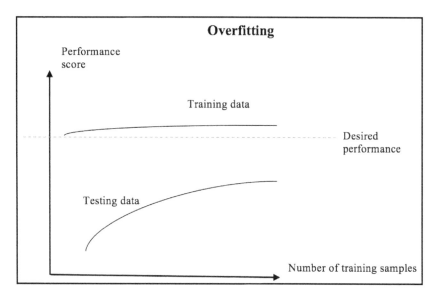

The learning curve for an underfitted model may look like the following diagram:

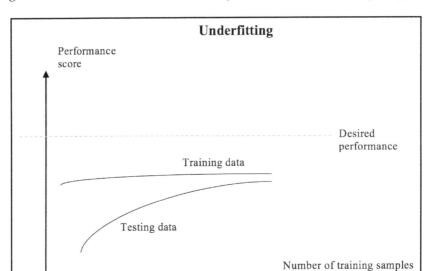

To generate the learning curve, we can utilize the `learning_curve` package from `scikit-learn`, and the `plot_learning_curve` function defined in `http://scikit-learn.org/stable/auto_examples/model_selection/plot_learning_curve.html`.

Best practice 18 – modeling on large-scale datasets

We have gained experience working with large datasets in Chapter 8, *Scaling Up Prediction to Terabyte Click Logs*. There are a few tips that can help you model on large-scale data more efficiently.

First, start with a small subset, for instance, a subset that can fit on your local machine. This can help speed up early experimentation. Obviously, you don't want to train on the entire dataset just to find out whether SVM or random forest works better. Instead, you can randomly sample data points and quickly run a few models on the selected set.

The second tip is choosing scalable algorithms, such as logistic regression, linear SVM, and SGD-based optimization. This is quite intuitive.

Once you figure out which model works best, you can fine-tune it using more data points and eventually train on the entire dataset. After that, don't forget to save the trained model. This is the third tip. Training on a large dataset takes a long time, which you would want to avoid redoing, if possible. We will explore saving and loading models in detail in the *Best practice 19 – saving, loading, and reusing* section later in this chapter.

Best practices in the deployment and monitoring stage

After performing all of the processes in the previous three stages, we now have a well-established data preprocessing pipeline and a correctly trained prediction model. The last stage of a machine learning system involves saving those resulting models from previous stages and deploying them on new data, as well as monitoring the performance, and updating the prediction models regularly.

Best practice 19 – saving, loading, and reusing models

When machine learning is deployed, new data should go through the same data preprocessing procedures (scaling, feature engineering, feature selection, dimensionality reduction, and so on) as in previous stages. The preprocessed data is then fed in the trained model. We simply cannot rerun the entire process and retrain the model every time new data comes in. Instead, we should save the established preprocessing models and trained prediction models after corresponding stages have been completed. In deployment mode, these models are loaded in advance, and are used to produce the prediction results of the new data.

We illustrate it via the diabetes example where we standardize the data and employ an SVR model, as follows:

```
>>> dataset = datasets.load_diabetes()
>>> X, y = dataset.data, dataset.target
>>> num_new = 30 # the last 30 samples as new data set
>>> X_train = X[:-num_new, :]
>>> y_train = y[:-num_new]
>>> X_new = X[-num_new:, :]
>>> y_new = y[-num_new:]
```

Preprocess the training data with scaling, as shown in the following commands:

```
>>> from sklearn.preprocessing import StandardScaler
>>> scaler = StandardScaler()
>>> scaler.fit(X_train)
```

Now save the established standardizer, the `scaler` object with `pickle`, as follows:

```
>>> import pickle
>>> pickle.dump(scaler, open("scaler.p", "wb" ))
```

This generates the `scaler.p` file.

Move on with training a SVR model on the scaled data, as follows:

```
>>> X_scaled_train = scaler.transform(X_train)
>>> from sklearn.svm import SVR
>>> regressor = SVR(C=20)
>>> regressor.fit(X_scaled_train, y_train)
```

Save the trained `regressor` object with `pickle`, as follows:

```
>>> pickle.dump(regressor, open("regressor.p", "wb"))
```

This generates the `regressor.p` file.

In the deployment stage, we first load the saved standardizer and `regressor` object from the preceding two files, as follows:

```
>>> my_scaler = pickle.load(open("scaler.p", "rb" ))
>>> my_regressor = pickle.load(open("regressor.p", "rb"))
```

Then preprocess the new data using the standardizer and make prediction with the `regressor` object just loaded, as follows:

```
>>> X_scaled_new = my_scaler.transform(X_new)
>>> predictions = my_regressor.predict(X_scaled_new)
```

We also demonstrate how to save and restore models in TensorFlow as a bonus session. As an example, we train a simple logistic regression model on the cancer dataset, as follows:

```
>>> import tensorflow as tf
>>> from sklearn import datasets
>>> cancer_data = datasets.load_breast_cancer()
>>> X = cancer_data.data
>>> Y = cancer_data.target
>>> n_features = int(X.shape[1])
>>> learning_rate = 0.005
```

```
>>> n_iter = 200
>>> x = tf.placeholder(tf.float32, shape=[None, n_features])
>>> y = tf.placeholder(tf.float32, shape=[None])
>>> W = tf.Variable(tf.zeros([n_features, 1]), name='W')
>>> b = tf.Variable(tf.zeros([1]), name='b')
>>> logits = tf.add(tf.matmul(x, W), b)[:, 0]
>>> cost = tf.reduce_mean(
        tf.nn.sigmoid_cross_entropy_with_logits(labels=y, logits=logits))
>>> optimizer = tf.train.AdamOptimizer(learning_rate).minimize(cost)
>>> sess = tf.Session()
>>> sess.run(tf.global_variables_initializer())
>>> for i in range(1, n_iter+1):
...     _, c = sess.run([optimizer, cost], feed_dict={x: X, y: Y})
...     if i % 10 == 0:
...         print('Iteration %i, training loss: %f' % (i, c))
Iteration 10, training loss: 0.744104
Iteration 20, training loss: 0.299996
Iteration 30, training loss: 0.278439
...
...
...
Iteration 180, training loss: 0.189589
Iteration 190, training loss: 0.186912
Iteration 200, training loss: 0.184381
```

Hopefully, these all look familiar to you. If not, feel free to review our TensorFlow implementation of logistic regression in Chapter 7, *Predicting Online Ads Click-through with Logistic Regression*. Now here comes the model saving part. Let's see how it is done by performing the following steps:

1. First we create a `saver` object in TensorFlow, as follows:

```
>>> saver = tf.train.Saver()
```

2. Save the model (or more specifically, the weight and bias variables) in a local file, as follows:

```
>>> file_path = './model_tf'
>>> saved_path = saver.save(sess, file_path)
>>> print('model saved in path: {}'.format(saved_path))
model saved in path: ./model_tf
```

3. Then we can restore the saved model. Before that, let's delete the current graph so it is more clear that we are actually loading a model from a file, as follows:

```
>>> tf.reset_default_graph()
```

4. Now we import the graph and see all tensors in the graph, as follows:

```
>>> imported_graph = tf.train.import_meta_graph(file_path+'.meta')
```

5. Finally, run a session and restore the model, as follows:

```
>>> with tf.Session() as sess:
...        imported_graph.restore(sess, file_path)
...        W_loaded, b_loaded = sess.run(['W:0','b:0'])
...        print('Saved W = ', W_loaded)
...        print('Saved b = ', b_loaded)
Saved W = [[ 7.76923299e-02]
 [ 1.78780090e-02]
 [ 6.56032786e-02]
 [ 1.02017745e-02]
 ...
 ...
 ...
 [-2.42149338e-01]
 [ 1.18054114e-02]
 [-1.14070164e-04]]
Saved b = [0.13216525]
```

We print out the weight and bias of the trained and saved model.

Best practice 20 – monitoring model performance

The machine learning system is now up and running. To make sure everything is on the right track, we need to conduct a performance check on a regular basis. To do so, besides making a prediction in real time, we should record the ground truth at the same time.

Continue the previous diabetes example with a performance check as follows:

```
>>> from sklearn.metrics import r2_score
>>> print('Health check on the model, R^2:
               {0:.3f}'.format(r2_score(y_new, predictions)))
Health check on the model, R^2: 0.613
```

We should log the performance and set an alert for a decayed performance.

Best practice 21 – updating models regularly

If the performance is getting worse, chances are that the pattern of data has changed. We can work around this by updating the model. Depending on whether online learning is feasible or not with the model, the model can be modernized with the new set of data (online updating), or retrained completely with the most recent data.

Summary

The purpose of the last chapter of this book is to prepare ourselves for real-world machine learning problems. We started with the general workflow that a machine learning solution follows: data preparation, training sets generation, algorithm training, evaluation and selection, and finally, system deployment and monitoring. We then went through in depth the typical tasks, common challenges, and best practices for each of these four stages.

Practice makes perfect. The most important best practice is practice itself. Get started with a real-world project to deepen your understanding and apply what we have learned throughout the entire book.

Exercises

- Can you use word embedding to extract text features and redo the newsgroup classification project in Chapter 5, *Classifying Newsgroup Topics with Support Vector Machines*? (note that you might not be able to get better results with word embedding than tf-idf, but it is good practice.)
- Can you find several challenges in Kaggle (www.kaggle.com) and practice what you have learned throughout the entire book?

Other Books You May Enjoy

If you enjoyed this book, you may be interested in these other books by Packt:

Building Machine Learning Systems with Python - Third Edition
Luis Pedro Coelho, Willi Richert, Matthieu Brucher

ISBN: 978-1-78862-322-3

- Build a classification system that can be applied to text, images, and sound
- Employ Amazon Web Services (AWS) to run analysis on the cloud
- Solve problems related to regression using scikit-learn and TensorFlow
- Recommend products to users based on their past purchases
- Understand different ways to apply deep neural networks on structured data
- Address recent developments in the field of computer vision and reinforcement learning

Machine Learning Algorithms - Second Edition
Giuseppe Bonaccorso

ISBN: 978-1-78934-799-9

- Study feature selection and the feature engineering process
- Assess performance and error trade-offs for linear regression
- Build a data model and understand how it works by using different types of algorithm
- Learn to tune the parameters of Support Vector Machines (SVM)
- Explore the concept of natural language processing (NLP) and recommendation systems
- Create a machine learning architecture from scratch

Leave a review - let other readers know what you think

Please share your thoughts on this book with others by leaving a review on the site that you bought it from. If you purchased the book from Amazon, please leave us an honest review on this book's Amazon page. This is vital so that other potential readers can see and use your unbiased opinion to make purchasing decisions, we can understand what our customers think about our products, and our authors can see your feedback on the title that they have worked with Packt to create. It will only take a few minutes of your time, but is valuable to other potential customers, our authors, and Packt. Thank you!

Index

CPSIA information can be obtained
at www.ICGtesting.com
Printed in the USA
BVHW010233120620
581397BV00007B/257